WHO'S AFRAID OF ADAM SMITH?

WHO'S AFRAID OF ADAM SMITH?

HOW THE MARKET GOT ITS SOUL

PETER J. DOUGHERTY

JOHN WILEY & SONS, INC.

Published by John Wiley & Sons, Inc., Hoboken, New Jersey.
Published simultaneously in Canada.

For general information on our other products and services, or technical support, please contact our Customer Care Department within the United States at 800-762-2974, outside the United States at 317-572-3993 or fax 317-572-4002.

Wiley also publishes its books in a variety of electronic formats. Some content that appears in print may not be available in electronic books.

Library of Congress Cataloging-in-Publication Data:

Dougherty, Peter J.
    Who's afraid of Adam Smith? : how the market got its soul / Peter J. Dougherty.
      p.   cm.
    Includes bibliographical references and index.
    ISBN 0-471-18477-2 (cloth : alk. paper)
    1. Smith, Adam, 1723–1790. 2. Capitalism—Moral and ethical aspects. 3.
Economics—Moral and ethical aspects. 4. Globalization—Moral and ethical aspects. 5.
Business ethics. I. Title.

HB501 D673 2002
330.15′3—dc21

2002072551

Printed in the United States of America.

10 9 8 7 6 5 4 3 2 1

"However selfish soever man may be supposed, there are evidently some principles in his nature, which interest him in the fortune of others, and render their happiness necessary to him, though he derives nothing from it except the pleasure of seeing it."

Adam Smith, *The Theory of Moral Sentiments*

We must encourage capitalism, it being the hope for the poor of the world and being in any case what we are, but our capitalism need not be hedonistic or monadic, and certainly not unethical. An aristocratic, country-club capitalism, well satisfied with itself, or a peasant, grasping capitalism, hating itself, are both lacking in the virtues. And neither works. They lead to monopoly and economic failure, alienation and revolution. We need a capitalism that nurtures communities of good townsfolk, in South Central LA as much as in Iowa City.

Deirdre N. McCloskey

Socialism is not the only enemy of the market economy. Another enemy, all the more powerful for its recent global triumph, is the market economy itself. When everything that matters can be bought and sold, when commitments can be broken because they are no longer to our advantage, when shopping becomes salvation and advertising slogans become our litany, when our worth is measured by how much we earn and spend, then the market is destroying the very virtues on which in the long run it depends.

Jonathan Sacks

Preface: Sympathy for the Dismal

Morals and metaphysics, politics and political economy, the way to make the most of all the modifications of smoke, gas, and paper currency; you have all these to learn from us; in short, all the arts and sciences. We are the modern Athenians.

Thomas Love Peacock

No real Englishman, in his secret soul, was ever sorry for the death of a political economist.

Walter Bagehot

In January 1985, in my capacity as an editor of economics books, I attended the annual New Year's meeting of the American Economic Association (AEA), held that year in Dallas. The events coordinator of the Dallas Convention Center, the same venue that had hosted the Republican National Convention a year earlier, must have been the wickedest wit—or most witless wonder—in the West, for he or she had booked, into one side of the Center, 5,000 dismal scientists—economists—and into the other, the National Cheerleaders Association.

In nearly 20 years of dragging my holiday-weary bones to the AEA meetings, I've never enjoyed any economists' convocation quite so much as this one. Every so often, having tired of meeting, greeting, and talking textbooks with the predominantly middle-aged, overwhelmingly male, relentlessly gray-suited economists, I could stroll behind the movable wall that split the convention center beyond the dismal din, and there sample, if only momentarily, the neon universe of cheerleaders—all bouncing pom-poms and gleaming smiles, and not a gray suit anywhere.

And yet, in the generation since I've been working with economists to publish their books, if there is a group in our society that deserves to flash a toothsome grin and maybe even wave a pom-pom or two, it is the dismal doctors of economics themselves. Whatever may befall us in the decades to come, the past several have been a time of triumph for economists, their students, their clients, and, most of all, their ideas. Even during recession, the world expects capitalism to bounce back more or less according to the economists' playbook—which is dramatically more than could have been asked for only a few generations ago, when competing economic systems were still very much in view. Darwin, for the time being, can take a back seat: We live foursquare in the age of Adam Smith, author of the two foundational works of modern economic society: *The Wealth of Nations* and *The Theory of Moral Sentiments*.

Market Wrap

The transition from central planning to markets, the restructuring of corporations, the liberalization of world trade, the surge in technological innovation, the spread of the international division of labor, the revolution in finance, the privatization of many public services, the rise of strategic management, the changing economic status of women, and the coming of a multinational commercial culture—what economists term the second great globalization—have generally conformed to the canon of modern economics.[1]

Add this recent record to the remarkable rise in living standards achieved throughout commercial society since the Industrial Revolution, and the relative stability of the major western economies since World War

II, and even the most stoic, cloistered, test-tube economist has reason to feel pride in the legacy of Adam Smith. To an impressive degree, the world now runs according to his rules, revised and updated for the changing times. To paraphrase a prominent economist, economic reality has come to resemble the model.[2]

The economists' recent run of success would seem to give more powerful credence than ever to the prophetic words of that most eloquent of self-described academic scribblers, John Maynard Keynes, who noted: "Practical men . . . are usually the slaves of some defunct economist."[3] Defunct or otherwise, economists have had not only their day, but, of late, an entire era. There is little reason to expect their influence to wane, much less to end. If economic events take a turn for the worse, the demand for economists and their ideas will only increase, and their influence will only improve. Economists, while not being wholly dismal, do hold an option on gloom.

An Undismal Dispatch

This book is a personal report from an observer on the economists' side of the convention floor, the gray-garbed assemblage that has produced some of the multichrome ideas that have influenced and will continue to influence the lives of practical men and women—and even blessedly impractical cheerleaders—everywhere.

Economic ideas in the tradition of Adam Smith are to democratic capitalism what an operating system is to a computer. The possibilities for capitalism, as for computing, are prodigious, depending on what we make of them; but they are only as good as the instructions that drive the respective systems.

In the chapters that follow, I hope to persuade you that our society will continue to benefit from the instructive economic legacy of Adam Smith, but also—dare I say more so—from contemporary economists' recently revived transfiguration of Smith's lesser known, yet surpassingly powerful, civic, social, and cultural legacy, lodged in the phrase "moral sentiments." This moral dimension of Adam Smith gives market society its soul, and this soul could very well reveal itself in unanticipated and exciting ways in the decades to come. How it came into being, faded from center stage in the theater of ideas, and returned to meet the challenges of our day, is the subject of my story.

Accounts Payable

I admire the British bibliographic practice of restricting acknowledgments to a spartan few, and I will be happy to abide by that tradition if ever I write another book. However, in this case, I have too many debts to pay in full.

Typically, a first-time author dedicates his or her book to a family member. It is only a small stretch to say that Peter L. Bernstein, to whom this book is dedicated, comes under this definition. I honor the day in the late 1980s when, in my capacity as a book editor at The Free Press, I called Peter, a celebrated Wall Street economist, to ask him about his book-writing plans. Since then, I have edited three of his marvelous, best-selling books.

Several years ago, after I had given a talk at the University of California, San Diego, on my approach to social science publishing, which I called "Recombinant Ideas and Enlightenment Ideals: Making Capitalism Work," I sent a copy of the talk to Peter. Peter liked the talk and featured it in his newsletter, *Economics and Portfolio Strategy*. Moreover, he saw in it the possibility of a book—specifically, this book. Peter urged me to talk to his editor, Myles Thompson, then a publisher at John Wiley & Sons, about developing the talk into a book proposal, which I did.

After I began to write this book, Peter Bernstein pushed, prodded, poked, and pulled the chapters out of their primordial maw. He combined his knowledge of economic history and macroeconomics with his shrewd literary sensibility—and his seemingly bottomless red pen—and delivered advice with what I can describe only as a father's sensitivity. He got me, a book editor, to learn the book-writing process as an author. Peter is my dear friend and I am eternally grateful to him.

In the late 'Eighties, I was also introduced to another invaluable associate and friend who ultimately had a hugely formative influence on this book. While at The Free Press, I had the good luck to sign the distinguished author and historian, Jerry Z. Muller. While working with him on his 1993 book, *Adam Smith in His Time and Ours: Designing the*

Decent Society, Jerry opened my eyes and my imagination to the work of the great philosopher Adam Smith.

My experience with Jerry made me appreciate Smith's style of thinking—namely, that Smith had puzzled out a progressive concept of society and retrofitted it with the incentive structures necessary to achieve a broadly humane vision. This intellectual style has conditioned my own thinking and informed my efforts to reckon the lofty ideas of social philosophers with the flintier prescriptions of economists in my publishing. Jerry did not read this book in its manuscript form, but I hope that when he reads it in published form, he will see his ideas as being effectively served. I am deeply indebted to him.

Robert K. Merton, with whom I had the great privilege of working some 20 years ago (he was my adviser during my days as a yearling social science editor), also played a direct and an indirect role in the publication of this book, for which I am grateful. When I sent Bob a copy of the aforementioned San Diego talk, he was kind enough to forward it to Jonathan Imber, who, much to my gratitude, published it in the Fall 1997 issue of *The American Sociologist.* Indirectly, Bob Merton's intellectual influence, resonant with the Smithian principle that form follows function in the way we attempt to shape our destiny, has governed my own way of thinking as well as my publishing—and, certainly, this book. The example of this great man has never left me since the summer day in 1979 when I met him in the Oak Room of the Plaza Hotel.

Several friends, authors, and associates read drafts of this manuscript, and I am most thankful to them for their criticisms and observations. Richard Swedberg, Shlomo Maital, James Meehan, Mike Elia, Romesh Vaitilingam, and, especially, Daniel Chirot (who read two drafts) sent me valuable comments on the chapters. I hope I have done them proud in rendering their wisdom in my revisions. Shlomo was generous in inviting me to deliver my first chapter as a talk at the June 2001 meetings of the Society for the Advancement of Behavioral Economics, which he organized, with Hugh Schwartz, at George Washington University in Washington, DC.

My own loving family, Elizabeth Hock and Colman Dougherty, had their patience tested well beyond reasonable saintliness as they watched me litter my home office and our den with files, books, articles, diskettes, and bad nerves in the preparation of this volume. Liz did double duty by lavishing her considerable editorial skills on the final draft.

Cole did yeoman's work by constantly reassuring me that I hadn't lost this chapter or that file in the remote recesses of my computers. My mother, Vera Dougherty, is hardly an enthusiast of Enlightenment ideas, but having raised three sons in extraordinarily trying circumstances, she exhibited, and continues to exhibit, the kind of moral sentiments that even Adam Smith would have regarded as heroic. So, too, did my late father, Joseph A. Dougherty—soldier, barkeeper, and family man—whose memory daily inspires my better sentiments.

As they awaited the completion of this manuscript, Jeanne Glasser, Joan O'Neil, and Jeff Brown, of John Wiley & Sons, displayed a level of patience that only a fellow publisher could appreciate. I hope that the finished product meets their expectations and those of my original editor and great friend, Myles Thompson. To Grady Klein, cunning designer, my thanks for a jacket that so beautifully captures the spirit of this work, and to the staff of Publications Development Company for their skillful and patient transformation of my manuscript into a book.

Finally, I wish to thank my authors of the past 20 years, whose books have enriched my life so greatly. Most of my authors and advisers are economists, and much of this book represents my attempt to do justice to their ideas, individually and collectively. This book does not purport to be a work of economics, nor economic history, nor economic theory, nor, God knows, empirical economics. As noted above, it is a "personal report" from an observer who spends his days within the culture of economics and social science, and who hopes to convey to his readers the potent and remarkably salutary ways in which economics can transform the culture for the better. Any and all mistakes are mine alone.

PETER J. DOUGHERTY

Princeton, New Jersey
July 2002

Contents

1

Letter Man

Present-day economists may know more than medieval astronomers, but they too are captives of a single overarching idea: that most people in everyday life are rational calculators of their own self-interest—that they are, in economic jargon, maximizers of utility. Given a sufficient imagination, they will come to the logically correct decision every time.

Alan Ehrenhalt

The man of systems seems to imagine that he can arrange the different members of a great society with as much ease as the hand arranges different pieces of a chess-board; he does not consider that the pieces of a chess-board have no other principles of motion besides that which the hand impresses on them; but that, in the great chess-board of human society, every single piece has a principle of motion of its own different from that which the legislature might seem to impress on it.

Adam Smith

I have spent the better part of my adult life as an editor of economists and their books. I am not an economist, nor do I play one on TV, but I know some of the profession's secrets. In fact, one of their bigger secrets has helped to shape the way I think about ideas and the ways in which those ideas can serve the useful purpose of making the world a better place—ways that I might not have anticipated only a few years ago.

This secret is lodged in the hidden identity of the philosopher Adam Smith, an identity I was lucky enough to discover during my education as an economics editor.

The Circle Game

Like so many of my fellow baby boomers, I was in the first generation of my family to go to college. College meant many things—penury, sideburns, medium-rare spaghetti—and, not least, a first exposure to economics. In the academic year 1968 to 1969, I survived, however barely, two hard, dreary semesters of economic principles. What little I learned about indifference curves, the GNP price deflator, the multiplier effect, and other such worldly wonders was more or less forgotten at exactly the moment I learned it. I sought relief in my courses on medieval history, the short story, politics, and film. Thus, when I began my adult life, it was hardly as an economic philosopher. A year after graduation, I got my first real job: a college textbook salesman at what was then Harcourt Brace Jovanovich.

Eventually, through hard work and luck, I was promoted to the position of textbook editor in the social sciences. In those days, only a few years out of college, I figured I would (a) live forever and (b) work for Harcourt forever. Then, in 1981, Harcourt having left its ancestral East Side New York City headquarters for new West Coast digs in San Diego, I decided to forgo California and accepted the job of economics editor crosstown at McGraw-Hill. It is a millenial understatement to admit that I took this job less for the lure of economics than for the want of gainful employment in my accidental, but by now beloved, field of book publishing. Upon arriving, I received new business cards that described me (with sublime unbelievability, to my way of thinking) as "Economics Editor."

Immediately after settling in on one of the twenty-something floors of McGraw-Hill's Rockfeller Center offices, I confronted anew what I remembered as the sawdust science of Adam Smith, including the Rube Goldberg-like figure I had earlier encountered in my economics principles textbook: the circular flow diagram of the economy. That diagram, whose provenance remains unknown to me still, is exactly what its name describes: A diagram that illustrates how each sector of the economy—

households, businesses, governments, the international sector—is connected with the others through the flow of capital. It appears in 1950s-era cartoon drawings in the first pages of most elementary economics textbooks; little houses and smokestack factories and banks and national capitols illustrate each respective sector of the economy, and fat little arrows connect them all around.

A colleague tells me that a famous mid-twentieth-century economist, Abba Lerner, once tried to build a water-powered plastic version of the circular flow model. Eventually, it was relegated to the basement of the Berkeley economics department, where it apparently has conducted very little water but collected much dust.[1] At any rate, the circular flow diagram has about as much intellectual sex appeal as, say, orthopedic shoes. And yet, there it was again, in all of its mechanical trappings, in the McGraw-Hill textbooks that I'd be working on as an editor. Right then and there, I decided that I would tread dismal water for a couple of years at most, and eventually move into an editorial field that would better honor my loftier humanistic pretensions; something like history or social theory—fields blessedly devoid of stylized contraptions like the circular flow diagram; fields more appropriate to a self-fashioned gentleman of letters like me.

But, unbeknownst to me at the time, I had started to absorb economics—not from divining its diagrams, but rather from talking to, and doing business with, its practitioners. The managers of McGraw-Hill seemed to be saying to me, though not in so many words, "Hey you, you're 30, collecting a salary, and wearing a tie—go up to MIT and negotiate contracts with some of the Nobel prize winners who defined the economics of negotiation!" Looking back on those days, economics—what I eventually discovered to be the rather more stylish science of Adam Smith—was all there in tiny fragments: signaling, asymmetric information, "cheap talk," cooperative and noncooperative strategies, reputation effects, oligopolistic competition—the whole nine yards. These clever economists I was dealing with thought like—well, come to think of it—they thought like economists. Clearly, there was more to this stuff than the funky circular flow. For all intents and purposes, I was back in Economics 101 and not minding it all that much this time around.

Within a year of starting my job—in December 1981, to be exact—I had my first meeting with the venerable economist and celebrated author

Paul Samuelson. I discovered him to be what I know him to be today: a fine gentleman and a great scholar. But I got a big lesson in economics the following day during an acceptance speech that Paul gave at a dinner celebrating the publication of *Paul Samuelson and Modern Economic Theory,* a book of essays in his honor. In his talk, which was attended mostly by MIT economists and McGraw-Hill executives, Paul turned to us, the publishers, and referred to us as "the cartel." "Cartel!?" I thought. To my mind, this was awfully harsh. OPEC was a cartel, not us. But it was true. We were indeed a cartel. So, did I discover, were economists. We publishers collectively dominated our market by doing our best to keep our costs low and our profits high. Economists, for their part, shared publishing stories for the sake of gaining competitive advantage in their dealings with us, the folks who published their books. They fought the cartel by acting like a cartel. It was, as the saying goes, only business.

What impressed me that evening was that, even in his acceptance speech, this most knowing of economists took the trouble to remind us that the facts of economic life are always with us. We're nice guys, we publishers, but we're also a cartel. Good neighbors make good fences. Acknowledging this economic fact brought definition and clarity to our affairs. In fact, it made the usually friendly partnership of author and publisher possible in the first place.

The inevitability of economics in life, so well obfuscated by the economists' circular flow diagram and a jargon that would gag an army of code crackers, is fundamental—or so I discovered. The eminent Victorian economist Alfred Marshall talked about it when he described economics as "the study of mankind in the ordinary business of life."[2] But until you've let it marinate a while, you don't really *know* it. And so it is equally important—no, necessary—to develop a way of thinking about it, of reconciling it with the world. That way of thinking is economics.

It's Not Personal

It wasn't long before I began to take in the atmospherics of economic inevitability all around me. I was imbibing the culture. For example, I found the film *The Godfather* to be a great tutorial in economics. In one of its most famous scenes, godfather-in-waiting Michael Corleone echoes the point about economic inevitability as he seeks to reaffirm his family's position in the New York crime cartel by planning to avenge his father's murderous competitors. Michael, played by a young and humorless Al Pacino, turns to his brother Santino, a hyperagitated James Caan, and intones the classic Mafia refrain: "It's not personal, Sonny. It's strictly business." This chilling incantation conveys but one of the many powerful economic tropes of this film. It makes me wonder why economists don't show *The Godfather* in the first week of classes, rather than the circular flow diagram. Soaked in the blood-drenched tones of Mafia history, rational action takes on an intensity that is irresistible even to the least amenable economics student.[3]

The Godfather would also serve to help economists make a surpassingly important point about capitalism, the particular economic culture in which most of us live and in which free markets are deployed to help feed and clothe us and spread the wealth of nations. The point is this: The morality of a tragic and lawless subculture like the Mafia, in which economic inevitability is enforced at the business end of a gun, is different from that of our mainstream commercial culture because we have insisted on the civilizing features that make our economic culture distinct.

In our culture, even the most ruthless economic exchanges usually lead to civilized outcomes—the blood left on the boardroom floor is ketchup. These outcomes are the legacy of painstakingly evolved civilizing institutions, including, but not limited to, law, social norms, good government, engaged citizenship, public service, and professionalism. We do not always get these institutions right—consider the number of lousy laws on the books—but these noneconomic institutions are as important to the maintenance and expansion of a healthy capitalism as are the economic machinery of stock markets and collective bargaining agreements.

I've Got a Secret

If we are to make the world a better place, we need to strengthen and enrich these noneconomic institutions, for they, along with more purely economic structures, are the hope for the future. Economics matters in this effort because economic life is so intimately implicated in the other spheres of living from which these institutions—cultural, political, and social—spring that it is folly to leave it out. By the same token, skillfully designed civic institutions are, as economists have been discovering in greater dimension, vital to economic progress. This leads me to the economists' big secret.

Adam Smith, stone-faced architect of the economics of prices, factories, and free trade (and, much as I hate to admit it, probably the culprit behind the circular flow diagram), had some big ideas about making noneconomic institutions work, as well. He was, in addition to being the father of economics, the designer of a grand cultural system built around the very civilizing institutions that we tend to look past when we think of the grinding economic machinery of capitalism.

Smith keynoted his broad attitude toward a civilized market society by insisting:

> . . . He is certainly not a good citizen who does not wish to promote, by every means of his power, the welfare of the whole society of his fellow citizens.[4]

These words hardly describe the money-grubbing *homo economicus* subscribed to by the critics—and even some of the apologists—of capitalism. On the contrary, they suggest that modern economics, at its very heart in the work of its founder Adam Smith, amounts to a good deal more than the usual batter of land, labor, and capital than a casual observer might think. Economics is also part of a larger civilizing project, and Smith's original effort to understand it was an exercise in soulcraft—one that has continued since his time and will not end today. This soulful side of Adam Smith is also, typically, the last thing one learns—or, at least one of the last things that I learned—in an economics education.

The Sidewalk Science of Adam Smith

By the early 'Nineties, having finessed my way around the circular flow a few dozen times, I had earned an editorial reputation worthy of my business card. I had racked up a string of impressive books by the likes of Nobel laureates Robert C. Merton and Harry Markowitz, the late great finance economist Fischer Black, and celebrated behavioral economist Richard Thaler, not to mention the distinguished Wall Street economist and writer Peter L. Bernstein. And by then, I had also become increasingly interested in the arcane civilizing side of Adam Smith, largely through the work of some prominent noneconomists.

After the fall of the Soviet Union and in the wake of the Reagan and Thatcher reformations, a handful of prominent intellectuals had begun to scratch their heads about the importance of civil society as a component of successful market democracy. Civil society describes the small-scale ordinary structures of life, including schools, neighborhoods, restaurants and small businesses, churches, local media and libraries, workplace cultures, pubs, families, sports and recreation groups—the "little platoons" that operate in the shadow of gigantic impersonal forces such as the state and the corporation. Analysts seemed to be recognizing that these small-scale structures play a much bigger role in incubating success than anyone had thought for a long time. Through these mediating structures, real progress, social and economic, finds its fire.

As the story goes, the "complex web of associations, networks, and contacts" that comprise civil society animates the shared expectations, the reciprocity, and, most valuably, the levels of trust essential to the smooth commerce of everyday life in a market democracy.[5] Trust and its accompanying norms are vital ingredients in this account. Social scientists, in their attempt to get to the heart of what makes a vibrant civil society tick, have given them a slightly souped-up name: Collectively, they call them *social capital* because, like economic capital—money, machines, and property—the more social capital a society holds, the more efficiently and productively it tends to work.

When there is a lot of social capital on the street—where people know and trust one another and the social networks work; where there is history and a strong collective culture—things get done relatively easily (or with low transactions costs, as the economists would say), all else being equal. Social capital appears to be most productive where it is most heavily concentrated: in towns, villages, and cities. Indeed, the industrial cities of Italy's *mezzogiorno* have been extolled as the world capitals of social capital because of their rich cross-pollination of democratically organized associations ranging from football clubs to choral societies to political groups.[6] Today's expositors of social capital trace the origins of the idea to that most perspicacious of political observers, Alexis de Tocqueville, who identified it in his musings on early America. According to the peripatetic French chronicler:

> Americans of all ages, all stations of life, and all dispositions are forever forming associations. There are not only commercial and industrial associations in which all take part, but others of a thousand different types—religious, moral, serious, futile, very general and very limited, immensely large and very minute. . . . Thus, the most democratic country in the world now is that in which men have in our time carried to the highest perfection the art of pursuing in common the objects of common desires and have applied this new technique to the greatest number of purposes.[7]

Contemporary political scientist Robert Putnam echoes de Tocqueville when he notes: "Whereas physical capital refers to objects and human capital refers to properties of individuals, social capital refers to connections among individuals—social networks and the norms of reciprocity that arise from them. . . . 'Social capital' calls attention to the fact that civic virtue is most powerful when embedded in a dense network of reciprocal social relations."[8] The great Jane Jacobs, a worldly philosopher in her own right, anticipated today's interest in social capital in her classic 1961 book, *The Death and Life of Great American Cities*. Referring to the social networks that unify city neighborhoods, she noted: "These networks are a city's irreplaceable social capital. Whenever the capital is lost, from whatever cause, the income from it disappears, never to return until and unless new capital is slowly and chancily accumulated."[9]

Although many economists dismiss the idea of social capital as too touchy-feely to be of any serious analytical use, it has gained a certain pride of place in the field's recent history. Glenn Loury, widely regarded as the first prominent economist since Victorian Alfred Marshall to use the term social capital, noted, in his work on racial inequality:

> . . . the fact is that each and every one of us is embedded in a complex web of associations, networks, and contacts. We live in families, we belong in communities, and we are members of collectivities of one kind or another. . . . Opportunity travels along the synapses of these

networks. . . . These kinds of opportunity-enhancing associations are not just out there in the marketplace to be purchased by the highest bidder. Nor are they allocated randomly so as to create some kind of level playing field.[10]

Robert Putnam, in his acclaimed book about contemporary America, *Bowling Alone,* observes a directly inverse correlation between the amount of social capital in an area and the distance that separates the places where people live, work, and shop. Other things being held equal, the smaller the triangle, the stronger the degree of social capital. If space matters thus, then much of contemporary America is the Bermuda Triangle of social capital.[11]

Streetcorner Serenade

My enthusiasm for the idea of civil society (and its life force, social capital) arises in part from the mists of my personal history. Having grown up in a smallish triangle in a big eastern city, and having seen there the bursting beauty of a commercially lively, ethnically heterogeneous, culturally robust, economically mixed civil society at work, I welcomed this embrace of the civilizing science of Tocqueville and Adam Smith with some self-satisfaction. Nobody would ever confuse the medley of soul music, seersucker, and saints' days of my West Philadelphia youth with the splendor of Tuscany, but the Philadelphia neighborhood now known as University City breathed a gentility and a vitality that I've since lamented as the world we have lost.

Admittedly, the West Philadelphia of my youth was forged, as are all places, by powerful historical forces such as the state and the corporation, and it was just as rudely undone by a conspiracy of these same forces. But what made it special were the small things—the mingling of a university, businesses, bars, shops, schools and churches, cafés, museums, black and brown and white subcultures, professors and bootblacks—the intimate cultural chemistry that resided within, yet also beyond, big government and big companies.

West Philadelphia was both liberal and conservative, in the best sense of both words. Liberal, in that it freed those of us in each of its many ethnic and economic enclaves to know and explore other subcultures; conservative, in that its institutions—its schools, libraries, small businesses, and establishments (we had our own chocolatier, haberdasher, and milliner!)—managed for a while to remain dignified and stable citadels despite the ever-changing social composition swirling about us.

Given the state of our society today—stretched by suburban sprawl, split by cultural polarities, and soaked by electronic images—I welcomed this return to a picture of the past that I knew and liked: a conception of a sidewalk society exemplified by the ties that bind instead of the pulverizing forces that set us apart. This vision of society, redolent of a more citified, even European past, is a tough sell to a generation weaned on SUVs and CRTs. It brings to mind comedian Buddy Hackett's comment that until he left his mother's kitchen, he had never known that there was such a thing in life as not having heartburn. By the same token, perhaps the wired generation will learn one day that there is also more to life than traffic jams, cell-phone bleeps, unsolicited marketers, e-mail pileups, and other sources of postmodern heartburn. A little Tuscany wouldn't hurt—even a little West Philly.

And yet, however promising this new wave of civic philosophizing seemed, initially it created a dilemma for me as a fellow traveler in economics because so many of the leading expositors of civil society also turned out to be such severe critics of markets and, by implication, of my economists. In article after article, the same intellectuals who extolled the virtues of civil society would deride economists as "Keepers of the Dismal Faith," condemn them for their poverty of vision, and intone wishful (and wistful) disciplinary obituaries with titles like *The End of Economics* and *The Death of Economics,* and "The Puzzling Failure of Economics." A Web site for "post-autistic" economics called economists to task for having become an army of mathematical vampires determined to suck the life out of the human institutions they purported to study. Apparently, someone besides me had had a bad date with the circular flow diagram.[12]

But in the meantime, my continuing education as an economics editor had reinforced in me the knowledge that most of the latter-day philosophic exponents of civil society appeared to have overlooked: Adam Smith, economist *par excellence,* knew a thing or two about civil society, and his civic ideas mattered as much as his economic ideas.

Cents and Sensibility

In many ways, Adam Smith was every bit the equal of Alexis de Tocqueville in drawing the contours of civil society because Smith had fitted
the realities of economic inevitability so hardheadedly into his larger
moral system—the same system that eventually helped to define contemporary capitalism. He suggested this connection obliquely when he
noted: "Whenever dealings are frequent, a man does not expect to gain so
much by any one contract as by probity and punctuality in the whole, and
a prudent dealer, who is sensible of his real interest, would rather choose
to lose what he has a right to than give any ground for suspicion. . . .
When the greater part of people are merchants they always bring probity
and punctuality into fashion, and these are the principal virtues of commercial nations."[13]

In other words, Smith built his civilizing project around the assumption that we are not angels, but rather the very self-interested beings
whom we know ourselves to be, and that we need institutions that channel our self-interest into service of the common interest while curbing its
more destructive elements. For Smith, the market accomplished much of
this service of the common interest by bringing buyers and sellers, owners
and workers together "as if by some Invisible Hand." But in his much-
neglected classic, *The Theory of Moral Sentiments,* as well as in other
writings, Smith emphasized the essential connection between strong,
trust-building social institutions and the productive economic machinery
of markets, a relation designed not only to expand wealth, but to instill
virtue—to multiply fiscal as well as social capital.

Smith's original conception of a healthy commercial society had two
big parts. In the first, Smith argued that the pursuit of self-interest, mediated by economic institutions such as the market, would not only increase
wealth, but would tend to inculcate good habits such as "economy, industry, discretion, attention and application of thought," as well as the working virtues.[14]

In the second, Smith argued that the development of self-esteem in
people, incubated in noneconomic institutions such as a village (or, say, a
family), would tend to result in greater civility, benevolence, and altruism—and thereby remove some of spikier edges of the market from the

rough-and-tumble of commercial society. As the saying goes, it takes a village, but not just any village—and certainly not the village of Corleone on the outskirts of Palermo, Sicily! The civic village is rich in reciprocity and reflects Adam Smith's design for a system of countervailing institutions.

Prosperous and vibrant communities owe their good fortune not only to the butcher, the baker, the candlestick maker, and other local employers, but also to the noneconomic activities of the rest of the villagers. Social capital complements economic capital, and vice versa. We tend to know social capital when we see it, and we see it clearly in bustling locales—from the Claphams and Hammersmiths of London to the micro-hamlets of Los Angeles, the industrial cities of Italy, and the urban canyons of Hong Kong.

If we want to sample social capital in its most gruesome absence, we needn't travel all the way to Corleone. An excursion into the highly uncivil streets of downtown Camden, New Jersey, provides an excellent object lesson. In Camden, we see people, but if we look a little harder, we also see ghosts—the ghosts of a lost civic culture and institutional tissue that would otherwise conjoin citizens, build collective activity, create reciprocity, and provide the basis for a brighter future for the generations of Camdenites to come—the ghosts of moral sentiments. These are the ghosts that Jane Jacobs warned us about and that Robert Putnam and Glenn Loury want to exorcise.

That these ghosts live among us in a society as rich and resourceful as ours is an indication of our greatest imperfection. The ghosts challenge economists and leaders alike to design new strategies for injecting economic capital and social capital into places where neither exists in any substantial measure. These ghosts call forth the legacy of Adam Smith, philosopher of wealth as well as sentiments, designer of civil society, big-idea economist.

One of Adam Smith's expositors neatly captures Smith's taste for the cause of the masses when he notes that, in Smith's own time, the great philosopher attempted to construct a system that worked for all orders of society. In Smith's design, according to this analyst, "Direct domination by political elites would be replaced by a network of institutions which promoted self-control among politically free citizens, while the rising level of material comfort would make it possible to expand sympathy and concern for others. It was this philosophy that lay behind Smith's advocacy of higher wages, mass education, and other policies that conflicted with the conventional wisdom of the upper classes to whom his books were addressed."[15]

It is remarkable how the spirit of Adam Smith—an odd duck of a man, who died two centuries ago—continues to exert its influences, large and small, over the increasingly technical ideas that govern our cyber-charged world. But it does, and society is better off for it. One economist notes that, "As Smith showed us over 200 years ago, the pursuit of one's enlightened self-interest, far from reducing the public welfare, leads to general prosperity provided governments set the proper rules of the game."[16] What we tend to debate these days are the rules, not the nature, of the game—a testament to Smith's capacious and enduring vision. Witness the debate over that stickiest of public problems, the delivery of health care. Invariably, both private and government structures are included in the discussion because both are needed. The rub is not to choose one over the other, but to figure out the right combination of elements from both. The same holds for everything from the zoning changes needed to revive cities to the financial architecture needed to revive developing nations.

Both Sides Now

As capitalism covers the globe and marinates in the world's diverse cultures and changing technologies, ironically it becomes a more, not a less, urgent concern for social philosophers. If they are to succeed in delineating compelling directions for society, thinkers and leaders alike require a firmer grasp of how the cost curves and repeated games of economic theory fit within social imperatives of commercial life. As the market dynamics that propel capitalism forward grow more feverish and forceful, the moral questions that accompany this economic progress take on new and unpredictable shapes, and loom larger.

Fresh issues abound: Whose kids get access to the best schools, and why? Whose parents get access to the best elder care? What becomes of a city after a corporation restructures its way out of—or into—town? Can small-town and main-street businesses coexist with cybercommerce? Will aging urban neighborhoods ever regain the vitality that once made them—

and us—great? Can families survive the dislocations of constantly changing job demands? Will the inner city ever be a safe, inviting place? What happens if I live 30 years past my retirement? Will the world's emerging economies ever really emerge? What leverage do the poor have over the powerful? Is the world turning into one huge Quarter Pounder with Fries? Can people of differing cultural backgrounds get along in a world awash in the restless movement of capital, labor, and ideas? Will the rich only get richer, and the poor, poorer? Can I find a place to park?

Adam Smith worried ceaselessly about the cultural conundrums of market society. His greatness stemmed not only from his defense of markets, but from his work at the intersection of the economic and moral, as well as the political and psychological, spheres in addressing these kinds of concerns. The Wealth of Nations and The Theory of Moral Sentiments were, respectively, about how the pursuit of self-interest serves the public interest and makes us more civil and decent toward each other. To paraphrase historian Jerry Muller, Smith labored a lifetime to show how institutions and incentives could be structured to make us better producers and consumers as well as better neighbors.

Figuring out how the sometimes seemingly incongruous parts of his puzzle fit together, and how they can be sustained, fortified, and expanded in an eruptive capitalist world, remains a seminal challenge for Adam Smith's main intellectual offspring: economists. And applying their lessons is a challenge for those who lead the society—executives, policymakers, and yes, even those without much of an appetite for economics.

If the best new ideas of economists make it into the realm of public policy and commercial practice in the years ahead, Adam Smith's influence will, if anything, move firmly into the new millennium. But the Smith we get to know in the years to come will be broader and more multifaceted a presence than the one we think we know. The Adam Smith of the market-clearing prices, fluid economic equilibria, fat-free tariff laws, profit maximization, and high-stepping labor markets that have come to define the dynamic economic system of our day is the hard-nosed fellow associated primarily with The Wealth of Nations—the guy on the neckties.

But his purely economic vision has been challenged and eclipsed by several generations of economists, from Joseph Schumpeter through Joseph Stiglitz, in investigations of market failure, oligopoly, and newly defined economies of scale. Smith's famed Invisible Hand may still be with us, but it has had its knuckles wrapped, its palm slapped, and its fingers pulled. Ironically, Smith's lesser known moral sensibility—the soul of the market—has endured. I think we will be hearing much more from this other Adam Smith—the philosopher, that is—as capitalism continues to evolve.[17]

A Sentimental Sampler

Economists, long authorities on Smith's *Wealth of Nations,* recently appear to be intrigued by the nonmarket aspects of Adam Smith's civilizing project. In fact, some have been doing exciting work in this realm, albeit quietly, for a while.

In the first instance, contemporary economists have started to replenish the recipe for moral sentiments, some two centuries after Smith coined it. New definitions abound. One economist recently realigned the characterization of moral sentiments with what she calls the "bourgeois virtues"—the virtues fit for a society not of silk-stocking elitists or hairshirt Marxists, but of the bubbling commercial culture in which most of us participate. Noting that markets promote virtue, not vice, this economist declaims that ". . . we all take happily what the market gives—polite, accommodating, energetic, enterprising, risk-taking people; not bad people, or else we complain to the management or take our business elsewhere. . . . The way a salesperson in an American store greets customers makes the point: 'How can I help you?' The phrase startles foreigners. It is an instance in miniature of the bourgeois virtues."[18]

Another economist frames the discussion of moral sentiments by defining the characteristics of an "inclusive economy." He stresses: "In inclusive economies there is no incompatibility between the functioning of markets and the existence of shared values, collective activity and institutions, and broadly accepted concepts of fairness. . . . Only if we dispose of the notion that the functioning of markets depends on the base and contemptible aspects of human behaviour will we create a market economy that commands wide and continuing support."[19]

These definitions, and those of other economists, resonate powerfully with the concept of civil society exemplified in the networks that produce social capital. But just what does a new civic economics look like? As I enter my third decade as an economics editor, I see civic economics breaking down into the following four broad directions:

1. The construction of civic infrastructure that attracts and stimulates markets in underdeveloped economies;
2. The economics of large-scale public enterprises;
3. The economics of expanded asset and property ownership;
4. A newly imagined urban economics.

Robert Putnam has called for a "new era of civic inventiveness" to promote social capital and enlarge the reach of civil society.[20] Economists are contributing, if somewhat indirectly (maybe even unwittingly), to this enterprise, and their influence is sure to grow, especially on the aforementioned fronts in the following ways.

Adam Smith's Modern Quartet

Promising theoretical work is being done toward the provision of greater "civic infrastructure," especially in emerging economies, thereby enabling more societies to participate in expanding global economic activity. This infrastructure includes institutions from commercial law through enhanced property rights, efficient regulatory regimes, and transparent accounting rules, as well as constitutional and political institutions conducive to the efficient functioning of markets. If markets provide the muscle for a successful commercial society, and human ingenuity constitutes its brain, then civic infrastructure serves as its bones—the skeletal structure needed to support a vibrant democratic capitalism. An invisible hand without good bone structure isn't worth much, as economists have come to learn.

This style of theorizing took root in the 'Sixties when Kenneth Arrow, Ronald Coase, and Douglass North, each one now a card-carrying Nobel laureate, were resurrecting economists' interest in the institutional prerequisites of economic performance. These great economists set the stage for the systematic reconsideration of civic structures designed to support, not subvert, economic vitality and social progress. The adoption of these structures is particularly urgent. They serve to secure the emerging markets needed for the expansion of economic growth and world trade—and, perhaps ultimately, world peace—and they are essential to the prosperity and social progress of developing nations.

As Hernando de Soto attests in his fine book, *The Mystery of Capital*, the gains from trade in these newly understood forms of social capital will be greatest in the developing world. According to de Soto, "The poor . . . do have things, but they lack the process to represent their property and create capital. They have houses but not titles; crops but not deeds; businesses but not statutes of incorporation." Economists are now seeking ways to create the features needed to kickstart this capital. One hopes that the lessons now being learned in what was formerly East Berlin can be grafted into East St. Louis and East Timur.[21]

Intriguing new economic thinking is being brought to bear on large-scale public enterprise, especially the advancement of knowledge, so vital to an ever-expanding economic pie. These initiatives include the cultivation of applied technological research, new educational delivery systems, and new approaches to the problems of poverty and social depredation.

The era of big government may indeed be over, but the era of big challenges is harder to eulogize away. National, regional, and even global conundrums—from delivering health care and nutrition, to providing cleaner air and water, creating a sturdier physical infrastructure, eliminating pockets of hard-core unemployment and deprivation—require large-scale public solutions in which new ideas increasingly play the lead. That this kind of "big think" elicits little moral support these days redounds to society's loss of faith in large-scale government projects in the wake of a well-intentioned, but often inefficient, welfare state, and, more generally, to the miserable failure of state socialism. Indeed, the lack of resolve that accompanies this retreat from the public square itself constitutes a deficit in social capital.

I'm not quite old enough to remember the victory culture that followed the Second World War, but the can-do public spirit that suffused it and provided the mood music for growth-enhancing initiatives as bold as the G.I. Bill and veterans' housing is precisely what's absent in our prosperous, if atomized, society. The new challenge would be to leverage the grand ambition of Normandy invasions, Apollo space shots, and inter-state highway systems with the ingenuity and cost efficiency characteristic of private initiative toward the solution of pressing large-scale public chal-lenges. In the spirit of Adam Smith, a fundamental challenge is to get the incentives right. As he said, "Publick services are never better performed than when their reward comes only in consequence of their being per-formed, and is proportioned to the diligence employed in performing them." Getting the incentives right in public enterprise is a design chal-lenge that economists are now coming to grips with.[22]

Another compelling research initiative is the work being done by econ-omists on the expansion of ownership and assets throughout the society. Adam Smith talked, not idly, of the necessity of making "every man a merchant," by which he meant, to a first approximation, making every-one a full participant in the economy. Alfred Marshall argued that public economic support for the disenfranchised was a political, as well as a hu-manitarian necessity, if the poor were to partake in the society as fully fledged citizens.

The architects of the welfare state attempted to provide this support through the economics of income transfers. But in a system like ours, based decidedly on free markets and on the politics of civic engagement, assets, not merely redistributed income, are increasingly the coin of the realm. Expanded assets enhance not only economic capital, but also so-cial capital by strengthening ties across race and class lines, and by giving more people a greater stake, and a bigger voice, in the politics of their own communities. Finance economists are on the case.

Economists are enlarging the civilizing mantle of Adam Smith in the imperative of a new urban economics. To the extent that economic prog-ress is conditioned on new ideas, the restoration of cities is important be-cause, historically, cities are the great incubators of ideas—economic, scientific, and cultural. They nurture knowledge spillovers that fuel eco-nomic prosperity. Cities serve as the main turbines of capital because they bring the vast variety of human creative resources together in an ongoing spontaneous and combustible mix. But the centripedal forces of a mobile society such as ours can and do work against the vitality of cities, so econ-omists are needed to draw up blueprints for the revival of cities—not only megacities like New York, London, and Tokyo—but also smaller, more specialized centers of urban life, as well.

For years, in my job, I've seen a need for the next great book in urban economics, but I've come up empty so far. Over time, I've come to believe that economists, despite excellent new work (particularly by some younger researchers), have yet to grasp the transformative potential of a book in the monumental mode established by Jane Jacobs in the early 'Sixties. Unfortunately, the requirements of economic science sometimes force economists into talking about cities in the same way that psychologists talk about sex. They take the fun out of it. But cities are as much about passion as they are about capital investment and labor supply. An important way for economists to serve the greater intellectual goal of civic renewal is to put the passion back into this field, which does not mean retreating from the research frontier. It means marrying thought to feeling and thereby helping to reaffirm the exciting connections that unite the historic wisdom of Adam Smith with city life.

Prometheus Unplugged

During my years as an economics editor, I have been privileged to watch economists expand impressively on the technical side of Adam Smith's legacy. Continuing breakthroughs in the analytical apparatus of fields such as finance, strategy, growth, organizations, trade, and money promise to charge the wealth of nations in untold ways, to fuel the fire of economic growth that began in the Industrial Revolution and outstripped anything like it in earlier human history. I am hopeful, as I think Adam Smith would have been, that, more than anything, these breakthroughs, by uniting markets with people in new and imaginative ways, will contribute rapid relief to parts of the world that desperately need economic development. But this technical progress, potentially so impressive and far-reaching, begs the question of what new kinds of concerns, cultural and social, will occupy the economic agenda in the years to come.

As a veteran economics editor who has learned the value of insurance and long discounts, I'll hedge by ending this chapter not with my words, but with the words of an economist: ". . . I may do well," said John Maynard Keynes in 1926, "to remind you, in conclusion, that the fiercest contests and the most deeply felt divisions of opinion are likely to be waged in the coming years not round technical questions, where the arguments on either side are mainly economic, but round those which, for want of better words, may be called psychological or, perhaps, moral."[23]

More on Keynes later; but first, to the bookstore for a look at two of the scriptural statements that have defined modern economics. As we will see, capitalism comes with Instructions; it also comes with a Warning.

2

The Instructions

As a pragmatist, were Smith alive today, he might well say, "People are entitled to make their own mistakes in many matters, but it is unrealistic to believe that every sane adult should be treated as a sovereign will. As humans, conscious that we are imperfect, aware in this post-Freudian world that our impulses can sometimes mislead us, we shall sparingly, for good cause, and with due process, democratically place restrictions on our own behavior. So again, laissez-faire perfect competition would not inevitably be the ideal."

Paul A. Samuelson and William D. Nordhaus

Not since Alfred Marshall's Principles, *which went through eight editions at a time when two editions were unusual, has a single book dominated the teaching of economics. The influence of Samuelson's text has been so great that when a group of radical economists in the 1970s put together a critique of economics as it is taught today, they titled their two-volume effort,* The Anti-Samuelson.

William Breit and Roger L. Ransom

In a scene from the black comedy *Raising Arizona*, Nicholas Cage and Holly Hunter play a married couple who cannot conceive a child, and so decide to steal one. They drive at night to the home of another couple who, according to the newspapers, has just delivered quintuplets. Cage mounts a ladder, climbs into the second-story bedroom of the infants, and grabs one of the babies. As he exits the bedroom window he tucks little Nathan, football-style, under one arm, sees a copy of Dr. Spock's book on child rearing perched on a night table, and sticks the book in the back pocket of his jeans. After descending the ladder, he races to the car where Holly Hunter is poised behind the wheel, ready to drive off with the treasured infant. Cage hands the baby to Hunter. Then, as he hustles into the passenger seat, he remembers the pilfered copy of Dr. Spock, removes it from his pocket, and hands it to his wife, saying, "Oh, yeah, here are the instructions."[1]

For the past half-century, cagey economics professors at colleges and universities near and far have been giving The Instructions to freshmen and sophomores in the form of economics principles textbooks. The book that set the standard for this ritual—the Dr. Spock of economics instruction—was first published in 1948 under the title *Economics: An Introductory Analysis* by a brash and brilliant young MIT professor—Paul Samuelson. Imitators, emulators, pretenders, probably a few impostors, and other composers of variants on the theme have come and gone since then. But Samuelson's textbook (later, its name was trimmed to the more economical *Economics*, but, invariably, admirers, detractors, and mere innocent bystanders refer to it simply as *Samuelson*) made the mold from which all others have been stamped.

In today's parlance, Samuelson became to economics what Windows is to operating systems. Along with its many successors, the Samuelson book has served, for better than a half-century, as The Instructions for understanding and navigating the brave new world of contemporary capitalism. No consideration of the technical legacy or language of Adam Smith's *Wealth of Nations* is possible without it or one of its spawn.

Samuelson Is What Economists Do

Economist Jacob Viner once defined economics as "what economists do."[2] To the extent that this is true, most of the tools of the trade have been explained in Samuelson. Todd Bucholz, an economist and writer with a knack for funny and telling phrases, notes that economics has produced only five important books in its history (a contention that, by the bye, stops the heart of economics book editors): (1) Smith's *Wealth of Nations*,

(2) John Stuart Mill's *Principles of Political Economy,* (3) David Ricardo's *Principles,* (4) Alfred Marshall's *Principles of Economics,* and (5) Samuelson's *Economics,* the one that resonates with most recent generations. Samuelson's antecedents indeed hearken back to Adam Smith, and his own book supplanted the eighth edition of Alfred Marshall's great *Principles* text, which first saw the light of publication in 1890.[3]

Paul Samuelson, in the wake of his Keynesian teacher Alvin Hansen, developed and distilled the economic ideas of John Maynard Keynes into a testable set of pedagogical principles for economists and, more importantly, for students. He constructed and elucidated a system of rules that described the efficient manner in which the Invisible Hand governs the market in good times, and the policy measures necessary to right it in bad times. Indeed, Samuelson's great achievement was to explain how the tools of macroeconomic management exposited by Keynes—countercyclical monetary policy and taxation—could be used to guide the economy through the gyrations of the business cycle, thereby allowing Smith's Invisible Hand to function smoothly the rest of the time. Samuelson, drawing on Smith, Marshall, Keynes, Hansen, and others, had produced an economics of the Golden Mean. One recent observer grabs its essence:

> Samuelson offered a balanced brand of economics that found mainstream support. While Samuelson (especially in the earlier editions) favored heavy involvement in "stabilizing" the economy as a whole, he appeared relatively laissez-faire in the microsphere, defending free trade, competition and free markets in agriculture. He was critical of Marx, weighed the burdens of the national debt, denied that war and price controls were good for the economy, wrote eloquently on the virtues of a "mixed" free-enterprise economy, suggested that big business may sometimes be benevolent . . . and questioned whether labor unions could raise wages. . . . This advice could often be summarized as an injunction to rely broadly on markets, but also to be aware that markets might fail in many cases, thus creating a situation where government intervention could be justified.[4]

Thus, was born the elaborate "neoclassical synthesis," a dynamic combination of free markets and government stabilization policy that reigns to this day as the controlling brain of modern economic society. When well-dressed investment bankers prattle on, in TV interviews, about what the

Fed ought or ought not do, macroeconomic stabilization policy is what they're talking about. What distinguished the neoclassical synthesis from all earlier systems was that Samuelson wrote it in the high-precision code of mathematics, which had previously been relegated to back-of-the-envelope status in explaining economic ideas. Thus, Paul Samuelson updated and refined economics, raising it from its high-buckle Scottish Enlightenment origins to a bow-tie Boston-based science, and demystifying and democratizing its principles for application by businesses and governments everywhere. As *The Economist* noted after the great book's fiftieth anniversary:

> It is difficult to exaggerate the worldwide impact of Mr. Samuelson's "Economics." . . . Although Mr. Samuelson claimed that he had no great message to impart in his first textbook, he was actually introducing, explaining, and advocating the then revolutionary economics of John Maynard Keynes. Hence the book reflected a belief in the need for active government and scepticism about market outcomes. Although it has evolved enormously over 15 editions, that tone remains.[5]

The fiercely smart young economist's book replaced all comers as the operative text in modern economics after the Second World War. But if that were all there was to this success story, it would be relatively unremarkable, given that economics is but one subject among many in the smorgasbord of academic offerings, and great textbooks abound throughout the fields that make up academia.

Making Book

Samuelson's maiden year, 1948, was a banner year for the textbook business. The troops who returned from the war were going to colleges and universities; they needed textbooks, and publishers were only too happy to oblige. Several classic textbooks were published: Ernest Hilgard's *Introduction to Psychology,* Garrett Hardin's *Biology,* Kingsley Davis's *Human Societies,* and perhaps the longest-delayed revision of all time, the second edition of Alfred Kroeber's *Anthropology* (its first edition had been published in 1923). Even those otherworldly philosophers, the anthropologists, seemed to be responding to incentives, as the economists might well have predicted.

Fueled by government spending and postwar scientific research, academic publishing was a literary boomtown. But even amid the gold rush, Samuelson's economics book carved out a singular, extraordinary, and enduring place for itself. Why? The answer goes beyond the timeliness of Samuelson's neoclassical synthesis and the widely acclaimed brilliance of his presentation. Economics, perhaps alone among all the social sciences, had come of age as a modern subject, and it constituted knowledge that was useful, to boot. Read my lips: *It helped make ends meet.* This may sound unscholastic, but for those intent on raising the civic discourse, it is vital to note that moral sentiments and money go hand in hand. As a million fundraisers, charity drives, and collection baskets attest, and as Adam Smith prophesied, wealth greases the wheels of benevolence.

No matter how handy the history books were in helping students understand their past—or the psychology books, their minds; the biology books, their bodies; the politics books, their leaders; the sociology books, their neighbors—economics was the one subject with something explicit to say about their wallets. The opportunities for making ends meet—and then some—were growing in the postwar prosperity, and the premium placed on big brains as opposed to big backs had grown as well. Samuelson helped provide—well, The Instructions—for making one's way in the professions and in the world.

Since the 1940s, workers of the industrial world have steadily abandoned their blue collars for white ones, their plowshares for calculators, their small towns for cities, their tractors for autos, and their rent checks for mortgage payments.[6] As this transformation has progressed, professionals, tradespeople, and bureaucrats have had to learn to speak two languages: English and economics. The fields of management, law, finance, government, small business, health care, transportation, communications—and the related professions such as civil and environmental engineering—are based explicitly, in part, on economics. The better developed these professions have become, the more explicitly their economic foundations have revealed themselves. Beneath every acronym-studded institutional variation—SEP, IDA, HMO, BBC, NBA, WTO, ESOP, NRA—is an undercurrent of economic principles. Even civic participation increasingly requires some appreciation of the basic ideas and terminology of economics. Woe betide the politician who can't talk the market patter. Recall, if you will, a certain campaign slogan: "It's the economy, stupid."[7]

What Paul Samuelson provided was not only a theoretical primer for this billowing economic culture, but a grammar, a lexicon, a rhetoric, a handbook, a daily missal for market communicants. Some academic fields come and go like fads and fancies, but no cohort of students since the new gold rush of 1948 has ventured forth without The Instructions of Samuelson or one of his many variants. The rival textbooks have been shorter and longer; harder and easier; duller and livelier; more Keynesian and less Keynesian, but Samuelson's was and remains the standard by which all successors and competitors are judged.

Mad Hatters

As I mentioned previously, when I was a newly minted economics editor at McGraw-Hill, a group of my colleagues and I traveled to Boston to celebrate the publication of a book of essays collected by Paul Samuelson's colleagues and former students—the Jedi Knights of economics. That event in suburban Boston, at MIT's Endicott House, inspired us to recall the history of this most famous of modern textbooks, a history that goes to the essence of the publishing culture—itself a part of the Samuelson story.

William Styron, who served briefly as a McGraw-Hill editor in 1947, painted a colorless picture of his employer in his autobiographical novel, Sophie's Choice. According to Styron's self-same narrator Stingo, McGraw-Hill was an "archconservative . . . paradigm of American business," and every employee who worked in the building (called "the Green Monster" though far from Fenway Park) on Forty-Second Street was outfitted in a gray flannel Weber & Heilbroner suit, an Arrow button-down shirt, and—the most important part of the uniform—a soft-brimmed businessman's hat.[8]

Decades later, McGraw-Hill's reputation for sound, conservative business management was still intact. The men still wore their gray suits and buttondowns, but their hats had long been off to Paul Samuelson, whose book laid the foundation for the publisher's impressive record of success in economics and related fields.

Styron's characterization of his employer bespeaks a company in which publishers took the business side of publishing every bit as seriously as they did the artistic side. The history of McGraw-Hill paralleled the rise of American industry and technology from the early twentieth century onward, even as its books and other publications told its story. As technology progressed and business prospered, so did the fortunes of McGraw-Hill. Yet, never was this publisher's fortune greater than in 1945, when its sales representative in Boston—one Basil Dandison, no doubt turned out in his flannels and hat—discovered a proposed book from a young MIT assistant professor.

Curtis Benjamin, the McGraw-Hill executive who signed the Samuelson contract, hardly could have foreseen the seismic impact this author and his book would have on his firm, any more than the administrators of MIT might have been able to predict the glory Samuelson would produce for what was then a backwater department of "industrial economics." MIT economics would later take its place at the top of the field, claiming among its graduates a remarkably disproportionate share of economic leaders from Washington to Wall Street to Westminster to Warsaw. Samuelson not only changed a science and our way of looking at the world, but, by making both his department and his publisher synonymous with economics, he changed the very institutions that sow the seeds of knowledge—the institutions that perennially deliver The Instructions—and the institutions of business and government in which The Instructions are applied and tested.

Speaking in Tongues

Samuelson's powerful impact became clear by 1950, the second anniversary of his book's life and the year in which his publisher boasted publication of two other famous if totally unrelated works: *Boswell's London Journal, 1762–1763,* and *The Betty Crocker Picture Cookbook* (the Dr. Spock—or Samuelson—of homemaking). The Samuelson textbook had been adopted in more than 200 colleges and universities.

Upshifting its way into the next decade, *Economics* entered its fourth edition and had sold more than 750,000 copies in nine countries. In 1959,

Business Week published a three-page retrospective, "The Economist with a Best-seller," citing the by-now–commonplace litany of superlatives to describe the book, its history, and its illustrious author. What is remarkable is that the article used the very language popularized by Samuelson—terms such as inflation, unemployment, and fiscal and monetary policy—in its discussion of the author and book. The man from MIT had laid claim to our vernacular, without our realizing it.[9]

Meanwhile, McGraw-Hill's fleet of economics textbooks was growing into a full-fledged navy. Samuelson's book was both its flagship and aircraft carrier. Dozens of other publishers got into the swim, but make no mistake—Samuelson was the set of Instructions by which all others were judged.

In 1967, *The New York Times Book Review* published a lengthy article to mark the coming of Samuelson's eighth edition. The author of the article, a freelance writer named Bennett Kremen, described the nearly unanimous familiarity he discovered Samuelson's book to have enjoyed among a group of young customers at a bar on New York's Upper East Side, and then posited this insight: The book that had earlier influenced a culture had effectively become an artifact of that culture. He buttressed his point by citing another article in which the author had noted that Samuelson's *Economics,* having been translated into some 20 languages, had given the entire world a second language—economics.[10] Indeed, as recently as 1959, at a world conference of economists, the only common tongue spoken was the text of Samuelson. Samuelson had become the lingua franca.

The Revision Thing

Foremost among the economics lessons Samuelson taught his publisher was the old economist's saw: There is no free lunch. The editors, designers, and production people who worked with Samuelson to bring out one successful edition after another spoke a language of their own, comprising four words: "Let's get it done." Stories of Samuelson's cliff-hanger schedules might never have been translated into Japanese or Russian or Spanish, but within the folklore of publishing, they are as legendary as the book that spawned them. Michael Elia, the editor who managed several editions into publication during the 1970s, to this day shows interested parties the "Samuelson Revision Tool," a handle from a department store suit box that he would use when carrying packages crammed with manuscript and proof, always rushing from New York to Boston, publisher to compositor, taxi to airport.[11]

In 1998, long after now-antiquated devices like the Samuelson Revision Tool had given way to the instantaneous communications technology of the Internet, the *Wall Street Journal* announced the publication of a great new economics textbook by yet another tweedy, bespectacled Boston-based economist, N. Gregory Mankiw. Mankiw, who received his PhD from the same MIT economics department made famous by Samuelson, had earned a well-deserved stellar reputation by updating, extending, and refining the self-same neoclassical synthesis that Samuelson had raised to public prominence a half-century before. Mankiw's book was heralded for its combination of intellectual virtuosity and clarity.

Soon after its publication, Mankiw's work became a most popular and widely adopted book. Its success spread from North America throughout the world, even into places where the message of modern economics was but a faint murmur as recently as a generation ago.

After a half century, the basic principles of economic science, as etched by Paul Samuelson and honed by two generations of his successors, had become thoroughly embedded in the language of commerce and government. The Instructions, it seemed, were working.

3

The Warning

For my part, I think that Capitalism, wisely managed, can probably be
made more efficient for attaining economic ends than any alternative system yet in sight, but that in itself it is in many ways extremely objec-
tionable. Our problem is to work out a social organization which shall be
as efficient as possible without offending our notion of a satisfactory way
of life.

John Maynard Keynes

If socialism failed, it was for political, more than economic, reasons; and
if capitalism is to succeed it will be because it finds the political will and
means to tame its economic forces.

Robert Heilbroner

The rites of autumn, for roughly the past half century, have included
the successful outfitting of fresh-faced college students with their
copies of The Instructions—Samuelson's *Economics* or one of its
offspring. But these rites are never complete without sweatshirts, backpacks, and at least one other economics book, Robert L. Heilbroner's *The
Worldly Philosophers,* yet another paean to Adam Smith's legacy. First
published in 1953, and now long familiar in its paperback edition, the
Heilbroner book provides the historical reply to Samuelson's scientific
song. In recounting the evolution of economic thought, Heilbroner inter-
weaves stories of the giants of the field, beginning with Adam Smith.

Like Samuelson's book, which is estimated to have sold well over 4,000,000 copies and been translated into 41 languages since its appearance (not counting the bootlegged editions), Heilbroner's has achieved gaudy sales numbers, having broken the 2,000,000 copies milestone when its sixth edition was published in the 1990s.[1] And, like Samuelson himself, Mr. Heilbroner—an octogenarian economist at the New School for Social Research in his native New York City, and a resident of the same Upper East Side neighborhood where the pub revelers all know their Samuelson—has achieved celebrity through the popular reputation of his book. As Heilbroner says, *The Worldly Philosophers* ". . . has lured, I am told, tens of thousands of unsuspecting victims into a course on economics."[2]

Unlike Samuelson, whose text is an acrobatic combination of words, graphs, equations, and sub- and superscripts suspended over a bed of tightly packed footnotes, Heilbroner is all smooth prose, laid gracefully over a rolling account of lives, events, and ideas. Adam Smith, David Ricardo, John Stuart Mill, Karl Marx, Alfred Marshall, and others stride forcefully across Heilbroner's story like the giants they are. But this is where the reverie ends, because what booksellers don't tell you when you walk away with your new books, backpacks, laptops, and T-shirts is this: Samuelson provides the means to a technical mastery of economic principles—The Instructions—but Heilbroner issues a Warning: Capitalism throughout its history and despite the herculean visions of worldly philosophers since Adam Smith, inevitably contains the seeds of its own disintegration. Accordingly,

> The scenarios of the worldly philosophers are time-bound. Smith's vision . . . holds not the slightest hint of the industrial capitalism that was to replace the pin factory with the steel mill. Ricardo's remarkable model . . . did not envisage the England of Alred Marshall's time, fifty years into the future. . . . By the time of Mill's death in 1870, it was already clear that his imagined stationary state was only a figment. . . . Marx's prognosis was more resistive to the erosion of events, but . . . one could see in the Great Depression both the confirmation of his scenario and its disconfirmation. . . . Keynes lived almost long enough to discover that buttressed capitalism would develop its own dysfunction. . . . Schumpeter's general predictions, although still relevant, already show signs of becoming obsolete.[3]

The World We Have Found

Robert Heilbroner delights in capitalism, but regards it as an ever-mutating and self-mutilating creature—a cursed wonder that, for all its grandeur, still rewards too few and punishes too many; a hopeful monster fraught with dread. He sees each of its epochs—mercantile, preindustrial, industrial, state supported, and technological—as pulverizing the very foundations and assumptions that brought it into being. Each new phase frames an emergent set of difficulties for which economics and its kindred social sciences must scramble to provide answers. Heilbroner regards those answers as increasingly pale and conditional because each set of answers has ever-diminishing social value. His prognosis for the market for future worldly philosophers is not encouraging.

In the end, Heilbroner, a charming storyteller, is a dark messenger. The moral of his history is that The Instructions, no matter how cleverly packaged by Samuelson and his scientific offspring, by all the king's theorists and all the king's quants, are but an inadequate and evanescent reply to the violent and ever-shifting undertow of capitalism. In a Heilbroner world, economists, like some benighted technocratic warriors of the night, are always fighting the last battle. *The Worldly Philosophers* is not the angriest attack on capitalism, nor the deepest, boldest, or most profound, but it is probably the most widely read and the most enduring. Polanyi and Veblen, Galbraith and Lange, have receded into the library stacks. But copies of Heilbroner are still stacked up at the bookstores, still leaving with the freshmen, along with the backpacks and sweat socks.

House of Nerds

To read the many books that Robert Heilbroner has written since *The Worldly Philosophers* is to sense a man saying not only, "I told you so," but also wondering why no one seems to be paying any attention to the social and political dilemmas that continue to beset capitalism—such as deepening inequality in the presence of soaring affluence. These dilemmas are brought about by the very success of economics, by its slavish obsession with the details set out in The Instructions at the expense of a more expansive and critical worldly philosophy.

Heilbroner and his colleague William Milberg excoriate their colleagues for "the extraordinary combination of arrogance and innocence with which mainstream economics has approached the problems of a nation that has experienced twenty years of declining real wages, forty percent of whose children live in 'absolute' poverty, and which has endured an unprecedented erosion of health, vacation, and pension benefits."[4]

Critics who scorn economics because of its too-easy embrace of the property rights, efficient markets, free trade, and chips-fall-where-they-may ethic, herald Heilbroner's admonition and echo it. Mainstream economists, only slightly bemused by this criticism from within the ranks, stick for the most part to their scientific knitting. Indeed, one prominent economist has fired back at Heilbroner for failing to recognize that the subject matter of economics has little to do with capitalism per se, and more to do with the broader analysis of human behavior under any set of social conditions, of which capitalism is only one.[5]

Once More, with Feeling

Yet Heilbroner's Warning does not recede quite so easily. Capitalism today stands as the triumphant engine of productivity around the world. At the same time, as critics such as Heilbroner are only too quick to note, it is still feared, hated, resented, and castigated as heartless by those injured or left behind by the swift pace of development. Much of the world goes to bed hungry at night. In the debate over free trade—perhaps the central pillar of modern economics and a rallying flag for supporters of Adam Smith—restless protesters, no matter how wrong-headed in their economics, remind the industrialized nations that capitalism is, at best, a work in progress. Witness, at the millenium, the Battle of Seattle; the trouble at the World Trade Organization and in Genoa; the opposition to trade with China; and demonstrations by environmentalists in Europe who declare, with their placards, "Capitalism is death."

Beyond the huddled masses, even capitalism's greatest beneficiaries, the well-scrubbed classes of the well-off nations, suffer the low-grade side effects of its success: mindless consumerism, rampant materialism, an unquenchable desire for bigger boats and better toys, and the reduction of so many of life's vital decisions to mere calculations in an Excel spreadsheet.

Note the number of rich and middle-class kids who still head to the psychic hinterlands or into drugs or sex or music in search of Meaning or something that closely resembles it.

For all its pungency, this dilemma is nothing new. Over 200 years ago, Adam Smith wrote—and kept rewriting—*The Theory of Moral Sentiments*. He was driven by concern that commercial society's relentless drive for profit would be so destructive to justice that its productive miracles would ultimately succumb to public outrage. In his book, Robert Heilbroner titles a chapter "The Wonderful World of Adam Smith." Smith himself didn't always think it was wonderful.

The economic engine of capitalism brings too many good things to life, in seemingly miraculous ways, for us even to consider shackling, much less replacing it. Comparable grand designs—communism, socialism, corporatism, and other variations on the theme of central planning—have ended in wreckage. Capitalism works only because it has managed to create and sustain institutions that balance the service of self-interest with the greater good, broadly construed. Still, in its darker hours, it appears no more than a plant closing or a dot-com crash away from the edge of immorality produced by other, more dysfunctional systems.

Robert Heilbroner worries about this state of affairs and laments the abandonment of economic society's collective center. He sees the common good and the social order left to the reckless impulse of the market, which has its pedal to the floor and is asleep at the wheel. He perceives a "crisis of vision" in economic direction, and he turns to the Visible Hand of government intervention at the national level to check the lurching machinery of the market. His unnamed hero seems to be a new John Stuart Mill, maybe even a new Karl Marx, who finally gets the economics of socialism to work.

Heilbroner is right to insist that capitalism requires, or even demands, the unrelenting attention of would-be worldly philosophers working in the realm of large-scale solutions. Yet his pessimism about the reduction of economics to a house of technically obsessed microspooks blind to The Big Picture is badly overstated. He is missing the trees for the forest. While we may have seen the last of titans like Adam Smith, the reconstitution of capitalism as both a moral and a market system is, in my view, well within the grasp of the often remote, if not quite invisible, hands of today's economists—with a little help from their more philosophic friends.

Given his contempt for those he considers the equation-obsessed followers of Samuelson, Robert Heilbroner sees little likelihood that a new worldly philosophy is in the offing. But he does not consider the possibility that many of today's challenges—from the expansion of health care, through the preservation of the environment, the revival of the cities and civic life, and the reconstruction of developing and transitional societies—might yield less to the gestures of gigantic central economic programs deployed at the national level than to new and daring smaller-scale economic policy initiatives designed to expand capitalism's bounty, developed and tested in a thousand different cultural settings, and channeled to ever larger and more diverse segments of society.

For all the good that national governments can and must do to support the general welfare, at the end of the day the primary engine of social progress may reside in the intellectual DNA of capitalism itself—that is, in the wealth of economic notions that, when properly deployed, coordinate human striving and sympathy. If Robert Heilbroner teaches us anything, it is that the power of commercial society comes not solely from the material magic of the market's Invisible Hand, nor from the guiding hand of government, but from the minds of his heroes and their successors. Locating the code of these ideas is the real challenge for the next worldly philosophers. Their best role model remains Adam Smith.

4

Little Platoons

*All the members of human society stand in need of each other's assis-
tance, and are likewise exposed to mutual injuries. Where necessary assistance is reciprocally afforded from love, from gratitude, from friendship,
and esteem, the society flourishes and is happy. All the different members of it are bound by the agreeable hands of love and affection, and are,
as it were, drawn to one common centre of mutual good offices.*

Adam Smith

*The reality of economic life is that pure individualistic market exchange
invoked in the usual defense of laissez-faire has been supplanted by many
institutions that allow collective action. Each of these institutions represents an attempt to take advantage of the opportunities for mutually beneficial coordinated action that are presented by the world in which we
live. . . . Each builds on or emulates at least some of the strengths of the
market: the push to do better that comes from competing against rivals,
the pull that comes from opportunities for individual gain, the diversity
that comes from having many individuals and organizations working in
parallel to achieve a given end, and the discipline that comes from clearly
enforced criteria for success and failure.*

Paul M. Romer

In his 1991 epilogue to the sixth edition of *The Worldly Philosophers*,
Robert Heilbroner noted that the next epoch of capitalism will be
global and technological.[1] Don't blink. His prediction has taken shape

before our very eyes. The tools that are especially relevant to economic activity now are "weightless," to borrow a term made popular by economist and writer Diane Coyle. The communications and information economy—all beeps, blips, pulses, and pips—has taken the high ground.[2]

When we think of the forces that trigger contemporary economic progress, our minds quicken to cascading innovations such as the highly sophisticated, financially engineered range of investment technologies that have provided many millions of people with the opportunity to convert the bounty of economic prosperity into greater well-being for themselves and their families.

We also think of computer-augmented systems of production that streamline the creation and distribution of new products—from baseball gloves designed in Osaka and manufactured in Malaysia, to stadiums in Baltimore, to games telecast through a cyberspace that is being sliced and sold to the telecoms by way of newly implemented economic auctions engineered by economists who cut their intellectual teeth on Samuelson's Instructions. Nor should we forget the profoundly critical role information technology is playing in the stimulation and spread of research that will gradually—or more rapidly, we hope—help to reduce the levels of illness, hunger, disease, pollution, and deprivation around the globe, and address some of the concerns registered in Heilbroner's Warning.

Not coincidentally, all this high-tech high-stepping finds its antecedents in the time-encrusted eighteenth-century metaphors of Adam Smith and his fellow worldly philosophers. The garages and offices and labs that incubate today's wealth of nations, and upon which our society must depend for a continued expansion of prosperity, have evolved from a seemingly archaic and exceedingly humble exercise—namely, Adam Smith's discussion of how to make *pins,* of all things! A quick tour of Smith's pin factory provides us with a point of entry for connecting the central insight of his economic system with his discussion of "the contagious effects of good company," his civic sociology.

Land of a Thousand Pins

If Adam Smith had stopped writing his long and labyrinthine *Wealth of Nations* after the first chapter, his contribution to the economic prosperity of commercial society would still be secured forever because his opening pages contain such a gigantic insight into the infrastructure of capitalism: the division of labor. Authors of economics books seeking to engage readers should dwell on this most potent of sentences: "The greatest improvement in the productive powers of labour, and the greatest part of the skill, dexterity, and judgment with which it is anywhere directed, or applied, seems to have been the effects of the division of labour."[3]

Smith instructed his readers in something taken so thoroughly for granted today that it seems second nature to us: the specialization of work. He explained that a score of workers, each specializing in some small aspect of the pin-making process, could make more pins in a given time period than one poor soul charged with mining the ore, building the furnace, firing the smelter, making the alloy, crafting the mold, pouring the tin, and waiting until he has made the pin, and then selling it—and all without a Web site.

Smith's conception of the division of labor, exemplified by the pin factory, has helped to define much of modern economic life. Abetted by the codification, in law, of secure property rights, the division of labor governs the activities of corporations, industries, bureaucracies, trading regions, lemonade stands, and kindred institutions all over the world. It allows the products of our labor to be leveraged efficiently into economic growth through the global network of product and capital markets. Countries that long resisted joining the international division of labor, opting instead for the Leviathan-like central planning orthodoxy of Lenin, now clamor to get on board. But while Smith's division of labor—his pin factory—is perhaps the most famous social invention to have emerged in modern commercial society and been captured, codified, and studied by economists, it is not the only such force.

Similar social inventions have long proved market society's most compelling catalysts: grist for both Samuelson's scientific models and Heilbroner's worldly philosophy. An oddity is that these social inventions have, until recently, gotten so little ink. The lessons of economic progress usually flow from stories of physical inventions—everything from horse stirrups to printing presses to gunpowder to iron smelters to microchips. But hardware innovations such as these deliver little payoff to the wealth of nations if they lack the necessary accompanying social software:

- *Contracts,* developed in the letters of introduction that allowed mutually anonymous medieval merchants to conduct commerce across unfamiliar cultures and provided the basis for commercial law and, indeed, the modern trading state;[4]
- *Insurance,* including the technologies of risk management reflected in the early bonds and other instruments that enabled venturesome entrepreneurs to surround the globe and connect previously strange cultures;[5]
- *Patents,* encoded in the system of property rights that provides the architecture for the orderly dissemination of modern ideas;
- *Transparent accounting principles,* built into the generally accepted business and financial rules that enable vastly different—and distant—societies to partake in the global financial system;
- *Titles,* and the accompanying array of legal instruments, from home mortgages through retirement accounts, designed to enable average citizens to amass transferable, tradable wealth;[6]
- *Corporate charters,* which grew out of the joint stock companies of Smith's time and enable businesses to undertake risky enterprises while protecting individual shareholders from financial calamity;
- *Research and development initiatives*—universities, military and corporate research divisions, private R&D departments—which provide support and structure for the application of new technologies that are necessary to nurture social and economic progress.

To the same degree as the physical production technologies which have harnessed the power of oil, steam, coal, steel, and silicon into economically useful products, these social inventions catalyze new ideas into economic processes and thereby constitute market society's intellectual working capital. Deriving new social inventions—such as electronic spectrum auctions, or markets in pollution rights, or employee stock ownership plans, or vouchers for the conversion of communistic methods to market enterprise—is the grand obsession of many of today's finest economists and is the truly weightless legacy of Adam Smith.

Such inventions both animate and thrive on that single most vital of forces: economic growth. As economist Paul Romer has said of the connection between innovation and growth, "No amount of savings and investment, no policy of macroeconomic finetuning, no set of tax and spending incentives can generate sustained economic growth unless it is accompanied by the countless large and small discoveries that are required to create more value. . . ."[7] Along with the stuff of steel and silicon, these inventions include strategy, teamwork, cooperation, and leadership. Though partisans who debate public issues inevitably haggle over having more—or less—government in the distribution of goods and services, history instructs us that the real leaps forward—those that yield true progress—come from new intellectual breakthroughs, not political logrolling.[8]

What They Didn't Tell You, 101

Because the social inventions embodied in the image of the pin factory matter so greatly to the expansion of capitalism, so do the knowledge-producing enterprises that cultivate them. Increasingly, vital social as well as physical inventions are incubated in the ever-evolving global web of information and technological industries, universities and foundations, R&D labs and consulting firms, media outlets and communications enterprises—and other such institutions that constitute the floating pin factories of the weightless world. These enterprises also reflect an invaluable source of social capital in the form of new applied knowledge.

However, the activity that spawns these "countless large and small discoveries" of useful knowledge does not occur in isolation behind the glass doors of high-tech firms or the gated walls of scientific establishments. It depends on even deeper foundations. These structures are the markers of civil society: the arts councils, classrooms, parish halls, baseball fields, choirs, soup kitchens, and corner stores where the earliest lessons of "skill, dexterity, and judgment," to use Smith's terms—traits vital to the execution of knowledge-based operations—are taught. These structures help catalyze the basic materials of social capital into economic activity of the competitive and cooperative kind. They complement the metal-on-metal industrial mechanisms of economic progress in the same way that the second strand of the double helix completes the evolutionary structure of genetic material.

Economics à la Samuelson may provide the operating system for the economics of capitalism. Economics à la Heilbroner may sound a useful warning of capitalism's episodic fragility. But capitalism is not only about economics—nor has it ever been—any more than business is only about greed. Capitalism is also about culture. It comprises norms, mores, attitudes, folkways, and codes of conduct. Max Weber, a German economist and social philosopher who lived a century after Smith but didn't make the cut as one of Heilbroner's worldly philosophers, captured the *cultural* character of capitalism in this passage from his classic work, *The Protestant Ethic and the Spirit of Capitalism:*

> The impulse to acquisition, the pursuit of gain, of money, of the greatest possible amount of money, has itself nothing to do with capitalism. This pursuit exists and has existed among waiters, physicians, coachmen, artists, prostitutes, dishonest officials, soldiers, brigands, crusaders, gamblers, and beggars—among "all sorts and conditions of men," in all times and in every land on earth where the objective possibility of it has existed or exists. This naïve conception of capitalism ought to be given up once and for all in the nursery school of cultural history. Unbridled avarice is not in the least the equivalent of capitalism, still less of its "spirit." Capitalism may actually amount to restraint, or at least rational tempering, of this irrational impulse.[9]

A vibrant and expansive capitalism depends to a large extent on public policies designed to support the network of mediating institutions that cultivate this "rational tempering" of the acquisitive urge, or, in Smith's term, "self-command." As reflected in the investigations of Tocqueville, Weber, Jane Jacobs, Robert Putnam, and Glenn Loury, these mediating structures provide the civic circuitry necessary for the cultivation and maintenance of the virtues reflected in notions such as "rational tempering." As Putnam notes, referring to his well-scrutinized Italian cities:

> Some regions of Italy, such as Emilia-Romagna and Tuscany, have many active community organizations. Citizens in these regions are engaged by public issues, not by patronage. They trust one another to act fairly and obey the law. Leaders in these communities are relatively honest and committed to equality. Social and political networks are organized horizontally, not hierarchically. These "civic communities" value solidarity, civic participation, and integrity. And here democracy works.[10]

These mediating structures help to build the foundations of reciprocity, self-governance, and shared values: how to give as well as take, to pass as well as shoot, to hit as well as catch, to act as well as sing, to lose as well as win. Any executive worth his or her salt knows that the really hard lessons of teamwork and leadership emerge not full-sprung from the boardroom but gradually from the classroom, the dining room, and the locker room.

Mediating structures did not escape the philosophical sights, or the poetic scope, of Adam Smith and his Enlightenment contemporaries. Smith's explorations of nonmarket institutions, and of the social virtues they propagate, are massive, and they are woven into his conception of economic society. He wrote extensively on the place of family, schools, town, city, church, and government in his blueprint for commercial society. But it was his admirer and fellow philosopher Edmund Burke who bestowed upon these mediating structures the memorable name "little platoons." They are civic counterparts of Smith's pin factories.[11]

Burke's Law

The pin factories of today's industrial capitalism, from corporate organizations through executive seminars through R&D labs, are highly progressive in character, but, ironically, the mediating institutions of civil society are rather more traditional in cast. Capitalism deploys its economic activity around the globe and into outer space, but the social networks, the "moral communities," upon which it depends, conduct their incubating work largely at the local level. Despite the breathtaking modernist protestations of worldly philosophers from Karl Marx onward, we human beings, no more Promethean today than we were at the dawn of Enlightenment, still need informal channels and local connections to sustain us.[12] This connectivity unites places as wildly different as my old West Philadelphia stomping grounds, Putnam's rather sexier Tuscan districts, brave new precincts like Silicon Valley, and other, more distant villages.

Bucolic images notwithstanding, why do such homespun "moral" institutions matter so greatly to the locomotive commercial society? Because, absent the social capital engendered by local mediating institutions and encoded in laws and moral norms passed from one generation to the next, the Invisible Hand (as noted earlier) may just as well be the Black Hand.

For Smith, the mediating institutions of community conditioned a person's ability to develop the habits necessary for effective participation in commercial society. According to Smith:

> This natural disposition to accommodate and assimilate, as much as we can, our own sentiments, principles, and feelings, to those which we see fixed and rooted in persons whom we are obliged to live and converse with, is the cause of the contagious effects of good and bad company. The man who associates chiefly with the wise and the virtuous, though he may not himself become either wise or virtuous, cannot help conceiving a certain respect at least for wisdom and virtue. . . .[13]

To the extent that "the contagious effects of good . . . company" in Smith's commercial society have survived the travails of two centuries, they have provided capitalism with a lifeline not only for economic prosperity, but for sustaining the civic wherewithal necessary for enlarging that success around the world—even in some of its colder corners, as the denizens of the former Soviet world are now learning. These contagious effects are, if anything, even more important to working-class and poorer communities than to already wealthy communities because they provide the poorer communities with the social capital they need for improving the lot of their offspring, complementing infusions of material resources. Indeed, Smith spoke explicitly about the responsibilities of the owners of businesses toward their workers as exemplars of behavior: "The owners of the great mercantile capitals are necessarily the leaders and conductors of the whole industry of every nation, and their example has a much greater influence upon the manners of the whole industrial part of it than any other order of men."[14] Tell that to the executives at Enron.

One contemporary observer puts it more positively when he says: "Law, contract, and economic rationality . . . must be leavened with reciprocity, moral obligation, duty to community, and trust, which are based in habit rather than rational calculation. The latter are not anachronisms in a modern society, but rather the sine qua non of the latter's success."[15]

Another critic—this one, an economist—is more direct and almost downright insistent on the matter: "I am proposing, in other words, that we stop sneering at the bourgeoisie, stop being ashamed of being middle class, and stop defining a participant in an economy as an amoral brute. . . . Even economists have learned by now that moral sentiments must ground a market."[16]

The Indiana Jones Dissent

Many—perhaps, most—economists have a hard time accepting the idea that the social capital has anything meaningful to do with the thrust of economic activity. Facts and figures at the ready, these economists typically argue that the standard factors of production—land, labor, capital, and, increasingly, technology—are much more reliable than folk tales about ways in which civic values or group psychology or some other such sociological green cheese either created or destroyed some episode of economic progress. The image that invariably comes to my mind in these exchanges is that of movie archaeologist Indiana Jones (in this case, an economist) confronting the saber-wielding swordsman (the social philosopher). Jones is momentarily dazzled by the swordsman's display of saberly showmanship, but then remembers he has a revolver, casually draws it, and blows the shrouded avenger away with cool efficiency.

For all the intellectual firepower they bring to these confrontations, economists protest too much. In the first place, certain economists have come to recognize the remarkable influence of noneconomic institutions in leveraging the factors of production that contribute to economic success or failure. For example, it's pretty widely agreed among economists that a subculture that puts a high premium on good schooling is likely to be economically successful in a commercial environment that rewards highly educated people. Economists of all political stripes single out education as a paramount antidote for poor and minority children seeking to mount the ladder of economic equity. Economists call this educational advantage *human capital*.

Thanks to University of Chicago economist and Nobel prize winner Gary Becker, work in human capital, from family dynamics through schooling, has been given strong pride of place on the economic research agenda.[17] Adam Smith would have approved. But, unless I'm mistaken, human capital finds impressive complements in social capital through the mediating functions of civic institutions such as schools and stable families—the contagious effects of good company, by any other name. It is also increasingly clear to economists that, in developing countries, the construction of legal systems, educational and health care systems, and honest, effective governments—all ingredients of social capital—is necessary to attract and retain economic capital.[18]

Secondly, economists sometimes overlook the tremendous amount of social capital that they hold as a profession. As high as the general level of technical competency is among economists, and as clear as the norms of scientific performance are, it would be hard to imagine that the actual quality and amount of the profession's academic output would be as great if it were not supported by a system of higher education and research like the American university culture that has been so effective in attracting and rewarding scientific talent.

For all their belief in private markets, many fine economists work to great effect in public institutions. Fiercely competitive as economists are, they display impressive collegiality and cooperation through their international system of working papers, seminars, and research networks. Their academic culture is a workshop culture, united by a common mathematical and conceptual language and connected by a wide-ranging and dense professional network stretching around the world—the National Bureau of Economic Research, the Centre for Economic Policy Research, and on and on. Alexis de Tocqueville would have been *very* impressed.

Finally, many economists have turned to the explicit study of the political, social, and organizational foundations of economic performance in their research. Scratch the New Political Economy, or the New Organizational Economics, or Law and Economics, and what you will find is the connective tissue of social capital.

Economists remain skeptical of the analytical concept of social capital, partly because it is tougher to run through the econometric data-grinder than raw demographic, production, and financial information—the more quantifiable products of economic activity. Social capital doesn't show up in the circular flow diagram. It's hard to reconcile with Samuelson's Instructions and Heilbroner's Warning. However, that no more means that economists should dismiss it as irrelevant than they would deny the social philosophy of Adam Smith.

As I think Smith himself would have appreciated, in our fluid and fast-breaking global marketplace, public policies and business strategies that connect the mediating and market institutions of modern capitalism are vital to today's worldly philosophy. The old trade-off between a progressive market culture and traditional social networks—cyberspace and the public square—seems a false choice. Although economists have not yet connected the dots within their theoretical models, these spheres exist as complements, not contenders. The key to an expansive capitalism is not in denying the importance of social capital, but in constantly seeking new ways to preserve and expand it within the structure of fiscal capital.

A Bridge Too Far?

The busy bridge that unites the pin factories of economic production and the little platoons of social capital is home to much interesting action found in today's leading economic research. *The Economist,* commenting on a wave of research being done by up-and-coming economists on everything from crime prevention to school choice to city living, notes that, "today's impressive young academics are using the tools of economics in fields on or beyond the traditional borders of their discipline." This research includes new and exciting investigations into health care, scientific research, street gangs, the cultivation of property ownership among the poor, voting and political representation, religious affiliation and membership, and investigations into the use of drugs, alcohol, guns, and media violence.[19]

This engagement with the full range of civic institutions has not sent economists off on a wild goose chase, but returned them to their roots: not to bury the incentive structure of capitalism, but to bend it toward more broadly civic ends, and to the stereoscopic vision of Adam Smith.

5

Enlightenment Wonk

To be amiable and to be meritorious; that is, to deserve love and to deserve reward, are the great character of virtue; and to be odious and punishable, of vice. But all these characters have an immediate reference to the sentiments of others. Virtue is not said to be amiable, or to be meritorious, because it is the object of its own love, or of its own gratitude; but because it excites those sentiments in other men.

Adam Smith, *The Theory of Moral Sentiments*

It is not from the benevolence of the butcher, the brewer, or the baker that we expect our dinner, but from their regard to their own interest. We address ourselves not to their humanity but to their self-love, and never talk of our own necessities but of their advantages. Nobody but a beggar chuses to depend chiefly upon the benevolence of his fellow-citizens.

Adam Smith, *The Wealth of Nations*

If Paul Samuelson and his successors have supplied the economic Instructions for operating capitalism and Robert Heilbroner has provided the Warning for interrogating it, Adam Smith gave capitalism its Bible, from which to draw its moral and material possibilities. His books, *The Wealth of Nations* and *The Theory of Moral Sentiments*, reside at the center of the capitalist canon like a pair of venerable stone tablets in an ancient sanctuary.

As is true of most enduring iconic doctrines, Smith's work is steeped in a mystery: How do individual people, each pursuing his or her own interests, contribute to the common good? This mystery has become a mantra: the market unites private interest and public welfare. This mantra has launched a thousand theses, arguments, policies, and reforms; started a couple of revolutions; and sold an awful lot of Adam Smith ties, to say nothing of books, and at least one television series. I'd like to have been his editor, if not his tailor.

Understanding Smith's mantra—the enigmatic proposition that the service of self-interested behavior is necessary to the greater good and in enhancing its reach—propels the worldly philosophy forward. No reflection on economics—technical, journalistic, or otherwise—is complete without a consideration of the manic Scotsman whose words color the ongoing composition of capitalism.

The Anti-Anti-Hero

Within the pantheon of modern social philosophers—thinkers concerned with society's moral and political texture—it would be difficult to rate Adam Smith high on the style scale. Smith would have been a publicist's disaster and a casting director's nightmare. No leading man in Hollywood would ever fill the bill—unless you can imagine Rodney Dangerfield in buckle shoes, a flat hat, and knee breeches. An odd duck by just about any measure, Smith was a lifelong bachelor who lived with his mother. He was unsightly, with a bulbous nose, a fat lower lip, bulging eyes, twisted front teeth, a speech impediment, a nervous twitch, and a penchant for talking to himself in public. As he said endearingly of himself, "I am a beau only in my books."[1]

Adam Smith would have made for a psychiatrist's field day. He was almost dangerously absent-minded. He once tried to make a cup of tea from a pencil; on another occasion, he fell into a tanning pit while trying to explain an idea to a friend. On yet a third star turn, while walking through Edinburgh with a friend, Smith was saluted by a Scottish guard who presented him his pike. The suddenly mesmerized Smith returned the gesture by duplicating exactly the guard's every step and gesture with his cane. When he finally rejoined the real world, Smith was standing atop a long set of stairs and continued his chat with his friend as if nothing had happened. On another auspicious occasion, he walked the freezing beaches of his native Scotland for 15 miles, clad only in his nightshirt but spellbound and oblivious to the world.[2]

Adam Smith had little of the insurrectionist fervor of Karl Marx, even less of the dark liberating insight of Sigmund Freud, and none of the revolutionary rage of Vladimir Lenin. Smith's idea of economic emancipation was to encourage people to trade goods and services with one another. His notion of psychological freedom was to propose ways of turning the passions toward virtuous social behavior through the disciplinary power of the market and corresponding social institutions. Political freedom for Smith was best supported by an efficient government structured to promote the common good by clearly defined incentives.

Nevertheless, he has left us a legacy more enduring than any from his more firebrand philosophical brethren. Much as Adam Smith's insights into the economic system are central to economic thought, his insights into the relevance of social institutions—including, but not limited to, the market—and their part in shaping the virtues necessary for serving the common good, are too often overlooked. In fact, the true architect of the modern conception of commercial humanism—the original social capitalist—is none other than Smith himself.

Philosopher Wonk

In his effort to raise both the prosperity and the moral quality of society, Adam Smith combined the panoramic vision of an Enlightenment philosopher with the tireless attention to detail of a Beltway policy wonk. His intellectual style stands as the best available model for contemporary thinkers interested in hatching new ideas to integrate the economic institutions of a lively capitalism with the social virtues of a civil society.

Adam Smith's unique and lasting contribution to modern social thought is twofold. First, he assumed that people spend most of their time serving their own grubby self-interest; that is, he treated people as they really are, not as they are supposed to be. (The latter assumption was a stumbling block for clerical thinkers before him and has remained one for collectivists since.) Smith recognized, in humans, "a desire of bettering our condition, a desire which, though generally calm and dispassionate, comes with us from the womb, and never leaves us until the grave," and an equally compelling penchant to "truck, barter, and exchange."[3]

Second, Smith revealed himself to be an advocate of the common people—*all* of the common people—a sentiment unheard of before his time and badly implemented on many occasions in his wake. His policy prescriptions are structured to promote the greatest happiness for the masses—to cultivate, in his words, "that universal opulence which extends itself to the lowest ranks of the people."[4]

In exhaustive detail, Smith elucidated the incentive structures needed to exploit the self-interest of each person for the betterment of all, and the unanticipated consequences of perverse incentives that would end up serving none.

And it is Smith's plan, with its revolutionary implications, and his message and method (minus the nightshirt) that continue to provide the most invaluable intellectual template for today's most promising policy intellectuals, particularly the leaders of civic revival.

The Nebbish of the North

Adam Smith was born in Kirkcaldy, on the east coast of Scotland, in 1723. His father, who bore the same name, had been the Comptroller of Customs for Kirkcaldy until he died two months before the birth of his only son. Smith the younger was raised by his mother, whom he "loved and respected more than I ever shall love or respect any other person." Scotland in the eighteenth century comprised a strange brew of rural poverty with urban striving and intellectual firepower. Influenced by Calvinism, Roman law, and the French Enlightenment, Scottish intellectuals of Smith's time were a rare species. Labeled somewhat incongruously as "provincial cosmopolitans" by one observer, these Scots, owing to their truly multicultural intellectual universe, were more sophisticated thinkers than their English counterparts, and more influential. Adam Smith and his friend David Hume were leading lights of the Scottish Enlightenment.[5]

Smith entered the University of Glasgow when he was fourteen. There he made his first steps in moral philosophy under the influence of

Francis Hutcheson and was first exposed to the ideas of Hume and Bernard Mandeville, whose poem of 1714, "The Fable of the Bees," had stirred interest in the tantalizing notion that the pursuit of individual self-interest, "private vices," would lead to the betterment of society, "publick virtues." Smith would later expand, deepen, and modify this paradoxical relation as a central tenet of *The Wealth of Nations,* thereby laying the foundation for much of social science and policy analysis.

Smith went on to study at Oxford, where he read voraciously in Latin and Greek, in modern European literature, and in philosophy. The main product of his Oxford years was a paper on the psychological formation of the scientific mind. Consistent with the burgeoning culture of rationality that had come to dominate European thought since Isaac Newton, Smith attributed the scientific attitude to the quest for order within nature, a condition that he himself would seek in trying to understand social relations.[6]

And it was at Oxford that Smith registered his first revealing account of the unanticipated consequences of an incentive structure. He complained about a decline in the quality of education offered at the university and observed that Oxford and Cambridge had become havens in which "exploded systems and obsolete prejudices found shelter and protection, after they had been hunted out of every other corner of the world."[7]

Noting that the faculty made few demands of their students, Smith attributed this poor pedagogical atmosphere to the fact that faculty salaries had been endowed by wealthy benefactors, thus removing any incentive from the activity of teaching. This was in fact the first instance cited by Smith in which the incentive structure of an institution would have a profound and, in this case, deleterious latent effect on behavior.[8]

Smith returned to Scotland in 1748 and gave, in Edinburgh, a series of celebrated lectures on topics in philosophy. In 1751, he was granted the chair in moral philosophy at the University of Glasgow; in 1759, his first book, *The Theory of Moral Sentiments,* which derived from his work on ethics, was published. Until then, Smith had been preoccupied with moral philosophy, but his focus would soon change. In 1762, he was elected a burgess of the city of Glasgow by the city's merchant elite. The burghers of this bustling town of 23,000 were making bushels of money by importing American-grown tobacco and reselling it throughout the British Isles.

In Glasgow, in his new role, Smith developed his earliest insights into the effects of protectionist—or mercantilist—legislation on the health of the larger economy, and on the wealth of nations.[9]

In 1763, Smith was induced by Charles Townshend, a member of the English Parliament, to leave Glasgow to tutor Townshend's stepson, the Duke of Buccleuch, a two-year assignment that required Smith to accompany the young Duke on the Grand Tour. In Paris, at the height of the Enlightenment, he met Benjamin Franklin and François Quesnay. Quesnay was the leader of the French Physiocrats, a school of political economists who believed that agricultural investment and not the amassing of gold and silver, was the prime source of national wealth. The Physiocrats also served as the inspiration for the original input/output models of state planning.[10]

Smith admired the Physiocrats and would later enrich their (at the time) novel insight by establishing the principle that labor and manufacturing were the surpassing sources of the wealth of nations. And as his own compass shifted to the direction of political economy, Adam Smith began researching taxation and national economic welfare for a new book that would change his life. Policy innovations claimed his interest. A Philosopher Wonk was born.

Adam Smith returned to England in 1766 and worked, for a decade, on his new book, which he published in that most auspicious of years, 1776. *The Wealth of Nations* was a great success; its first printing sold out in six months. Thereafter, his reputation soared and his counsel was sought by the highest officials in England. He was made Commissioner for Customs in Scotland, a post that he held until his death in 1790, and an unlikely job for the man most responsible for advising leaders against the ill-conceived and destructive policies of protectionism. But Smith was *not* against *all* taxes, just those that distorted the productive power of the market.

Despite his active engagement in the political sphere, and the ample income he earned from his tutor's pension and his salary as Commissioner, Adam Smith left only a small estate, having quietly given away much of his money to charity. How poignant and ironic an ending for a man who had effectively united his interests in an effort to improve the wealth and condition of common people with a lifelong concern for exemplary behavior.[11]

What a Wonderful World It Would Be

Smith's astonishing vision led him to identify mechanisms (such as the market) that would channel basic human drives into greater social well-being, and to posit that effective participation in a free society assumed not self-sacrifice but self-interest—or, as they called it in Smith's day, self-love. Accordingly:

> Whoever offers to another a bargain of any kind, proposes to do this. Give me that which I want, and you shall have that which you want, is the meaning of every such offer; and it is in this manner that we obtain from one another the far greater part of those good offices which we stand in need of.[12]

This seemingly paradoxical connection between self-love and universal opulence sat at the center of Smith's system of social philosophy and has survived more than two centuries of attack from a never-ending army of critics. For many of these critics, that Smith connected the pursuit of private interest to service of the public good is as mysterious as some of Harry Houdini's better tricks. Luckily for us, Smith's system is easier to test than Houdini's. What makes it work? The pin factory, introduced in the previous chapter, provides the key. Here he is on the division of labor:

> One man draws out the wire, another straightens it, a third cuts it, a fourth points it, a fifth grinds it at the top for receiving the head; to make the head requires two or three distinct operations; to put it on is a peculiar business; to whiten it is another; it is even a trade by itself to put them into paper. . . . I have seen a small manufactory of this kind where ten men only were employed and where some of them performed two or three distinct operations. But though they were very poor, and therefore but indifferently accommodated with the necessary machinery, they could, when they exerted themselves, make among them about twelve pounds of pins in a day. There are in a pound upwards of four thousand pins of a middling size. Those ten persons, therefore, could make among them upwards of forty-eight thousand pins in a day. . . . But if they had all wrought separately and independently . . . they certainly could not each of them make twenty . . . perhaps not one pin a day. . . ."[13]

Imagine Smith, a professor of philosophy, stumbling and bumbling his way through a factory full of workers twisting, pulling, and pounding pins only to emerge with a remarkable insight: that every pin maker, each serving his own self-interest by exchanging his work for pay, could, through a proper division of labor, produce a vastly greater volume of pins than each working alone, thereby supercharging the nation's economic output. Simply and succinctly, Smith linked the self-interest of individuals to the welfare of the society and reflected, in a passage from *The Wealth of Nations:*

> . . . every individual, therefore, endeavors as much as he can to employ his capital in the support of his domestic industry. . . . He generally, indeed, neither intends to promote the publick interest, nor knows how much he is promoting it . . . he intends only his own gain, and he is in this, as in many other cases, led by an invisible hand to promote an end which was no part of his intention. . . . By pursuing his own interest he frequently promotes that of the society more effectually than when he really intends to promote it.[14]

The division of labor yielded more than just more pins and widgets. As Smith's factory-floor observations suggest, it also promotes technologies, specialization, expertise, dexterity, and improved machinery, thereby creating greater wealth and enriching the productive potential of the society. Self-interest, mediated by the division of labor, multiplied economic goods and, with them, the appetites to consume them and the resources to afford them. Subsequent analysts would remark that the wealth produced by Smith's system would yield greater equity as well. As the division of labor multiplies and divides, so do risk-taking, invention, innovation, and the market itself, which brings into its radius exponentially larger sectors of society.[15]

Adam Smith prized the market not only for its power as an engine of wealth, but also as a system of signals for setting prices and wages, regulating the supply and demand of product flows (fewer pins now, more staples later), and inducing risk and invention (snap buttons and self-sealing tape). Even as the market raised the wages of the working class through the accumulation of wealth, the number of workers borne by higher wages and better living conditions would increase, and competition among them would thus drive the wage rate back down toward, but not to, a level of subsistence.

As long as the market was allowed to operate freely and accumulation proceeded accordingly, the economy would expand and evolve, leading to increasing productivity and more and more jobs. Smith could not have foreseen the troubles confronted by market society in the future, but his was a starting point, not a resting place. As one observer comments, "*The Wealth of Nations* is a program for action, not a blueprint for Utopia."[16]

Globalization, Enlightenment-Style

Ultimately, Smith's motivation and interest can be pinpointed in his defense of free trade among nations against the kind of protectionist laws instituted by the jolly mercantilist elites of Glasgow and, later, in the lobbies of Parliament. After all, as a wag has conjectured, "What good are 10,000 pins if they cannot be traded because of restrictions or high transportation costs?"[17]

What held for a single pin worker also held for towns, cities, and even nations: the market mechanism, operating freely around the world, could only help to increase the wealth of nations. Smith sealed the case with what seems, over two centuries later, a rather obvious point: nations would gain from trade if they imported, from outside their borders, certain goods that would cost more for them to make at home.

Smith used the example of his own overcoat to drive home the point that workers and resources from all around the world—shepherds through button-makers through merchants—were necessary suppliers in the creation of this useful product. Moreover, "none of these laborers had to know each other, know Smith, or know why Smith wanted a coat. All they had to know was that the wage for shepherding or dyeing was high enough to make their labor worthwhile. . . ." Substitute cars or computers for overcoats and the point emerges in vivid contemporary relief.[18]

As was his wont, Adam Smith set out to defend his beloved market system by making another counterintuitive argument: Protectionism was not really protection at all. To the contrary, *trade* spurs the wealth of nations, increases the commonweal, regulates prices and wages, and harmonizes the relations among nations. Seen against a historic backdrop that featured the crumbling remnants of a medieval economic system that had placed a premium on maintenance of social hierarchy, domination of the poor, accumulation of silver and gold, and protection of local industries through high tariffs, Adam Smith's prescriptions for a division of labor and a policy of free trade delivered a powder keg.

But if his novel economic principles were not enough, Smith's campaign for free trade also reflected the humanity of a moral philosopher, a thinker concerned with the social implications of economic incentives and sanctions. In urging an English political leader to lift trade restrictions on the oppressed country of Ireland, Smith insisted that "to crush the Industry of so great and so fine a province of the empire, in order to favour the monopoly of some particular towns in England and Scotland, is equally unjust and unpolitic. . . . Nothing, in my opinion, would be more highly advantageous to both countries than this mutual freedom of trade. It would help to break down that absurd monopoly which we have most absurdly established against ourselves in favour of almost all the different classes of our own manufacturers."[19]

Note that Smith grounded his moral arguments in the rhetoric of economic self-interest. He appealed to the wallet, not the heart. He used a similar style of argument to press for the abolition of slavery. In addressing well-heeled elites, he argued that slavery made for a costlier economy than free labor because while slaveholders were responsible for the maintenance of their slaves, free laborers were responsible for maintaining only themselves. These moral concerns suggest that Smith saw in the market a hidden function, a *civilizing* force. Wearing his philosopher's hat (probably with earmuffs), Smith considered that civilizing force with utmost care, but he is little remembered for that consideration.[20] Some economists, sporting their renewed interest in institutional design, are heading in that direction today.

Commercial Humanism

Despite his decade of counting pins, tabulating tax rates, codifying the contents of his overcoat, and indulging in other such wonkish obsessions, Smith managed to remain the consummate moral philosopher. He continually revised his first book, *The Theory of Moral Sentiments;* a sixth edition was published just before his death. As is true for all moral philosophers, Smith concerned himself first and foremost with the betterment of society, which, for Smith, meant social mechanisms intended to reduce unvirtuous behavior—everything from murder and theft to adultery and cheating—and to promote virtuous behavior—the suppression of self-interest in favor of commitment to others. Sympathy, fairness, self-control, and duty form the core of such moral behavior. They are the foundations of trust, the base metal of civil society.

But whereas most earlier thinkers struggled to figure out ways to encourage people occupying positions of high social status—usually the religious or political leaders—to exhort the masses to improve their moral behavior, Smith turned the tables on his philosophic forbears and demonstrated how social institutions, properly outfitted with effective incentive structures, could improve the moral behavior of all ranks of society. In the words of one of his most insightful expositors,

> His purpose was to make people more decent by designing social institutions which draw the passions toward socially and morally beneficial behavior. This is the thread that runs through all his works: how the market can be structured to make the pursuit of self-interest benefit consumers; how the passion for the approval of others can make us act more selflessly; how public institutions can be structured to ensure that they deliver the services they are mandated to provide; how our desires for sex and for progeny can be structured by the law to create family institutions that foster self-control. . . .[21]

In considering the moral potential of commercial society, it is vital to remember that until Adam Smith's era of Enlightenment and democratic political liberalization, the vast majority of people lived not under freedom and self-determination, but under the velvet heel of princes, bishops, and other sovereigns. Smith supported the newly emerging political freedom that accompanied liberalization, but cautioned that it would work only to the extent that society could create a substrata of institutions that would channel people's passions toward the behavior necessary to the cultivation of a healthy civil order. Control of the passions required the exercise of virtues such as "prudence, vigilance, circumspection, temperance, constancy, (and) firmness."[22]

Smith responded to the political ferment in places like the American colonies by designing a system of civilizing institutions to replace the punitive, hierarchical, political institutions that had long held the masses subject. He envisioned a society unified not by political force, but by a dense and extensive network of markets and economic exchange—a commercial, as opposed to a coercive, society. In Smith's thinking, the market was the institution that not only converted the pursuit of self-interest into the wealth of nations, but, by disciplining its participants, promoted positive social behavior, including "economy, industry, discretion, attention, and application of thought."[23] For example, a carpenter's livelihood depends on the reputation he establishes through information shared by his customers, who, collectively, comprise the market. Knowing that his business is founded on the reputation he has established for himself in the market, the carpenter is far less likely to show up on jobs drunk than if there was no market to test his reputation and penalize him for his indulgence.

Not bad for an institution that has been maligned by a steady parade of critics, from Marxists to muckrakers to moviemakers. Typically, we don't see a connection between virtues and an incentive-driven system of markets, but it would be hard to envision a successful modern society without it. The moralizing function of the market linked *The Wealth of Nations* and *The Theory of Moral Sentiments*.

The connection that unifies markets and social networks forms the foundation of commercial humanism. In his book, *Adam Smith in His Time and Ours,* Jerry Z. Muller explains this connection concisely:

> Smith valued the market most because it promoted the development of cooperative modes of behavior and because it made men more self-controlled and more likely to subordinate their asocial passions to the needs of others. . . .[24]

The market, which brought people together in mutually beneficial economic exchange, was the most important institutional mechanism in Smith's design for a benevolent commercial society. The market offered a firewall against coercive political domination and a platform for greater benevolence achieved through enhanced wealth. But the story did not stop with a shoeshine and a smile.

The Impartial Spectator

The moral dimension aside, it is a mistake to think that is all there was to Adam Smith, a position conveniently espoused by libertarians intent on praising Smith and collectivists intent on burying him. Smith conjectured that commercial society made everyone "in some measure a merchant," but he was well aware that markets alone could not promote a decent life for the society of his time, and that they would, in fact, need to be complemented and tempered by countervailing influences.

In *The Theory of Moral Sentiments,* Smith limned the origins of human sympathy and reasoned that eagerness to win the approval of others—a psychological process that stimulates pride—initially disposes the self-interested person toward virtuous social behavior.

According to Smith, the search for social approbation manifests itself through "the Impartial Spectator," the part of the psyche that checks our primal instincts and enables us to get along with others by putting ourselves in their position. This vital social-psychological feature would later be elaborated in social science by Charles Horton Cooley as the looking-glass self and consecrated by none other than Sigmund Freud as the super-ego.[25]

The Impartial Spectator is the compass by which we modulate sentiments, adjust our reactions, and get along with others in a society based on the exchange of mutual self-interest. This aspect of Adam Smith's philosophy makes its way into few economics books, but economic life as we know it is inconceivable without it—except maybe among gangsters who secure their dealings through the threat of violence, but are clever enough to call this "respect." There is honor among thieves at least up to the point where the rule of retaliation replaces the rule of law. The bad guys have yet to sacrifice their silk shirts for Adam Smith neckties.

Smith reasoned that moral sentiments, modulated by the Impartial Spectator, were latent within almost everybody, but he argued that these sentiments only emerged in full and healthy expression through myriad social networks—that is, in our dealings with parents, siblings, friends, clergy, and other people who occupy vital roles in our lives. This is why the family—not to mention the other little platoons of civil society—was so important in Smith's design. As a small society unto itself, the family served as the necessary training ground for developing moral sentiments in children. So it was, and thus it remains, a master institution within an inclusive economic order—perhaps even more important today because of the sometimes baleful influence of the media, the automobile, and other modern contrivances.

It is indeed odd that the socializing role of the family is so conspicuously absent from much contemporary discussion about how "social capital" is formed. It may "take a village" (to borrow a phrase from Hillary Rodham Clinton) to raise a child, but are families any less valuable in socializing children in our fast-break society?

Smith also believed that it takes a village. For him, the civilizing roles played by schooling and religion were vital in that they inculcated the behavior necessary for successful participation in commercial society. Alexis de Tocqueville would inveigh later with similar insights on the civilizing role of participatory associations, or "It takes the Elks Club." Though Adam Smith was not much of a family man (he lived with his mom), nor an avid churchgoer (a deist), he regarded these and other institutions as essential for their *functional* value as moralizing agents in a free society.

Contrary to the view of many of capitalism's critics, nowhere did Smith advocate uninhibited freedom as a means to a wonderful world. Human passions were to be effectively governed by the Impartial Spectator in personal affairs and constrained by the discipline of markets and social networks in public exchange. Only then would free people be able to exercise their self-interest in an orderly culture.

Heaven Can Wait

Attacks on commercial society as a den of thieves divorced from anything resembling Adam Smith's benign vision have been legion. However, Adam Smith's cathedral of commercial humanism has survived not only criticisms, but even political and military threats from such powerful and elaborate alternative systems as communism, which dominated huge portions of modern populations, promised a better life for all, and ended up in monetary and moral bankruptcy. Perhaps because Smith built his system of commercial humanism on such a cold-eyed acknowledgment of human imperfection, his vision still stands and wide-eyed utopian schemes have fallen.

Commenting on one strain of Adam Smith's legacy, nineteenth-century American capitalism, political scientist John C. Mueller captures the importance of an oft-lampooned norm of commercial humanism—honesty in business dealings. He puts this bourgeois virtue to a serious stress test by choosing as his subject no less notorious a practitioner of the craft of self-enrichment than the famed circus impresario P. T. Barnum:

> In his spirited pamphlet and popular lecture, "The Art of Money Getting," Barnum stresses that integrity "is more precious than diamonds or rubies" and argues that "the most difficult thing in life is to make money dishonestly" since "no man can be dishonest without soon being found out" and "when his lack of principle is discovered, nearly every avenue to success is closed against him forever."[26]

As for contemporary commercial society, Mueller notes:

> On the contrary, capitalism systematically—though not equally—encourages and rewards business behavior that is honest, fair, civil, and compassionate, and . . . heroic. . . . I will not assume that capitalists are saintly . . . but rather that they are essentially impelled as envisioned by their caricaturists; their highest goal . . . is the acquisition of wealth. . . .[27]

The unstated point in this claim is that legally constituted markets help not only to produce wealth but to discipline buyers and sellers. Participants are forced to treat each other with a modicum of decency or be marked as cheats, crooks, or charlatans and banished forever from capitalism's cookie jar. P. T. Barnum understood this. Legions of Adam Smith's critics, struck by utopian visions, have not.

If P. T. Barnum preached what he practiced, Adam Smith also practiced what he professed. When Smith retired from teaching at the University of Glasgow in midsemester to become a tutor for young Buccleuch, he offered, to each of his students, financial compensation for having deprived them of the balance of his lectures![28]

The Market for Government

Adam Smith knew that the world he had devised was wonderful only by comparison with the myriad tyrannies of the past and the mercantilist schemes that threatened to dominate and oppress nations in his day. Thus, he insisted on a role for government: helping to promote the provision of universal opulence.

Smith understood governments in their historical context and explained their rise as an outgrowth of commercial society itself. The story goes something like this. As trade brought about the growth of cities, the royal and religious elites, who looked after the poor in return for labor and tithes, began to acquire greater amounts of the worldly goods made available by commerce and the arts. Early versions of *Martha by Mail* clearly were reaching palaces and monasteries.

The more these elites spent, the more tribute they tried to exact from the increasingly alienated poor. Central authorities, intent on defending the interest of increasingly successful merchants in return for taxation, stepped into the breach, also inadvertently providing the masses with protection. Thus, did the market create the government.

No Pollyanna, Smith called them like he saw them. He regarded government as a necessary instrument for setting standards of public behavior, taxation, and defense, and for administering a public sector to ensure these standards. As he said, ". . . the government in a civilized country is much more expensive than in a barbarous one; and when we say that one government is more expensive than another, it is the same as if we said that one country is farther advanced in improvement than the other."[29]

Adam Smith would not be surprised by the size and complexity of governments in the industrial societies of our time, but he would part company with many a big-government enthusiast on the manner in which government should be used. Smith insisted upon the achievement of public policy aims through a variety of measures—some public, some private, but always designed to achieve maximum impact through the most cost-effective means.

Smith saw the primary role of government in public life in strategic terms. His views on education constitute a case in point. One of Smith's most radical proposals was for the public provision of universal education in order to ease and enrich the lives of ordinary people, most of whom made their living from very hard and punishing work.

Today's debates over school choice, as originally proposed in the 1950s by economics Nobel laureate and public philosopher Milton Friedman, revive Adam Smith's ideas on the strategic delivery of public service. Always, Smith preferred to apply incentive structures to the delivery of governmental service in order to guarantee the best service, at the lowest price, to the greatest number of people. There was little room for feather beds or pork barrels in the wonderful world of Adam Smith.

If our society has strayed from Adam Smith's original conception of efficient and honest government, it has done so most promiscuously along the line that leads competing interest groups to feed too greedily at the government trough for everything from favors to kickbacks to influence. But this pathology is as much a function (or malfunction) of democracy as it is of capitalism, and it festers because governments have so much power and spend and tax in such high volume. To "reinvent government" means nothing short of rediscovering the Strategic Adam Smith and the mixed system of incentives he regarded as necessary for serving the public interest. As Robert J. Samuelson noted in his article on *Adam Smith in His Time and Ours,* "Smith combined a lofty vision of a decent society with an exacting analysis of the means of attaining it. Our modern luminaries often assume their means are always up to their ends."[30]

What Ever Happened to Moral Sentiments?

Adam Smith spent a prodigious amount of time revising *The Theory of Moral Sentiments,* his first and last book, but it is a forgotten classic, dwarfed in its influence by *The Wealth of Nations.* In the past two centuries, economists have rabidly mined volumes of technical detail out of *The Wealth of Nations,* and the world is arguably a better place for all this hard work. But lost in the bounty of the A-primes and betas that stud economics is Smith's template of moral sentiments, the culture of commercial society, the soul of the market.

Until now, few economists since Smith have been as intent as he was to specify the moral or social implications of capitalism, and few have tried. Even the heroic efforts of Robert Heilbroner, John Kenneth Galbraith, and the more philosophically inclined John Maynard Keynes have been generally ignored by the mainstream. Yet a combined economic and moral picture of capitalism is not only possible but *necessary* in conceptualizing the problems of contemporary society—maybe even more so than in Smith's time. As Smith so persuasively demonstrated, economists and their work are essential parts of this picture. How their position in it has changed since Smith's time is suggestive of their status today.

6

Soul Survivors

For it is easier to make believe, even to oneself, that one looks down on wealth, than to work with energy in order to make wealth a thing of which the world may be proud. But in fact material resources enter of necessity so much into the thoughts and cares of nearly everybody that, if the world is not proud of its wealth, it cannot respect itself. Surely, then, it is worthwhile to make a great effort to enlist wealth in the service of the true glory of the world.

Alfred Marshall

It was as though he had to live two lives, one as a professional . . . who could talk tough about the bottom line, the other as an old buddy who could talk about what was bothering him. The two quite different languages coming from the same man was what most struck my friend. Not as though one were a private language, a language of the sentiments, and the other a professional language, the language of necessity, although that was certainly part of the picture. Rather, a strictly economic, business language has grown up without including within itself the moral, religious, even humane language appropriate to its own activities.

Michael Novak

Occasionally, in the university town where I live, I run into my friend Carlo. I see him at the supermarket, in the restaurants, in the pharmacy, on the street. Carlo, a distinguished historian and also a prominent man of the political Left, cares about books. Invariably, when he sees me, a twinkle enters his eye and he asks me what I've been up to; what I've been publishing. Just as readily, I pipe up with enthusiasm and tell him about a great new economics book I've just published in, say, game theory or finance or regulation. But the effect is always as if I just told him that one of my son's lizards died.

Invariably, Carlo laments what he considers the sad literary state of economics, and, just as surely, he always ends on the note that what we need is "a new Heilbroner." The glint in his eyes disappears. So does the lilt in his voice. So does he. He turns his cart and heads for the raisin bran.

A former boss of mine—an intensely political man and an intellectual of the Right—once came very close to throwing me out of an editorial meeting for having brought in one too many book proposals from economists. The fact that he had hired me to publish books written by economists was an irony lost on him during this particular tirade. Although he did not invoke the totemic Robert Heilbroner in casting me out along with my devil-economists, my right-wing boss was motivated by the same distaste for economists that moved my left-wing friend Carlo away from me and toward the breakfast foods. Intellectuals—most of them, anyway—do not love economics.

Economics, as one Nobel laureate once explained it to me, "tells you what you can't do." Intellectuals—elitists and activists, by definition—want to say not only what we, as a society, can do, but what we *should* do. Why let a bunch of rate-limiting variables, repeated games, and lagged co-efficients get in the way? C. P. Snow prefigured this state of affairs a century ago in "The Two Cultures," his article about the contending cultures of science and the humanities. Economics has fallen on the pocket calculator side of the divide. It ain't easy defending economic science in a world of intellectuals who identify their roots in humanist aspirations.

Hold the Check

As noted above, most intellectuals, especially those of a political stripe, don't like economics. Intellectuals like to ponder the possibility of society in their own terms, and economists are forever reminding them that there is no free lunch. Preoccupied by politics, these intellectuals often care more about what's on the menu than what the items cost; more sustenance, please—and hold the statistics.

Robert Putnam has written a landmark book on the restoration of civic life, the aforementioned *Bowling Alone*. Economists are no more popular in Putnam's bibliography than I am in the local Princeton grocery stores. He cites only a small handful of economists, despite the awesomely disproportionate influence economists, as opposed to other social scientists, have had in the shaping of public policy.[1] What is going on in a world of ideas where the wildly influential economists get so little respect among other intellectuals?

This breach between intellectuals and economists conditions the public debate about vital questions such as who will receive good education and health care, who will live on safe streets and in decent houses, who will enjoy the benefits of freedom and prosperity, who eats lunch and who doesn't. Virtually all issues, except perhaps matters of absolute good and evil, come into this debate.

Means and Ends

Tension between intellectuals and economists goes all the way back to none other than Adam Smith, who embodied it in the titles of his two books, *The Wealth of Nations* (the economists' holy writ) and *The Theory of Moral Sentiments* (a classic of social philosophy). The history of public ideas over the past two centuries is, in some respect, captured in this seemingly split Smithian personality. Admirably, Smith worked both sides of the street, which is partly why his framework persists to this day. Now, to my way of thinking, economists are beginning to close this gap.

Before economists turned to the technical terrain that led to the mathematical rendering of economics as a science of rational choice, plenty of ink was spilled over moral sentiments in the creation of market society. Four thinkers in particular—Edmund Burke, Karl Marx, Alfred Marshall, and Max Weber—kept the spirit of Smith's soulcraft humming. Despite the triumph of technical economics, the more philosophical ideas of this quartet continue to shape market society to this day. Their legacy speaks more directly to Heilbroner's Warning than to Samuelson's Instructions;

but in so speaking, it also engages the growing cadre of economists interested in nonmarket institutions.

Edmund Burke: Enlightenment Cheesehead

Edmund Burke was born in Dublin in 1756. He was not an economist, but was recently dubbed (by no less perceptive an economist than John Kay) as perhaps a philosopher of our time. Kay admires Burke precisely because he was so eloquent in defending civil society against the depredations of over-the-top radical ideas, whether of the Left or the Right.[2]

Burke was a great political thinker, a member of the English Parliament, and a friend and colleague of Smith. Burke supported commercial society, but nervously so. Like Smith, he celebrated political and economic institutions as means to a better society, not as ends in themselves. But unlike Smith, he worried that the novel social formations that accompanied modern market society—including capitalism and early revolutionary forms of unrestrained political freedom—would pulverize the hallowed civilizing institutions of the past, enshrined as they were in the *ancien régime* and in the religious and knightly order represented by European tradition. He was torn by the tension between the liberating effects of political democracy and economic liberalism on the one hand, and the tempering effects of traditional culture on the other.

Gimme Shelter

A vociferous supporter of freedom from political oppression, Edmund Burke regarded the French Revolution as the premier expression of the havoc latent in liberalized modern society. He denounced the Terror that followed political revolution in France as an exercise in unrestrained homicidal political license. Yet he was a passionate advocate of social progress, especially for the lower orders of society. The American Revolution was more to his liking because the American colonials were revolting to preserve the rights of citizenship established in constitutional authority, not to undermine the idea of established authority itself.

A social radical who spoke out forcefully in the English Parliament against the oppression of his fellow Irishmen, Burke nevertheless feared that the gains achieved by the political and economic enfranchisement of the masses would be offset by the damage done to the civil order and the cultural institutions he considered the very repositories of moral sentiments and of civilization. As the following words attest, Burke did not take political change lightly:

> The Age of Chivalry is gone. That of sophisters, economists, and calculators has succeeded; and the glory of Europe is extinguished for ever. Never, never more, shall we behold the generous loyalty to rank and sex, that proud submission, that dignified obedience, that subordination of the heart, which kept alive, even in servitude itself, the spirit of an exalted freedom. The unbought grace of life, the cheap defence of nations, the nurse of manly sentiment and heroic enterprize is gone![3]

Burke's remarks foreshadowed an anxiety about the fate of moral sentiments that has been embraced ever since by a parade of intellectual successors, most of whom have been fiercely protective of established social and political structures. Burke was, in this regard, the original "compassionate conservative." He was eager to promote and preserve communal order among families, neighborhoods, schools, churches, and civic associations—all those little platoons that are essential to society.

To that end, he would likely have supported policies that protected these little platoons not only from the depredations of an overweaning state, but from the corporate convulsions and upheavals that threaten the stability of small-scale social institutions. On the contrary, policies that disperse ownership among workers, and various family-centered forms of social insurance—from retirement accounts through long-term unemployment insurance, as well as portable job benefits and housing futures—would be Burke's cup of tea.

Burke also would likely have approved of the salutary economic effects of an efficient corporate sector on the general level of prosperity, but could be counted on to look askance at the culture of conspicuous consumption and envy that drives it. He hated financiers and would have had no time for Wall Street or corporate suites, especially those occupied by chief executives who have collected million-dollar bonuses while firing tens of thousands of employees. Lee Iacocca, who showed solidarity with his employees by refusing pay during the restructuring of Chrysler, would have been closer to Edmund Burke's ideal of the modern executive, as would the late Roberto Goizueta, the philanthropic head of Coca-Cola and one of the city of Atlanta's great benefactors.

Burke would have been bemused to discover that, in 1996, *Wall Street Journal* political columnist (and now editorial page editor) Paul Gigot dubbed him a retroactive fan of the Green Bay Packers football team. For Gigot, the locally owned, publicly held Green Bay Packers embody the Burkean values of communal conservatism unlike any other contemporary commercial enterprise.[4]

A bit of American football history is in order. In the early 1950s, the Packers, in return for a local citizen-financed rescue of the football franchise, agreed to stay in, and not stray from, the tiny and remote Wisconsin town of Green Bay. Gigot conjectures that this exercise in communal preservation would have warmed the heart of Edmund Burke. In contrast, Gigot notes that Burke would have frowned upon the economically rapacious Dallas Cowboys, who, in Gigot's view, stand for merely stripped-out commercial values, not truly conservative ones. The point is: A true Burkean conservatism places the values of community over those of commerce. Whether Edmund Burke would have donned a big yellow cheesehead and cheered for the Green Bay Packers is doubtful. But, given his concerns about the disruptive effects of modern commerce on civil society and social order, it is almost impossible to think of him as a proto-admirer of that corporate embodiment of commercial ferocity, the Dallas Cowboys.

Karl Marx: Praise the Masses and Pass the Moral Sentiments

If Edmund Burke registered his conservative criticisms of the moral shortcomings of commercial society at the time of its infancy in the eighteenth century, Karl Marx railed against it during its period of raging hormonal adolescence in the Industrial Revolution of the mid-nineteenth century. Marx, born in Trier, Germany, in 1818, wrote in the tradition of classically oriented economists such as Adam Smith and David Ricardo. But like his contemporary John Stuart Mill (1806–1873), Marx criticized capitalism for its skewed distribution of wealth and the market's punishing exploitation of the poor. Mill, both a moral philosopher and a political economist in the tradition of Adam Smith, balanced his criticisms of commerce with a respect for the fundamental productive efficiencies displayed by market forces. His writings also helped form the modern idea of liberty and the public emancipation of women. Marx was hardly so timid.

Karl Marx admired capitalism for its liberating power, but saw in its economic machinery an inherent self-mutilating dynamic that necessitated a whole new universe of repression and social injustice in order to maximize the return on capital that economic growth requires. He predicted the demise of free-market capitalism after it had completed its "historical task" of economic development. For Marx, and eventually for millions of his followers, the forces that brought about the world of bourgeois capitalism would devour the very market principles and moral sentiments on which this world was built.

After lending an admiring nod to the early dynamic effects of free enterprise, Marx later attempted to level the entire structure of commercial humanism—economics, morality, the whole ball of invisible hand wax—in favor of a workers' paradise. He satirized "reformers" in contrast to revolutionaries. Haunted by the inequities, poverty, and brutal working conditions produced in the smoke-belching furnaces and foundries of industrial England in the 1840s, Marx, along with his fellow radical Friedrich Engels, attacked their capital-driven society from an entirely different angle than that of Burke. The critical swath cut by Marx slashed across not only Adam Smith's commercial humanism, but also Edmund Burke's cultural conservatism and any remains of Europe's ancient institutions.

Determined to champion the interests of the working classes above those of princes and bishops (to say nothing of bankers and merchants), Marx set forth a theory of society in which he identified power—the ownership of the means of production through which the capitalist appropriates what the workers produce over and above their means of subsistence—as the animating force of all social organization and culture. He regarded class and the class system, spawned by incipient capitalism, as the circuit board that ran the power. He searched for ways of rewiring that circuitry through class struggle to socialize ownership of the means of production and transfer power to the masses.

Marx considered the market and virtually all social and civil institutions, especially the family and religion, as the collective structures that preserved and perpetuated capitalism's system of oppression, the incubators of class consciousness. According to Marx, this system, in turn, reproduced structures of power that further reinforced the interests of capitalists over those of the workers they employed, while impoverishing the most unfortunate around the world. When economic development is complete, said Marx, the capitalist system will overproduce, and the only way to absorb this great supply is to transfer ownership of the means of production to the masses, so that the entire product, including surplus value, would belong to them.

One of the great weaknesses of Karl Marx's system was that it contained no theory of culture.[5] Still, in the view of most Marxists, seemingly every aspect of culture, from prices to prayers to poems to proms, could be accounted for by the inequality bursting from its heaving economic substructure. This pervasive *cultural materialism,* as it is known, gave Marxism powerful leverage over all kinds of intellectuals in sympathy with the founder. It would enable generations of his followers, from economists through psychoanalysts and every manner of thinker in between, to draw deep ethical lessons about economic arrangements flowing from the inegalitarian exercise of power.

Power, derived from property relationships that determine class structure and are reflected in culture, became the be-all and the end-all in Marxian analysis. Springing from the famous maxim that wealth should be spread "from each according to his means, to each according to his needs," Marx, a philosopher with no apparent theory of culture, set into motion the most potent and sustained cultural critique of capitalism since the origins of modern commercial society. He would have dismissed the Green Bay Packers (to say nothing of the Dallas Cowboys) as social narcotics.

If Karl Marx created any lasting legacy, it was the analysis of power. Not that his is the last (nor the first) word on the subject. Adam Smith, for his part, took power seriously but came up with ways of taming it by offsetting one interest against another. "Setting power against power" was a major theme in the work of David Hume, Smith's friend and fellow Enlightenment thinker, and in the checks and balances designed by the American founders in the Constitution.[6] Later, it would be resurrected by John Kenneth Galbraith in his attempt to defend the role of big government against the corporation as an agent of countervailing power.

The great attraction of Marx's project was twofold: its penetrating analytical critique of the dynamics of capitalist production, which gave heart to all intellectuals wary that markets had simply replaced feudal structures as preferred instruments of oppression; and its insistence on the socialization of the means of production.

Adam Smith's concept of moral sentiments helped humanize a balanced system of countervailing social institutions that provided incentives to shape the behavior of free individuals in commercial society in socially benevolent ways. Marx's moral sentiments emerged in the liberation of workers from the very restraints imposed on them from the structures that ordered capitalist society. Marx's soaring appeal to egalitarian justice was captured in the words of the international socialist anthem, *The Internationale,* inspired by him and sung for a century in socialist centers around the world:

> Arise, ye prisoners of starvation,
> Arise, ye wretched of the earth,
> No more tradition's chains shall bind ye.
> A better world in birth.[7]

Words such as these would have struck fear in the heart of the traditionalist Edmund Burke, not because they served as a clarion call for the lower orders of society with whom Burke sympathized, but rather because they threatened to destroy the ancient governing traditions of the West that maintained Burke's beloved social order. For Burke, culture—moral sentiments—provided not chains, but only the delicate bindings by which one generation preserved civilization and passed it on to the next. Smith had hoped that a decent commercial order would break the chains of illegitimate primordial power, while preserving and even strengthening the ancient cultural ties of civil society—a balancing act fit for a wonderful world. Karl Marx, the "dark man of Trier," was buying none of it.[8]

The Chains of Freedom

Ultimately, Marxian systems of political economy collapsed not only because of the stubborn rigidity of their centrally administered nonmarket principles, but also because the allegedly liberating moral faculties of communism subverted the very social and civil institutions that sustain peoples' lives. Environmentalists critical of capitalism need only look at the physical wreckage left in the path of communist regimes to discover what true ecological degradation is all about. Communitarians, even those of the Left like Hillary Rodham Clinton, need only look at the destruction of such social institutions as the family for evidence of a society riddled by mistrust and deceit. The lesson is one of political arrogance and moral bankruptcy as well as of faulty institutional design—of subverting Burke's networks as well as ignoring Smith's markets.

Capitalism itself has had a long history of market failure, worker oppression, inequality, economic warfare, mass unemployment, urban abandonment, and worse. But it has managed to overcome its convulsions by three means: first, economic innovations that have supercharged growth; second, evolving social inventions, including the provision and expansion of new and better property rights, commercial law, risk management techniques, and scientific knowledge; and third, sustained moral sentiments, notably the cultivation of social capital based on historical foundations of democracy, religious tradition, family, and community. Capitalism has been able to absorb new ideas, adjust to new cultures, and innovate in the face of some seemingly insurmountable challenges. It has kept many of its pin factories and little platoons in harmony most, if not all, of the time, Heilbroner's Warning notwithstanding.

Institutional and technological innovation, as well as cultural resourcefulness, have conspired to carry Adam Smith through some very rough patches. Marx's legacy has had a tougher time of it. The commissars who dined—and dined well—in Leningrad served themselves the same high-quality vodka and caviar that was on the buffets of the pampered capitalists in London and New York, but the commissars lacked the market channels through which to transport the product of their ambition and initiative to the people in whose name they ruled.[9] Further, unlike their capitalist counterparts, the commissars comprised an elite that took no risks. They could not lose, and thus lost—and when they lost, they lost everything. They had all the advantages of an economic elite and none of the disciplinary restraints provided by markets or law. Economists in the tradition of Adam Smith, including Alfred Marshall, had no such illusions about a free Leninist lunch.

Alfred Marshall: Back to the Future

While Karl Marx and Friedrich Engels were hard at work penning *The Communist Manifesto* in Manchester during the 1840s, young Alfred Marshall, a worldly philosopher in the making, was studying *The Wealth of Nations* in London. In 1890, Marshall published the first edition of his *Principles of Economics,* a book that would introduce several generations of students to economics, and would serve as The Instructions until the first copy of Samuelson rolled off the press more than a half-century later. At the time, Victorian society was in full flower and Marshall's name had become synonymous with price-clearing classical economics.[10]

Departing from the critical strain of political economy forged by Marx and Engels, Marshall rejoined Adam Smith's extended family of market-oriented economists—which now included David Ricardo, J. B. Say, Vilfredo Pareto, Leon Walras, and William Stanley Jevons—in delineating the economic structure and dynamics of market society. Names such as these have never provoked so much as a snore, much less a storming of the barricades, but their long-term collective legacy is enormous.

Walras, a Swiss economist hailing from the University of Lausanne, had achieved a milestone in economic reasoning by introducing into the evolving classical model (prices, labor, land, and markets) the concept of equilibrium—the notion that markets clear and prices adjust as though subject to the judgment of a "blind auctioneer." Walras enabled theorists to assign definite numerical identities to economic values, thus opening the way for the manipulation of economic ideas through calculus. Meanwhile, Jevons, a Manchester-based economist, developed seminal ideas in utility theory, in which value could be established in terms of its marginal utility, that is, reflecting a subjective component in its estimation.

This combination of equilibrium analysis and marginal utility theory would catapult economics forward as the most rigorous of the newly emerging social sciences. Also, at this time, it became possible to integrate into economics a means of applying probability and statistical analysis to social life, much as Francis Galton had been doing in the physical world. The upshot would result in the concurrent rise and ongoing cross-fertilization of economic ideas and economic facts—what we know now as modern economic theory and econometrics, both very much going concerns today.[11]

Marshall contributed mightily to the mushrooming body of technical knowledge that shaped and defined the foundations of economic science by delineating the concept of supply and demand in a dynamic, equilibrating economy. He introduced the notion that a market economy was a self-correcting system and insisted that economic progress came about through slow, evolutionary processes that developed at the frontier of marginal costs and returns. Marshall was a genius; he would read the first and last chapters of mathematical treatises by the fireplace, and fill in the middle. He was in a hurry to explain a world that moved slowly.[12]

But Marshall, for all his acumen as an incipient scientist of economic society, had entered economics expressly to help address the problem of poverty. A bleeding-heart classicist, he went further than any of his fellow Victorian-era economists in attempting to retrofit the evolving science of economics with the moral foundations originally exposited by Adam Smith.

Contrary to the caricatured notion of the classical economist, Alfred Marshall was no libertarian. Indeed, in his youth, he was a socialist (as were so many subsequent leading economists who went on to distinguish themselves as market philosophers), and he always thought of himself as such. He even believed in promoting the widespread prosperity of common folk, the poor included. What united Marshall with John Stuart Mill, whom he admired, was his belief in the need for direct government intervention in the amelioration of poverty. Marshall displayed the mind of a social inventor—and interventionist—at work. Contrary to today's libertarians, Marshall saw the need for minimum wage laws, public relief, and welfare, to guarantee society's service to the poor. He noted that government in his time was less corrupt than in Adam Smith's time, and easier for people to police, so he proposed to use it in the interest of the poor.

Wake Up the Echoes

Marshall resurrected the dual material and moral sociology of capitalism in the unlikely sounding phrase "economic chivalry." Speaking to the Royal Economic Society in 1907 (his address was titled "Social Possibilities of Economic Chivalry"), Marshall cast a distant reply to market-wary Edmund Burke by insisting:

The Age of Chivalry is not over; we are learning how dependent the possibilities of leading a noble life are on physical and moral surroundings. However great may be our distrust of forcible socialism, we are rapidly getting to feel that no one can lay his head on his pillow at peace with himself, who is not giving some of his time and substance to diminish the number of those who can earn a reasonable income, and thus have an opportunity of living a noble life.[13]

Marshall argued that the goal of providing everyone in society with the "opportunity of living a noble life" could be best advanced by two means. The first of these was an ethic in commercial culture that cultivates "the fine pride of the warrior who esteems the spoils of a well fought battle, or the prizes of a tournament, mainly for the sake of the achievements to which they testify, and only in the second degree for the value at which they are appraised in the money of the market . . ." and, then, in the ideas of economists.

In this first instance, the chivalrous businessmen of Marshall's Victorian scheme would, in his conception, readily promote the best social use of wealth, display a public spirit, make generous public contributions of their wealth, volunteer their services for public causes, and encourage a moral ethic within their communities. This ethic has never been the main bill of fare in business schools; rather, it is inculcated at the dinner table, in literature classes, on scouting trips, in track meets, at Saturday synagogue services, and at Sunday mass. It is a matter of "habit, not rational calculation." It is about character and judgment—traits not necessarily associated with the fierce cut-and-thrust of capitalism. But it is a mistake to think of a healthy and effectively functioning capitalism without it. We saw it in the nineteenth century in P. T. Barnum. In our own day, this ethic is exemplified by "high-road" corporate leaders like Iacocca and Goizueta who, profit-driven as they may have been, displayed a genuine and generous concern for their productive and loyal employees and for the communities their companies called home.

In the second place, Marshall called on his fellow economists to help "distinguish that which is chivalrous and noble from that which is not . . . a task that needs care and thought and labour . . ." in order to secure the moral sentiments needed for capitalism to function properly. Marshall's call for "care and thought and labour" in the service of economic chivalry was an economist's equivalent of Winston Churchill's call, decades later, for blood, sweat, and tears. Designing institutions that would simultaneously balance the requirements of economic efficiency with those of moral sentiments was a tough challenge. It must have landed on pretty dead ears among this crop of incipient analytical economists who were gradually developing their field as a full-fledged science in the study of choice and scarcity.

Nevertheless, the sociological principles of perhaps the two greatest economic philosophers of all time—Adam Smith and Alfred Marshall—resonated tightly with one another. They remain intact today, captured in the notion that, in order to be effective, the modern principles of the market economy need to be complemented by moral norms of social behavior—moral sentiments, economic chivalry, bourgeois virtues, civic virtue, or whatever name we might wish to assign them—and to be supported by government, in order for the society to be worthy of the wealth that capitalism produces.

Not Happening

Robert Heilbroner points out, in *The Worldly Philosophers,* that Alfred Marshall, for all his brilliance in elaborating the classical theory of markets, was ultimately a buttoned-up man who lived in buttoned-up times—not a very interesting chap. True, Alfred Marshall was no hip-hop artist; he possessed none of the intellectual derring-do of Karl Marx nor the political passion of Edmund Burke. He had little of the incredible synthesizing range of Adam Smith, or even of Smith's endearing personal eccentricity.

But Marshall really was more a button-down kind of guy—a social scientist for the ages. As was true of other intellectuals in his famously restrained Victorian age, the man who coined the phrase "economic chivalry" understood the importance of balancing the dynamic activity of markets with the civilizing features of moral sentiments. According to Gertrude Himmelfarb, a leading historian of Marshall's period:

> As medieval chivalry had elicited an unselfish loyalty to prince or country, so economic chivalry would cultivate a spirit of public service. . . . Economists studying the behavior of businessmen would be

able to distinguish the chivalrous and the noble from the selfish and ig-
noble . . . and a business enterprise, even if it did not produce great
wealth, would be esteemed so long as it was honorable in its aims and
methods.[14]

This is a far cry from the greed-'n'-guts style of capitalism served up
in Hollywood images of businessmen. Even as Marshall gave a central role
to markets, property rights, and the capitalist division of labor as a means
of enlarging the economic pie, he called for the well-to-do to exercise
moderation and prudence in the disposition of their wealth. He cautioned:

> . . . there remains a vast expenditure which contributes very little to-
> ward social progress, and which does not confer any large and solid
> benefits on the spenders beyond the honour, the position, and the in-
> fluence which it buys for them in society . . . if the society could award
> this honour, position, and influence by methods less blind and less
> wasteful; and if it could at the same time maintain all that stimulus
> which the free enterprise of the strongest business men derives from
> present conditions, then the resources thus set free would open out to
> the mass of the people the new possibilities of a higher life. . . .[15]

Daniel Bell echoed this notion a century later:

> The conceit of Marxism was the thought that in Communism, eco-
> nomics would be "abolished." . . . But the point is that we still have to
> think about economics and probably always will. The question, then, is
> whether we can arrive at a set of normative rules which seek to protect
> liberty, reward achievement, and enhance the social good. . . .[16]

Now, there is an agenda. Alfred Marshall couldn't have stated it better
himself.

Compassionate Victorianism

Marshall propagated a Victorian work ethic—a set of cultural norms—
for preserving whatever gains in life the poor achieved through the work
they did. For the affluent, he favored norms for using wealth to promote

the greatest social gain—through savings, investment, and charity. Private charity in Britain reached an all-time per-capita high (in proportion to national wealth) during the Victorian era in which Marshall lived.[17]

Most likely dismissed by Marxists as peripheral to true social progress, the chivalrous Victorian businessmen of Marshall's day nonetheless helped keep society together, pulled at least some of the poor out of their predicament, and established many of the institutions that have helped the poor ever since. The much-discussed social safety net originated during this period in both England and Germany. As Adam Smith predicted—and as most of us overlook—widespread wealth and improving national income (achieved through the market) made the public's support of the welfare of the poor possible in the first place. Successful enterprise begets benevolence.

It Takes a Victorian

Marshall believed that a government safety net balanced by religious, social, and educational institutions would promote moral well-being and alleviate economic hardship. His were the shared values of the Victorian world. This is an exceedingly important notion for the discourse of our day, when critics on the Left seem to prefer government-directed economic redistribution to the poor with no moral mediation attached, and those on the Right opt for tough love with little or no economic help. Economic chivalry requires money *and* moral sentiments.

Alfred Marshall was able to discuss what it meant to uphold and nurture moral sentiments because his buttoned-up society possessed such a clear-cut idea of what constituted proper social behavior. Thus, Marshall was probably not the least bit reluctant to propose the idea that "economic chivalry" should be augmented by the public purse. He was confident that the recipients of welfare payments would live in a culture that secured the social standards of Victorian society. Some in that culture must have shirked these responsibilities, but their lack of response is almost beside the point because the moral standards themselves were firmly in place and commonly held.

Marshall would have been aghast at our current welfare laws, which have provided incentives for poor women to live apart from the men who father their children. He would have been even more horrified by the social example set by many affluent people who think that, in the name of free expression, they can do anything that pleases them and that their irresponsible behavior does not, in profound and far-reaching ways, affect the conduct, and damage the lives, of those less fortunate who emulate them.

Max Weber: From Virtue to Values

The marriage of moral sentiments and market economics in policy analysis suffered a setback at the moment of its triumph, the end of Marshall's Victorian era. At that time, the philosophical enterprise of Enlightenment, which had given birth to economics, spun off into a handful of designer fields, including a host of sparkling modern social sciences such as political science, sociology, anthropology, psychology, geography, and, last but certainly not least, economics itself.

Marshall's tribe, the "Respectable Professors of the Dismal Science," as Thomas Carlyle sarcastically dubbed them, eventually dropped the label "political economists" for the sleeker ID "economists," and strutted with price theory down the scientific side of the street, leaving politics and culture to others to ponder. The rest is Samuelson and The Instructions.[18]

With the exception of notables such as Alfred Marshall, who tried to maintain Adam Smith's dual focus on markets and moral sentiments, the newly emerging economics profession eventually proceeded to build its subject into an increasingly technical science. Market economists who promoted ideas such as free trade paid tribute to moral sentiments, but only insofar as these sentiments were established in the legacy of eighteenth-century political economy. Trade encouraged growth, and growth was linked to the free and prosperous economic conditions under which a healthy civil society flourishes. National incomes rose, and all orders of society, in various degrees, profited from that growth. But something had disappeared from the field of Smith and Marshall.

What had fallen out of economics in its broad embrace of price theory was any explicit interest in making sense of *noneconomic* civic institutions, or, by extension, the virtues that bound economic activity and civic culture together. It's not that economists had gradually become immoral (although many of their critics today accuse them of being morally tone-deaf); it's more that the field lost any direct interest in the kind of big, sprawling moral philosophizing done by Adam Smith and his closest colleagues and successors. Gone was the frank civilizing interest in institutional design advanced in the joint economic and sociological writings of the worldly philosophers.

Meanwhile, beyond the din of economic model-building, real markets in real life were being joined by a new and complex array of economic structures that collectively added flexibility and connective tissue to the institutions of democratized capitalism. Commercial and merchant banks, administrative courts and government agencies, the welfare state, joint stock companies, the research university, municipal governments, the limited-liability corporation, philanthropic societies, domestic and international transportation and communication systems, business groups and associations, and an encompassing latticework of commercial and civil law enriched the structure of market society in Europe and America.

On the other side of the divide separating C. P. Snow's two cultures of scholarship, philosophy was becoming a pin factor unto itself. Specialization had overtaken the study of society. While markets and money came under the economist's microscope, moral sentiments and economic chivalry, the soulful side of Adam Smith and Alfred Marshall, had drifted into the purview of sociologists, historians, political scientists, geographers, and other social philosophers. The thinker of this period who was most effective in placing capitalism under the moral microscope was the aforementioned Max Weber, the German economist and social philosopher and author of *The Protestant Ethic and the Spirit of Capitalism*.

Unlike Marshall, Max Weber was of the continental intellectual tradition. He was an economist—as was his countryman Marx—but not in the dynamic, price-clearing sense in which the profession was evolving within its classical Anglo-American context. Weber was a professor of law at the University of Heidelberg and a prodigiously wide-ranging scholar. He studied, taught, and wrote about economics, law, history, culture, ancient societies, agriculture, social structure, religion, and seemingly everything else. He is claimed as a role model by intellectuals in all of these fields, even to this day. But the sociology of religion was Weber's specialty and the focal point of his analysis of capitalism.

Moving alongside Smith and Marshall, whose philosophical commentaries on commercial society sought to tease out the moral and economic imperatives of a virtuous capitalist order, Weber approached capitalism primarily as a sociological subject and studied its value structure. He was interested in its folkways, mores, and customs—not unlike the way anthropologists had begun to study the codes and symbols of non-Western societies. Weber's island society was Europe, and the culture he dissected was that of hormonal capitalism. His penetrating insight was that "the Protestant ethic," more than any other animating force, was responsible for the emergence and proliferation of capitalism in Europe and throughout Western society.

Citing highly prized traits such as hard work, thrift, and industry—all anchored around the "inward asceticism" of the Protestant relationship between the individual and God—Max Weber used religion to explain why the rational structures of capitalism emerged in England and northern Europe. By the same token, he explained why they failed to evolve in other religious contexts around the world, including the Latin countries of Southern Europe.[19] In Italy, Spain, and even France, the still-reigning Catholic ethic, in which people communed with God not personally but through their priests, had produced other, more collectivist forms of economic and political engagement, underscored by cross-cutting alliances among elite landowners, businessmen, bureaucrats, and politicians. It persists in some parts of Latin America today.

Thus, Max Weber had framed a new cultural anthropology of modern social systems that would be applied by succeeding generations of sociologists around the world. His was a less wonderful world than Smith's, a less virtuous world than Burke's, a less revolutionary world than Marx's, and a less evolutionary world than Marshall's. But it was unparalleled in the breadth of its social conception. Contrary to Smith and Marshall, who had advocated ways of balancing market institutions with strong social institutions, and Marx, who attacked the whole works, Weber registered his reflections on market institutions by clinically exposing the bureaucratic machinery of commercial society. For Weber, the Protestant psychology of individual industriousness, together with the proliferating institutional superstructure of markets, formed a machinery of bureaucratic routine and institutional rule that regularized the culture while propelling the economy forward. The religious ethic of ascetic Protestantism was, for Weber, the ghost animating capitalism's clockwork. Weber's intent was neither to bury Adam Smith nor to praise him. Instead, he was interested in exposing the stress points and weak spots of the system.

If Marx had no theory of culture, Weber filled the breach with a panoramic one worthy of a George Lucas film. Weber tried to combine the economist's understanding of the maximizing behavior of self-interested individuals with the sociologist's understanding of the social and cultural influences on behavior to create a basis for a truly synthetic science of economic analysis—one that incorporated economic dynamics and social embeddedness into its investigations of society and its challenges.[20]

Moral Sentiments at the Margin

Framed by a lively middle-class culture, and bereft of the illusions of orthodox Marxism, market economics made great Victorian strides as a science of wealth through the end of the nineteenth century. And yet the economic system of Smith and Marshall would continue to draw critical fire as an inequity-and-poverty-belching homunculus while western imperial power spread throughout the world on the back of expanding capitalist industry.

These criticisms would come not only from Marxists, but, increasingly, from more mainstream critics, journalists, social democrats, and other intellectuals troubled by the exploitation of colonial workers and indigenous peoples, and by the structural instability within capitalism that bore witness to many volatile economic contusions, the worst of which was the Great Depression of the 1930s.

The first several generations of the twentieth century would leave economists with all the international turmoil they could handle. The reunification of wealth and sentiments, of economics and the quest for social capital, would have to wait. Economists had fiercer fish to fry.

7

Dragon Slayers

Richard Kahn, who was in the audience, felt he had to break the ice. "Is it your view," he asked Hayek, "that if I went out tomorrow and bought a new overcoat, that would increase unemployment?" "Yes," replied Hayek, turning to a blackboard full of triangles, "but it would take a very long mathematical argument to explain why."

Robert Skidelsky

Friedman donned the white robes of science to demonstrate the singular relevancy of neoclassical economics for contemporary problems. . . . Pragmatists like Samuelson and Lerner were met on their own ground by an economist of equal brilliance and persuasiveness. If a refurnished and reformed market economy survives the onslaught of the new economics, much of the credit will go to Friedman and the new neoclassicism.

William Breit and Roger Ransom

A famous, and apparently fatalistic, philosopher once said that civilization proceeds by geological consent.[1] It may also be said that civilization proceeds by macroeconomic consent. Our livelihoods, homes, health, and hope for the future depend on the economic and financial infrastructure that enables us to trade goods, grow and transport food, build schools, maintain hospitals, and pursue happiness in myriad ways. The condition of currencies in East Asia can have a hair-trigger effect on the level of Christmas shopping in Wales.

By the same token, without stable prices and money, the talents, skills, and habits of industry that we develop in our classrooms and kitchens, and implement in our lecture halls and offices, would be second-order stuff. They provide us with the means—the human and social capital—to perform the productive tasks that propel the world economy forward. There is no small-scale economic activity without large-scale economic momentum.

Clarifying the terms of macroeconomic direction is no easy task. Articulation of its superstructure—including protean forces such as money, unemployment, and inflation—remains the main challenge of most economists today. Much is still to be done.

John Maynard Keynes, Milton Friedman, and Paul A. Samuelson helped to define the conceptual architecture of today's wealth of nations and advanced the future possibilities of moral sentiments by illuminating the stabilizing power of macroeconomic economic policy. The right mix of fiscal and monetary measures comprises the so-called "neoclassical synthesis" of macroeconomic stabilization in the service of microeconomic productivity, but getting the macroeconomics right has long been a struggle.

Blueprints and Barricades

The awesome economic and political events of World War I and the depression of the 1930s sent the first generation of the twentieth century's economic thinkers hurtling toward their blackboards. The world's leading nations, having opted out of Adam Smith's and the classical economists' design for economic growth through free trade, tried to control international product markets through protectionist foreign policies. These policies, and misguided monetary management, helped lead to a world war and, eventually, a worldwide economic collapse.[2]

The struggles that ensued pressed early twentieth-century economists into defending the doctrine of free trade and eventually rehabilitating it as a cornerstone of national and international public policy. Beyond the imperative of free trade, a solution to mass unemployment, with all of its attendant human and political havoc, became the prime moving force behind the economists' urge to understand the functioning of capitalism from the turn of the twentieth century all the way through to the Cold War.

The race to divine the central economic problem of mass unemployment galvanized the interest of the best twentieth-century economists, beginning with John Maynard Keynes. Later, Milton Friedman would join the battle and fight against inflation and central planning. Paul Samuelson would contribute by creating a working consensus for addressing all the big questions bearing on the modern wealth of nations and by making modern economics more policy-friendly when problems of market failure had to be addressed.

Many other economists—Friedrich von Hayek notable among them—would contribute significantly to the effort defined by the dual dogs of war and unemployment. Joseph Schumpeter would illuminate the internal contradictions inherent in capitalist production by showing how the most dynamic of entrepreneurial enterprises contained the seeds of their own ossification; hence, "creative destruction." Kenneth Arrow would reveal the informational anatomy of markets as well as the dynamics of democratic decision making. But by connecting the circuitry from Keynes through Friedman and Samuelson—the trio that struggled to help clarify macroeconomic thinking during its period of greatest challenge—the contours of modern economic policy—its glory, its shortcomings, and its implications for the return of the civic side of Adam Smith—begin to emerge.

The main weapon these thinkers would apply in developing their economic models was formal logic, which, by the 1950s, would become the closed and barbed code of economics, thereafter to be joined by game theory, itself a mathematical language of strategic means and ends. The transformation of economics from a Victorian philosophical enterprise to a modern, largely American, rocket science, and the consequences for the culture of capitalism, thus began as a chalk-and-blackboard game.

Two Steps Back

Alfred Marshall and his fellow classical economists had succeeded in constructing a simple set of economic principles that shed light on the dynamics of economic equilibrium throughout the Victorian and Edwardian ages. But the classical economists lacked the political leverage, moral suasion, and policy skills needed to head off the West's descent into the protectionist hell that helped pave the path to war. Also, the classical economists were a tiny fraternity. Marshall noted that in 1907 there were 235 economics professors in the United States, and a Washington economist once mentioned to a mutual friend that, in the year 1900, the federal government allegedly employed only one economist—in the Ornithology Section of the U.S. Department of the Interior. Even if this is an urban legend it is remarkable.[3] (The American Economic Association now has about 25,000 members.)

Perhaps most critically, classical economists a century ago lacked the intellectual firepower needed to illuminate that most destructive of economic problems: unemployment. It dominated the industrialized world in the early decades of the twentieth century, and it affected the political and social stability of that world unlike any other force.

The problem of unemployment, which festered throughout the first decades of the twentieth century and then exploded in the Great Depression of the 1930s, would absorb the waking interests of economists in the years leading up to the Depression and through the end of World War II. A persuasive explanation of unemployment, and a concomitant set of policies to relieve it, constituted the Holy Grail of Edwardian-era economists.

To the extent that economists brandished a concern for moral sentiments during these decades, their sentiments were concentrated—lock, stock, and barrel—on solving the problem of unemployment. Their obsessions were justified, given the havoc these dark forces visited on the lives of people and on the commercial and political institutions that held societies together. Mission Control for their operation was the University of Cambridge, where Alfred Marshall was busy training the man who would surpass him as the world's leading economist: John Maynard Keynes.

The Sybaritic Cincinnatus

Robert Skidelsky aptly subtitled the second volume of his biography of Keynes as "The Economist as Savior." This is no exercise in flattery. In choosing to address the main structural problem of mass unemployment, Keynes, like Cincinnatus on the sieged banks of the Tiber, attempted no less than a rescue of England, of the West, and of modern democratic capitalism.[4]

Keynes was the great shining prize of English economics and perhaps the most influential policy intellectual of the modern era. He changed the world by analytically dissecting the brutal and protean force of unemployment like some throbbing crablike alien in a monster movie. And he addressed it in an original system of economics that could be learned and embellished by his colleagues—and, for better and sometimes for worse, aggressively applied by policymakers. But Keynes had to break free of the classical price-clearing assumptions developed by his teacher, Marshall, before he could make his mark. The sturdy stone house of Victorian economics was about to get some sexy Edwardian furniture.

A master of the clever reflection, Keynes famously intoned the point that "madmen in power who hear voices in the air are usually the slaves of some defunct economist a few years back." If he had been referring to himself as the economist in question, he would have been either uncharacteristically modest or just terribly British. In a life that bracketed two world wars, the Crash of 1929, the Great Depression, the abandonment of the gold standard, and the reconstruction of the international financial system, Keynes (1883–1947) revolutionized economics and the art of economic policymaking on a grand scale. An eminent modernist through and through, he did for economics what Freud did for psychology; Einstein, for physics; and Picasso, for art. He liberated it, and he knew what he was about.[5]

Originally a student of mathematics and probability, Keynes later shifted his attention to economics at the urging of Marshall, and quickly moved beyond the shadow of his father, John Neville Keynes, also an economist. The younger Keynes' great contribution to economics was to develop a powerful diagnosis of, and an associated means of attacking, the menace of depression, which, by the early 1930s, had driven dreaded unemployment to levels above 20 percent. Contrary to Marshall, who had devised a celestial machine-like model of the economy at full employment, Keynes was determined to understand the economy as it really was: stuck at various levels of unemployment.[6]

A crucial idea for Keynes was that an economy could be stalled, with no natural forces to set it right. Prosperity, in his world, was never just around the corner. Keynes reasoned that unemployment comes about during downturns in the business cycle, when people hoard their money and commercial activity contracts. This combination of conditions slows—

and in some extreme cases, critically depresses—economic activity. Consumers stop their spending, which forces businesses to stop producing and induces them to lay off workers, thereby creating a downwardly spiraling economy. The result is the feared liquidity trap in which people hoard money rather than spend it, and thus suffocate the market. Keynes argued that the most destructive side effect of economic recession—unemployment—could be rectified by government intervention.

Keynes demonstrated how government could stimulate demand by pumping more money into the economy (through a mix of monetary and fiscal policies) and by government spending. This policy initiative, if effective, would increase demand for products and services, which would then trigger productivity and put people and factories back to work, thus pulling the economy out of recession. Happy days, as the song goes, are here again.

Keynes' prescription had a dual power. He had exquisitely conjured a plausible solution to the menacing and perennial economic problem of unemployment, and he packaged it for user-friendly policy application. Rather than saying about recessions, "Let's keep a stiff upper lip, a steady supply of money, and wait this thing out," as his classical forebears may have done, Keynes gave policymakers their Excalibur and the instructions for wielding it: Take bold, positive countercyclical action at the bottom of the business cycle.

Inadvertently or not, he also gave them their Swiss Army knife for micromanaging every conceivable kind of policy problem through deficit spending or transfer payments. Keynes placed politicians center stage in the biggest theater of social action of them all—the economy. This placement has not been welcomed by all as an unadulterated blessing. In the words of one critic, "Since the publication of his 1936 masterwork, *The General Theory of Employment, Interest, and Money,* opponents of profligacy in government and state manipulation of the economy have had to contend not merely with the selfishness and cowardice of politicians, but also with the subversive power of Keynes's mordant and glittering mind."[7]

Keynes did not publish the full elaboration of his economic ideas until the depths of the Depression; *The General Theory* was completed in 1936. But his steadily developing ideas, spawned in the wake of World War I and conditioned by a grinding economic downturn in England during the late

1920s, anticipated the solution to the Great Depression. However inadvertently, governments, by the late 1930s, had played a full Keynesian hand by deploying the most tried and true of all public spending programs: military buildup. World War II thus provided the fiscal launching pad for the postwar boom and the serendipitous enshrinement of Keynesian demand management techniques as the governing principles of countercyclical macroeconomic policy.

Edwardian Economics

To use the name John Maynard Keynes in a word-association game today would still trigger a parade of edgy reactions, depending on who's playing: *decadent, aesthete, libertine, genius, radical, hero, scourge, subversive, savior, lover, stylist, prophet, menace* (even *Marxist,* as the slightly undiscriminating Herbert Hoover apparently identified Keynes). Any of these emotionally charged labels could be anticipated in response, and apparently none alone would capture a shadow of the man. Robert Skidelsky wisely observes that Keynes cannot be understood without reference to his time, and even then he gets through the fingers.

Keynes was born in 1882. His Edwardian England saw the modernist ethic of human liberation gradually replace the hidebound aristocratic and religious virtue of the Victorians as a guide to the good life and decent society. The ethos of self-restraint that had underpinned civil society through the age of Marshall had given way to a celebration, at least among the elites, of self-expression.

Cambridge laid legitimate claim to being the hot center of this liberating revolution in culture, and Keynes was a Cambridge giant. Together with the likes of G. E. Moore, Frank Ramsey, Ludwig Wittgenstein, and other luminaries, not to mention Keynes' artist friends in London's Bloomsbury Circle (among them, Duncan Grant and Virginia Woolf), Keynes attempted to cast off the fusty conservatism and piety of Marshall's world and strike a blow in the interest of cultural freedom and widespread material well-being.

The moral sentiments that had driven Alfred Marshall's Victorian conception of economic chivalry had been powerfully informed by Christian charity and classical liberalism—praise the Lord and pass the price theory. Marshall wanted not only to alleviate poverty, but also to raise the masses to a society of more gentle, God-fearing folk. Marshall regarded economic assistance—provided by government as well as private charity, in his rendering—as a necessary ingredient in enabling people to participate in the economy, through which they could achieve the means of living virtuous lives.[8]

This basic income was considered more than just relief; it was table stakes for partaking in democratic society. A measure of economic prosperity was both a necessary stimulus to civil society and a product of it. This notion is captured today in the contemporary policy term, "citizen's income."[9] Civility would recapitulate prosperity, and so on. Deferred gratification—expressed in the trinity of saving, thrift, and industry—in combination with Christian virtue, were crucial elements in Marshall's economic sociology.

But Keynes, unlike his teacher, had little time for these Victorian pieties. He was born into the world "after virtue," as Skidelsky notes, appropriating the title of Alasdair MacIntyre's famous book as the marker for modernism.[10] Human expression and its liberation from the constraints of an allegedly stultifying Victorian culture were, for Keynes, a large part of the intellectual agenda. He was no less sympathetic than was Marshall to the economic plight of most of his fellow Englishmen and the poor abroad. If anything, having read both Marx and Mill and having witnessed the horrors of modern industrial society on the grand scale, he must have been more acutely aware than was Marshall of the vicissitudes of social deprivation in their modern frame. But his intellectual orientation to the inequities of modern society was markedly different from those of his teacher.

Keynes cared not a lick for saving the souls of the poor or for turning Cockney ragamuffins into Cotswold squires. He had deep doubts about capitalism and was revolted by what he considered its most grotesque embodiment, America. He was a cultural elitist who located justice in the public manipulation of aggregate economic forces in the service of full employment, and moral sentiments in the celebration of the modern artistic temper.

For Keynes, the economic problem was a transitory "muddle." He wanted to get beyond money and to the ballet. As Skidelsky notes, Keynes' identity and outlook were formed within the improbable cultural crossroads of Whitehall and Bloomsbury.[11] Marshall's romance with the evolution of economic life over the long term gave way to Keynes' acid observation: "In the long run we are all dead." When, nearing the end of his life, he was asked what he would have done differently, Keynes replied that he would have drunk more champagne. He focused his attention on the development of policies for correcting the course of the economy in the short run. And it is lucky for the democratic world that he did.

Despite his demonstrable concern for the cruelties of a mindless laissez-faire system, and his revulsion at what he considered the crass embodiment of capitalism made flesh in America, Keynes was, by his own insistence, no Marxist, and he was always and ever clear in distinguishing his perspective from that of the followers of Marx. This is no small claim, considering that the Cambridge of his time was a hotbed of socialist activism and later a spawning ground of Soviet spies. Keynes dismissed *Das Kapital* as only he could have. In a letter to George Bernard Shaw, Keynes condemned the book by complaining: ". . . whatever the sociological value of [*Das Kapital*] I am sure that its contemporary *economic* value (apart from occasional but unconstructive [*sic*] and discontinuous flashes of insight) is *nil*."[12] Though sympathetic with the humane goals of socialism, he was less a born-again Marx than a modeling Mill—a market economist with a strong and pragmatic government interventionist bent.

The essence of the intellectual Keynes is distilled by economist Donald Moggridge, who, according to Skidelsky, describes him as an applied economist who invented theory in order to solve problems.[13] His great triumph rested in solving these problems by devising a body of technically rigorous theoretical principles that accounted for the short-term disequilibria that Marshall and his forbears failed to address. In the decades to come, these principles would absorb the mathematical elaboration and more than a little intramural mud wrestling among several generations of economists.

Keynes' time was a veritable highlight film of world-shaking national and international problems. Most of them were attached, in one way or another, to unemployment, his all-consuming interest. Propelled into the world of public policy as a member of the British Treasury following the First World War, Keynes was appalled by the punitive—and what he considered the manifestly impossible—schedule of reparations that the victorious Allies imposed on Germany after the war.

So disturbed was Keynes by what he perceived as the Allies' poor judgment in punishing the already defeated Germany, he resigned from the Treasury and went to work on *The Economic Consequences of the Peace*—a warning to policymakers and the public that their ill-contrived reparations plan would prevent the German economy from recovering, jeopardize its political stability, and set the stage for another war. The rest is Hitler and history: the Great Depression and World War II.

Similarly, Keynes was compelled by the high levels of unemployment that marred much of the late nineteenth and early twentieth centuries to address the question of how to govern a national economy on the grand scale. His approach revolved around the maintenance of full employment as exposited in *The General Theory of Money, Interest, and Employment,* a book written in elegant if often abstract English, and pregnant with profound analytical implications. This project consumed his professional life, not to mention the lives of a small army of fevered Cambridge economists, and culminated in the publication of *The General Theory,* the boldest and most controversial book since Adam Smith.

The General Theory laid out the theoretical case for the economy in disequilibrium and has helped define the research agenda for macroeconomists ever since. In the process, economics was becoming a battle royale of "my interpretation of the numbers versus yours." Its focus was imperceptibly but steadily inching away from the worldly philosophy of Adam Smith and the economic chivalry of Alfred Marshall, and toward the cathedral of technicalia that is today associated with the legacy of Keynes.

Suffering Fools Unsentimentally

The problems of the world, more than the requirements of theory, had coaxed *The General Theory* into existence. Society needed a savior in economist's tweeds, and Keynes obliged. He shared with Adam Smith a passion for influencing public policy; as Smith railed against mercantilism, so Keynes fought unemployment. But there was precious little sentimentality in Keynes' moral sentiments. The chivalry in Keynes was to be found in his blackboard analysis, trained squarely and sparely on the policy business at hand. But after his death in 1947, as the political elites emerged from the

Second World War, they simultaneously drew their newly acquired blade of Keynesian economic management and integrated deficit spending directly into workaday fiscal and monetary politics. What's more, Keynesian economic management dovetailed neatly with the victory culture.

The inclusive sense of national purpose that had defined the culture during the war remained intact to inform policy construction well after the last shot was fired. National planning, managed through Keynesian deficit spending, became the norm throughout industrialized societies; social inclusiveness and the socialization of risk became the main moral sentiments; and programs such as nationalized health insurance and public education became the preferred delivery systems. The Keynesian welfare state was the prime product of this marriage of victory culture and policy science.

Friedrich von Hayek and John Kenneth Galbraith—the former arguing in favor of fiscal austerity, monetary responsibility, and personal freedom, and the latter in favor of social planning—would fight the battle of the welfare state in a language intelligible—even appealing—to the public. But what they were really fighting over was economics according to Keynes—its perils and its promise—for Keynes had changed the way economists and political leaders think about the place of government in economic society.

In the decades following Keynes' death, the Galbraith camp won; victory came with the successful erection of the Keynesian-supported welfare state, a *fait accompli* throughout the Western democracies during the waning years of the Cold War. Democratically elected governments used the Keynesian Creed freely to build burgeoning welfare states and the deficits by which they were financed. Whether Keynes would have approved of the sometimes wanton application—to say nothing of the bold political exploitation—of his antirecessionary principles during relatively calm stretches of the business cycle, is doubtful.

In America, the powerful analytical structure of *The General Theory* would come to absorb mathematics like a parched towel soaks up water, and, along with it, the fevered attention of equation-wielding younger economists. Keynes' major legacy was an elaborate intellectual template that would serve for generations as the text of an ever-expanding technical conversation by economists attempting to unite theory, measurement, and public policy advice.

Slouching toward Bloomsbury

David Frum sharply criticizes Keynes' influence as Nietzschean in that he had provided policy elites with a means to achieve their will to power over society. Critics on the Right (such as Frum) tend to see Keynes as the intellectual progenitor of big government and the overweening welfare state, indifferent to the influence of the traditional social institutions that Smith, Burke, and Marshall considered so crucial to the sociology of classical liberalism. Perhaps. But a clue left late in his life, in a correspondence to a longtime Bloomsbury friend, suggests an intriguing ambivalence on the economist's part.[14]

According to Robert Skidelsky, Keynes confessed to Virginia Woolf his conviction that the world had lost something of great value in the abandonment of the Victorian virtue of Marshall's time. Keynes admitted with some regret that his generation of intellectuals, having demolished the Victorian worldview, nevertheless had profited from having been trained in it. "I begin to see that our generation—yours and mine . . . owed a great deal to our fathers' religion. And the young . . . who are brought up without it, will never get so much out of life. They're trivial: like dogs in their lust. We had the best of both worlds."[15]

That sentiment in mind, John Maynard Keynes probably would have been pleased to know that at least some of the civilizing ideas of his classical forbears—the best of both worlds—managed to survive the wars and economic convulsions of his own time and were revived by a future generation of economists and other intellectuals. Meanwhile, another decidedly twentieth-century dragon, fresh from the recombinant idea-lab of Enlightenment crypto-science, would have to be slain: Leninist communism. Field headquarters for this fight had shifted from the south of England to an unlikely encampment in Hyde Park, on the South Side of Chicago, Illinois, USA.

The Classical Liberal in Cold Warrior's Armor

A wag has put it thus: "While celebrations of the virtues of the market go back to the days of Adam Smith, the near-fatal dent in the market's reputation left by the great depression forced many market proponents to go underground, languish on the fringe of political discourse, or move to the University of Chicago."[16]

So powerful was the reconstruction of classical principles, from the 1930s onward, on the gray gothic grounds of the University of Chicago, that the two-centuries-old Scottish and English classical liberal entablature etched by Adam Smith would soon be replaced by a big neon American marquee bearing the name *The Chicago School*.

If enthusiastic Keynesian intellectual and political leaders—not to say Keynes himself—had succeeded, after the war years, in rerouting capitalism through the expanding precincts of the Welfare State, their trip hit rough track when it reached 63rd Street in Chicago's Hyde Park. There, at the head of the greeting party on the Midway, was the diminutive but fiercely brilliant and combative figure of Milton Friedman. Born in Brooklyn of Ruthenian immigrants in 1912, and educated at Rutgers, Columbia, and the University of Chicago shortly before and during the Great Depression, Friedman, in his younger years, was moved by many of the same convulsive international incidents as was the adult Keynes. Just as the Depression and mass unemployment provided Keynes with his philosopher's stone, so they did for the youthful Milton Friedman.

Milton Friedman would revive, for a new generation, the tradition of public philosophy forged by Adam Smith and Alfred Marshall. And he did so during a time when the spirit of Karl Marx was the favored guest at academic soirees near and far (well, maybe not so near to Chicago's economists). Friedman was, and is, first and foremost, an analytical economist of great accomplishment. He joined the public discourse on modern political economy and established his widespread reputation with his own distinctive view of what caused the Great Depression.

Friedman's economic focus is on money, that is, in the belief that the real economy can take care of itself only if its financial house is kept in order. He is unequivocal—to put it mildly—in his analysis of the causes of the Depression: It was the product of a failure of the U.S. Federal Reserve to inflate the money supply in time to stabilize the economy during the bank runs of 1931, period. His view was consistent with the classical doctrine that money is a medium of exchange, not a liquid asset; thus, a stable money supply is essential to the preservation of economic vitality and full employment. Furthermore, according to this classical view—and contrary to the Keynesian one that Friedman attacked—remedial government action in correcting economic perturbations, including recessions, should begin and end by stabilizing money.

According to Friedman, the Federal Reserve's failure to inflate the currency and thereby stabilize the money supply in 1931 fueled the downturn and exported it abroad, precipitating the international economic collapse and bringing on the Depression. Friedman sympathized with some of the actions employed by governmental leaders in their struggle against the effects of the Great Depression, especially the attempts made by President Franklin Roosevelt to stimulate the prosperity of Americans by authorizing large-scale public works projects in the form of the New Deal. But later, Friedman would fight tooth and nail against Keynesian demand management because it introduced delayed and unpredictable shocks into the economy which, he said, would have seriously destructive effects well after the problem at hand was addressed, to say nothing of its continuing gift to domineering politicians.[17]

As an intellectual who has strong libertarian credentials and places freedom above all other values, Friedman, like Hayek, regards more government as analogous with less *freedom,* the surpassing ingredient in the classical liberal's conception of civil society. He considers the Keynesian-financed expansion of government bureaucracy, and its accompanying social welfare programs, as nothing short of crypto-socialism, the road to serfdom perilously paved. Socialism, in its sinister totalitarian Soviet Communist form, was the enemy faced by the West during the Cold War, which began around the time of Keynes' death in 1947 and lasted until the end of the 1980s, thus bracketing the most creative professional years of Milton Friedman.

Just as Keynes had battled the twin-headed monster of world war and depression in the first part of the twentieth century, Friedman would direct his intellectual energy to combat the linked spread of inflation, central planning, and political repression in the second part. His crusade was directed against the unanticipated consequences and perverse incentives caused by economic hyperactivism.

Had he never written a word on monetary theory (the area of economics in which he gained worldwide fame), Milton Friedman would have made his mark by helping to place economics on a firmer statistical and econometric basis. By appropriating the ideas of mathematicians and statisticians in the interest of sound economics, and by putting to wise use the accumulating data on national economic aggregates, Friedman promulgated a style of economic scholarship—called *positive economics*—which fortified the principles of neoclassical microeconomics through scientific verification.

Friedman's first great contribution to the science of economic thinking was his 1957 book, *The Theory of the Consumption Function*. But he would make his most lasting mark with his work on the topic of money, the area in which Keynes had distinguished himself, and the part of the field that most profoundly affects national economic policy toward inflation and unemployment, the yardsticks of the wealth of nations.

Sentiments and Statistics

Monetary economics had united Friedman's interest in national policy, his love of classical political economy, his commitment to individual freedom, and his powerful command of mathematical economics. Along with economist Anna Schwartz of the National Bureau of Economic Research, Friedman wrote *A Monetary History of The United States,* a book that, in 1963, slashed through the growing theoretical thicket of Keynesian economics. Friedman and Schwartz made the bold empirical claim that there was a direct and irrefutable relationship between the stability of money and the strength of the American economy, and that the Great Depression represented a government-induced rupture in this relationship.

Friedman and Schwartz sent a signal—to policymakers in the democratic west and to incipient democratic leaders in the socialist east—that attempts to manage national economies through irresponsible Keynesian deficit-driven tax policies, or through activist monetary policies, was worse than misguided. These policies were downright dangerous in that they subverted the very social goals and habits of industry they claimed to promote, and they destabilized prosperity in the bargain.

Keynesian economists battled back through a set of mathematical arguments developed by James Tobin and others. These arguments supported Keynes' idea that the economy settled at various levels of disequilibrium and could be managed through fine tuning and other means of monetary and fiscal manipulation. Led by Paul Samuelson at MIT, and Tjalling Koopmans and other economists associated with the Cowles Foundation originally at Chicago and then at Yale, the opponents of monetarism would galvanize their econometric arguments to challenge Milton Friedman.

Meanwhile, back in England, Joan Robinson and other of Keynes' successors were taking the master's work in a decidedly leftward, even socialist direction, by substituting Keynesian fiscal management for blunt-edged central planning as a basis for democratic socialism. Herbert Hoover would have called it just about right this time.

The Economist as Popular Intellectual

Milton Friedman, echoing the classical liberal economist Friedrich von Hayek—whose best-selling book, *The Road to Serfdom,* made the powerful point that socialism would lead to the enslavement of the societies that embraced it—didn't settle for exchanging sweet mathematical scribblings with his fellow social scientists. Rather, he made a second career as a public—even popular—intellectual, through his powerful expression of libertarian moral sentiments and monetarist economics. It is possible that he perceived the popular media as the best means of influencing public policy during the Cold War; in any event, Friedman proceeded to take his libertarian case to the people through books, journalism, lectures, and television. His reputation as a popular economic philosopher and razor-sharp public debater would be rivaled only by that of John Kenneth Galbraith, whose brilliantly written political and economic tracts formed the blueprint of policy intellectuals on the Left.

Friedman gained a worldwide audience as a public intellectual with the 1970 publication of *Capitalism and Freedom.* Together with his economist wife, the former Rose Director, he achieved mass-market best-sellerdom with the publication, in 1978, of *Free to Choose,* a popularization of the free market philosophy at the heart of *Capitalism and Freedom.* Perfectly timed, *Free to Choose* was published just when the public's faith in the Welfare State was beginning to wear thin. It is hardly a coincidence that the Reagan and Thatcher elections, not to mention the demise of Soviet communism, followed hard on the heels of the success of *Free to Choose.*

At the same time, academic macroeconomics was undergoing yet another theoretical reconstruction. The leaders were Robert Lucas and

Thomas Sargent, whose idea of rational expectations—the notion that you can't fool all of the people all of the time through policy manipulation, and if you try, you'll cause more harm than good—cast new doubt on the Keynesian conceit that the economy could be managed by the manipulation of taxes and interest rates.

The Mandeville of the Midway

More than anything else, Friedman has argued that freedom is the highest of human values, and that the achievement of human freedom comes about through the liberation of market forces and the restraint of government. Friedman is at his most ingenious in demonstrating how otherwise well-intended government programs, such as welfare and centralized public education, undercut the very goals they are intended to support, while fattening the wallets, as well as the ranks, of government bureaucrats who thrive on programs designed to promote economic relief and justice.

Friedman argues that, because they drive up the cost of labor and cause further unemployment, laws supporting labor unions and the minimum wage subvert the greater interest of the very working people they are intended to serve. He contends that regulation increases the costs of business, thus compounding prices to consumers, and that rent control forces landlords and builders out of business, thereby reducing rental properties and increasing rents. His message is that government intervention helps only government; it hurts productivity and efficiency, and it subverts growth.

Friedman held the line for other economists whose work on public policy would leverage the efficient features of markets in service of socially redeeming goals. Well-designed employee-based pension fund schemes, urban reinvestment and tax abatement plans, credible work-to-welfare programs, individual medical and retirement accounts, school choice programs, and minority business incentives come to mind. The expansive capitalism embodied in initiatives such as these mimics the utopian dreams of Mill and Marx much more closely than the failed command economies of the Eastern bloc ever did. Power, as the 1960s saying goes, to the people.

A Hong Kong of the Mind

Milton Friedman's references to the classical economists are copious and frequent, and his revival of the works of Adam Smith is nothing less than heroic. There are many similarities in the intellectual styles of Friedman's libertarianism and Smith's classical liberalism, but there is a difference as well. Smith was concerned with showing how markets and other institutions, including government, were needed to devise strategic policies that would shape the society by regulating freedom through moral restraint.[18]

Friedman, on the other hand, has focused—to a much greater degree than his classical predecessors and his economist contemporaries—on the defense of liberty as an end in and of itself. His public arguments have concentrated on the defense of freedom, and he has delivered withering attacks on the denial of freedom under socialism and even under welfare-state capitalism. He has done less to argue a case for the cultural dividends paid by the countervailing social institutions of commercial society; that job is left to noneconomist neoconservative thinkers such as Irving Kristol, Michael Novak, and James Q. Wilson.

The difference is exemplified in their respective positions on drug policy. Whereas Milton Friedman supports the legalization of dangerous drugs on the grounds of personal liberty, it is hard to imagine that Adam Smith, Alfred Marshall, or any number of prominent neoconservatives (William Bennett comes to mind), dedicated as they have been to improving the overall moral well-being of the society through restraint of the passions, would agree.

Friedman would be in greater agreement with Smith in their *strategic* public approach toward the treatment of certain societal problems—specifically, poverty.[19] Contrary to his popular image as an apologist for the wealthy—an image that is unfortunately shared, in the public mind, along with Smith—Milton Friedman has steadily expressed great concern for people in poverty and more so than most economists, has continuously addressed the problem of poverty in his writings. However, his proposed policy prescription—a guaranteed national income—is decidedly unconventional by the standards of the cumbersome modern Welfare State and more in keeping with a classical conception of civil society.

Friedman would attack the problem of poverty by asking the government to guarantee a minimum income for all citizens, thereby providing society with a stable safety net. But that is all he would have the government do: substitute the guaranteed income scheme for the labyrinthine welfare bureaucracy that he regards as clumsy, ineffective, and preserved largely for the bureaucrats who make their living from administering it. Thus, by using the government primarily for strategic purposes and enabling the family, church, and school to assume the socializing function served by bureaucracy in the Nanny State, Friedman's approach is most certainly in keeping with Smith's style of policy prescription.

A pundit once made the tantalizing observation that whereas Sigmund Freud made too much of sex, Milton Friedman may have made too much of markets.[20] Given the literal content of his public pronouncements, it is hard to deny the nearly religious status that Friedman attributes to the market as the crowning social institution. As a scholar, there is no doubt whatsoever that Friedman elevated the study of markets to a higher, if not heavenly, level. The first Chicago economist to win the Nobel prize in economics, Friedman has been followed by no fewer than six of his fellow Chicagoans, all fellow free marketeers: George Stigler, Ronald Coase, Merton Miller, Gary Becker, Robert Fogel, and Robert Lucas.

Respectively, they have advanced knowledge in price theory, organizational economics, finance, human capital theory, economic history, and macroeconomics. With the exception of Coase, who eschewed the use of mathematics, each, in his own way, also has added power to the mathematical arsenal of modern economics, and has echoed, in his work, a connection with Milton Friedman, the economist.

As a public figure, Friedman almost single-handedly revived the tradition of classical liberalism that was associated with Adam Smith and was long since marginalized by the mostly Keynesian mainstream social scientists. Friedman returned the market, and its strategic role, to the center of the discussion of civil society.

Lester Thurow once said of John Kenneth Galbraith that he is a paradox: a brilliant economist outside the mainstream of economic thought, but squarely in the center of economic events.[21] Friedman is every bit as much a paradox, precisely because he has made his mark in both arenas *and* on a scale as great as that of any economist in the twentieth century. To the extent that he advanced the study of the market—based as it is on the self-interested behavior of rational individuals—he is a modernist through and through. But he is also a traditionalist insofar as he pried open the public discourse of freedom, a virtue laid low by the encroaching socialism of the twentieth-century state.

But the Modern State, though streamlined, has not withered away, nor will it. The job of calibrating it, honing it, and fitting it to serve the metrics of a society beset by uncertainty is an endless task—the province of economic science and economic chivalry, alike. It is why they pay economists and their fellow social scientists. Indeed, the only modern economist since Milton Friedman who contributed as mightily to the accelerating progress of contemporary economic science as a policy tool is a man who spent his undergraduate years at the University of Chicago under the spell of the Great Depression, and who was the first American to win the Nobel prize in economics: Paul Samuelson of MIT.

Svengali on the Charles

One June day in the late 1980s, when I was visiting MIT's economics department with an editorial colleague from England, Romesh Vaitilingam, we had the pleasure of spending a few minutes chatting with Professor Paul Samuelson in his office in the Alfred Sloan Building, which overlooks the Charles River. After leaving the professor's office, as we were making our way down the hall, Romesh turned to me and said, "Well, I just met God." In the culture of economics, this is just a slight overstatement.

If John Maynard Keynes and Milton Friedman helped to make economics a theoretically and empirically sophisticated social science, they also drew it in certain unmistakable political directions—Keynes toward social democracy, Friedman toward the minimal state. Samuelson simultaneously raised the scientific ante and split the political difference. He has tried to marry the countercyclical measures of Keynes with freely functioning markets embraced by Friedman. When he has made mention of this marriage, he has referred to his belief in the competitive market microeconomics of the nineteenth-century economist Leon Walras and other classicists, and the need for active government policies to promote full employment.[22]

Samuelson could have added that he was the most surpassingly scientific of economists of his generation. According to an economist who spent a year as a visiting professor at MIT during the 1970s, Samuelson was, at the lunch table, as conversant with the physicists, chemists, and engineers as he was with his fellow economists.[23]

Another economist, describing Samuelson as a "human mainframe," notes that, by the time he turned 25, the number of his published articles was greater than his years of age.[24] Through his distinctly scientific contribution to economics—in the formation of national policy, industrial and corporate organization, and the architecture of the international economic order—he made his enduring mark. Samuelson's economics is modernist social science of the high church variety.

In his first book, *Foundations of Economic Analysis,* published in 1945 and based on his Harvard dissertation, Paul Samuelson shed impressive light on the Walrasian-Keynesian connection. He put this body of knowledge— "the neoclassical synthesis," as it came to be known—on detailed mathematical grounds in *Foundations.* The neoclassical synthesis held that under conditions of full employment, classical economic principles took priority in policy decisions, whereas under less than full employment, Keynesian stimulus was needed to bring the economy back into shape. This proposition has defined the research agenda for macroeconomists for decades. Samuelson's subsequent contribution to economic scholarship, applied in virtually every aspect of the field, is unparalleled. Unlike any scholar before him, Samuelson invigorated the language and culture of economics through mathematics.

Born in Gary, Indiana, in 1915, Paul Anthony Samuelson was an undergraduate at the University of Chicago while Milton Friedman was a graduate student. In 1935, Samuelson was lured to Harvard for graduate school by the excitement surrounding Edward Chamberlain's work in monopolistic competition, and by a bucolic vision of a white-picket-fenced New England town. The latter image was dashed upon his arrival in Cambridge's Central Square, a hard-boiled cityscape more akin to Chicago's Hyde Park than to the verdant backs of the older, gentler English Cambridge of Keynes. Samuelson left Harvard for MIT in 1940—a move fueled, it is said, by a combination of anti-Semitism and intellectual jealousy on the part of some powerful members of the Harvard economics faculty. To say that Harvard's loss was MIT's gain is the great understatement of the modern history of economics.[25]

From his big, sunny MIT office overlooking Boston's Back Bay, Paul Samuelson has exported his mode of economics through an elite corps of students. His troops have traveled not only throughout the academic groves, in the work of fellow Nobel prize winners Lawrence Klein and James Tobin, but in the halls of Washington and Wall Street as well. His style of economic thinking has been carried beyond academic economics, notably through former students such as Nobel laureate Joseph Stiglitz, Chairman of the President's Council of Economic Advisors during the Clinton years; Nobel laureate Robert C. Merton, widely regarded as the leading finance economist in the world; and Robert Shiller, whose work on market volatility has helped to define modern applied economics. These are but a few of Samuelson's many students.

Samuelson proceeded to revolutionize economics through his work with fellow MIT faculty, including Nobel laureates Robert Solow and Franco Modigliani; through his many distinguished students; and through his prodigious scholarly output. The first five volumes of his collected papers contained nearly 5,000 pages. A sixth volume is now in preparation. However, nothing in the Samuelsonian oeuvre is as influential or as lasting as his textbook, *Economics,* discussed in Chapter 2.

Keynes found a general outlet for his influence in policy heroics during and after the Great Depression, and Friedman's fame grew in public writings and appearances. Samuelson reached the world through the undergraduate classroom. The economics learned by far-flung professors and waves of new students came straight out of Samuelson's text. The mid-twentieth-century generations of economists were perfectly prepped for the Keynesian-propelled New Frontier and Great Society and their social engineering crusade. The book, in its several editions, gave these economists the basic toolkit for governing the world through economic and social policy formation—itself very much a modernist project. The watchword for Samuelson in matters of policy is *moderation,* a norm intended to steer the economy through the shoals of inflation and unemployment by way of an active, but steady, hand guiding the fiscal and monetary controls.

Despite the long period of "stagflation" that followed the Vietnam War—a period that gave rise to a renewed Chicago attack on the Keynesian demand management in the form of rational expectations—the measured and moderating influence of Paul Samuelson's brand of economics, updated and extended notably by Alan Blinder, Paul Krugman, and N. Gregory Mankiw, among others, has served successfully to govern democratic capitalism ever since.

The Samuelson Revolution has been accompanied by a rapidly enlarging technical apparatus that has earned the economics profession a seemingly unshakable reputation as a legion of mathematically obsessed geeks. The more data economists have to process, the more they seem, to the outside world, to be data processors. Yet, the success of this analytical army of economists—Keynes, Friedman, Samuelson, and onward—has helped to stay, if not slay, the Depression-borne dragon of mass unemployment, and to slow its twin dragon, inflation.

The Golden Mean

For all of his considerable contribution to the expansion of economic knowledge, Paul Samuelson has largely made his mark without explicit reference to moral sentiments. Aside from some essays on liberalism that appear in his collected works, and the column in *Newsweek* that alternated with Milton Friedman in the 1960s and 1970s, Samuelson's moral and political views are best intuited from his various affiliations over the years. Though he made a point of never crossing the Potomac to participate in any particular administration, he did advise John F. Kennedy during his presidency. And many of his politically active students, who have occupied important government positions around the world for half a century, could be similarly described as hardheaded liberals.

To the extent that Samuelson has made a contribution to the moral sentiments side of the Smithian equation, it has been in his cultivation of useful principles of *knowledge,* the seedbed of future social inventions needed for the spread of market democracy. He has made an unceasing effort to provide commercial society with a systematic—if not downright scientific—means of managing its economic affairs at the level of national policymaking. An outstanding feature of this contribution is his work on market failure: defining when the government should act to correct problems of economic distribution and inequality, and calibrating the extent and nature of those interventions.

By applying his scientific standards unflinchingly throughout his career, Paul Samuelson has helped the economics profession to achieve its systematic understanding of the connection between economic theory and policy. The gradual, albeit steady, results are a narrowing of the differences between Keynesian and classical economists on matters of significant economic policy, and the establishment of a coherent language, if not a singular vision, for the adjudication of economic policy differences.

The language of mathematics championed by Samuelson has enabled a constructive conversation, during the past 30 years, between the freshwater free-market economists of Chicago and the salt-water Keynesian economists of Cambridge, and has led to a cautious truce between the two camps. One economist neatly summarizes this situation by noting that each side has declared "a brackish victory."[26]

Contrary to the views of most observers outside the discipline, virtually every cogent and fair-minded economist will say that there is more *agreement* among members of the profession on the big matters of fiscal and monetary policy than there is *disagreement*. Given that it is difficult to distinguish a Democrat economist from a Republican economist these days, or a Labour economist from a Conservative economist on the major questions of policy direction, the progress marked by those standouts whose heroic work has been discussed in this chapter speaks for itself.

Thus, has the war of wits—waged by American, British, and other economists from the democratic world—helped rescue, for many of us, the privileges of living in a civil society that would surely make Adam Smith proud and of struggling anew with the challenge of expanding it for the benefit of others. Macroeconomists will continue to sling mathematical symbols at one another, but not for any lack of effort toward consensus. The problems they address are so great that they will probably always elude definitive solution. Hence, solutions must always be sought.

8

Comeback Kid

Instead of looking for necessary and sufficient conditions of change, we must train ourselves to be on the lookout for unusual historical developments, rare constellations of favorable events, narrow paths, partial advances that may conceivably be followed by others and the like. We must think of the possible rather than the probable.

Albert O. Hirschman

When we are right—and have the clarity to prevail against the special interests and the quacks—we make an extraordinary contribution to the amelioration of poverty and the progress of humanity. . . . The intricate social cooperation that emerges when there is a sophisticated array of markets requires far better institutions and economic policies than most countries have.

Mancur Olson

In 1999, when summarizing the remarkable impact of twentieth-century monetary and macroeconomics on the functioning of today's capitalist economy, one economist made the following remark, and not without a touch of irony: "Decades ago, Paul Samuelson wrote of a 'neo-classical synthesis' in which the proper application of macroeconomic stabilization policy would create the full-employment conditions necessary to validate neoclassical microeconomics. Well, to a first approximation,

109

we have achieved that neoclassical synthesis in the United States. Thus, did the intellectual descendants of John Maynard Keynes pave the way for the worldwide comeback of Adam Smith."[1]

Now You See It

Despite the progress of macroeconomics, the return of Adam Smith had surprising implications for his descendants in the economics department. As economists developed more and more mathematical acumen, and better and better ways of capturing and combing data, they had come to be viewed, by critics, less as worldly philosophers and increasingly as airless technicians who were detached from the world that they had claimed, with such apparent arrogance, they could explain. The sterner strictures of *The Wealth of Nations,* it seemed, had trumped the sweeter nostrums of *The Theory of Moral Sentiments.* Adam Smith, in his contemporary guise, had been rendered a philosopher with a head full of numbers, a heart full of dust, and an invisible hand in everything. As one economist critical of his field conjectured, "Mathematics brought rigor to economics. Unfortunately, it also brought mortis!"[2]

Meanwhile, outside of economics, a generation of postwar political thinkers, historians, and philosophers—well represented in universities and in an array of publications from *Dissent* and *The Nation* to *The New Statesman and Society*—were intent upon reshaping market society along the lines of European-style democratic socialism. They seemed only too happy to reinforce the image of economists as engineers of an increasingly inflexible competitive corporate capitalism.

This chapter will not tell a story of one hand clapping. Quietly, beyond the din of macroeconomic debate, some economists chipped away at the stony image they had earned, not by abandoning their mathematical models, which became even more abstract as time wore on, but by expanding their scope and turning their sights to new and unlikely—but useful—civic purposes. The economist who has been most brilliant and influential in setting the agenda for this new wave, Nobel laureate Kenneth Arrow, captured the spirit of this research initiative incisively when he said:

There are all sorts of institutions in the economic world which depart from the simple price/market model. . . . There are all sorts of contractual relations between firms and individuals which do not conform to the simple price theory—profit-sharing schemes and so forth—and the explanation for these suddenly became clear. We now understand why these emerged and that they are based on differences in information in the economy.[3]

Economists in this new wave had begun to help integrate their understanding of economic institutions into a broader picture of society. Moving beyond the high church affairs of fiscal and monetary policy, increasing numbers of economists shifted their attention to the understanding of political and social structures, where economic and social capital mingle, where wealth and sentiments meet.

As noted in the first chapter herein, a high degree of social capital is inherently valuable in a market democracy because it embodies the society's cultural resourcefulness—the very quality Smith sought to promote in *The Theory of Moral Sentiments*. But, as the new wave of economists discovered, it also has implications for economic performance. For example, the effective functioning of organizations, from airlines to construction companies to insurance firms, depends on the amalgam of trust, sociability, knowledge, and shared ethical expectations contained in the experience of their employees and in the culture of their managements. It therefore conditions their ability to produce, grow, and innovate. Thus, social capital is also of consequence, literally, to the wealth of nations, and therefore to economists.

Adam Smith had indeed reappeared, but the Enlightenment *arriviste* who had returned to inspire the chalk-and-blackboard seminars of many of his economic offspring proved to be as interested in the promotion of civic institutions as in the production of wealth.

With Friends Like These

The renewed interest in civic institutions in economics did not happen overnight. Beyond the journals and café conversation of the Left, many middle-of-the-road political and cultural publications had effectively stopped paying attention to mainstream economics. They omitted from their pages all but the occasional economist (except for the ever dependable Robert Heilbroner and a few other kindred souls). To make matters worse, economics had begun to develop a peculiar cottage industry of in-house inquisitors and critics. Chief among them was MIT economist and popular writer Lester Thurow, who, in his widely read book, *Dangerous Currents,* took mainstream economists to task for their overreliance on mathematics and econometrics.[4] Later, prominent economic historian Deirdre McCloskey tore into the heart of her field—especially Paul Samuelson's hyperquantification of it—for its mathematical fetishism, and for "the insignificance of statistical significance."[5]

Not surprisingly, most of this criticism came from those on the field's political Left. They formed a loyal opposition and searched for an expanded role for the redistribution of wealth—a balm that would ease the problems of inequality as defined by any number of standards. (Race, class, and, increasingly, gender were the prime categories.) But even the usually sympathetic commentators on the Right—writers such as libertarian Paul Craig Roberts—condemned mainstream economists for what they regarded as a tepid, politically correct embrace of public policies (such as the minimum wage) and a failure to completely exorcise government from the economy.[6] Rodney Dangerfield would have understood.

Outside the Box

But all was not boards and brickbats. Perhaps the most perceptive—and most constructive—critique from within the field arrived courtesy of the late Mancur Olson, an economist who managed to combine his criticism of economic orthodoxy with an impressive penchant for partaking in some of the more avant-garde initiatives afoot in the field. Olson was one of those rare economists who always seemed to think outside the box. As interest began to mount on the civic side of economics, Olson reveled in the intellectual energy transfer he saw taking place.

Mancur Olson—a native North Dakotan who had pursued a distinguished career at the University of Maryland, and sadly died an untimely death in 1998 at age 66—was not quite a renegade economist, but almost.

Olson had long blazed a novel intellectual trail, not by denigrating economics but by ransacking it. Olson usurped economic thinking to explore the ways in which poorly designed civic and political institutions impeded economic progress.

In his 1965 book, *The Logic of Collective Action,* Olson explained that cartels were inherently faulty because of the ever-present incentive for some members to free-ride on the contributions of others. In *The Rise and Decline of Nations* (1982), Olson cautioned that interest groups, feeding at the public trough, would inevitably subvert economic progress in a democracy by corroding the political system with graft and patronage, thus bringing a stifling gridlock to the public square. The movement to create "term limits" for legislators is largely a policy outgrowth of Olson's critique. The economist from North Dakota expropriated his profession's preoccupation with incentives and sanctions to try to explain problems that had seemingly little economic content. He appears to have seen these forces, and the opportunity for using economic tools to understand them, whether he was trying to explain why things worked or why they failed to work. He was not highly regarded as a technical researcher, but a leading economic theorist once remarked to me, over lunch, while Olson was still alive, "The guy writes great books."[7]

Worldly Philosophers, with Beer and Mower

In the posthumously published 1999 book that he edited with Satu Kähkönen, *A Not-So-Dismal Science,* Olson and his coeditor likened the neoclassical core of the field to an aging inner city studded with abandoned, silent streets, and dark, imposing, classical skyscrapers. This characterization would have had fellow critics of economics nodding their heads in approval and calling for more—until they read on. For, according to Olson and Kähkönen, this snapshot of downtown, while accurate, was incomplete and therefore misleading. In their view, the action in economics had not disappeared. Economists had just piled into a station wagon and moved to the suburbs. Accordingly,

> . . . the suburbs of the subject are thriving and expanding. In the study
> of politics, economists and political scientists using economic-type

methods have had an extraordinary influence and created the substantial and growing field that is variously called collective (or public or social choice). In the study of law, ideas from economics have been the single most important source of intellectual change. . . . In history, the quantitative and theory-inspired approach of economics has had, partly through "cliometrics," a profound influence. In sociology, economics has had a smaller, but rapidly increasing influence through "rational choice sociology" and economists' study of demography, the family, and crime.[8]

I once used Mancur Olson's suburbanization analogy to explain the changing character of the dismal science to a group of noneconomist scholars, most of whom had little knowledge of, and even less interest in, economics. I began by noting that the economists' move—out of the classical precincts of the old city—had enabled them to exploit and enrich the connections among a host of neighboring "suburban" fields alluded to by Olson, including politics, law, organizations, psychology, sociology, philosophy, and even cultural analysis. Not uncoincidentally, these fields had some of their roots in *The Theory of Moral Sentiments,* and, as noted earlier, had split off from economics during the latter part of the nineteenth century. Moreover, the economists' sojourn to the suburbs had given the profession hope that the addition of new and more complex shadings to existing orthodox models would yield better accounts of economic reality, and thus better means of guiding policymakers.[9]

In my talk, I stressed to my dubious academic audience that what was new about Olson's suburban economics was not the recognition that civic institutions matter. What was new and encouraging was the economists' *explanations* of how institutions work, or fail to work, and how these political and civic institutions affect the quality of economic policy-making and thus the wealth of nations. Olson and other economists felt that their understanding of noneconomic institutions, based on observations founded on incentives and strategic considerations, brought new insight to the task of reforming these vital structures for the betterment of society.

As my talk continued, I told suburban stories. I noted that poverty economists had come to understand famines less as the result of natural disasters than as a failure of the purchasing power of the poor owing to political corruption or errant policy coordination.[10] Specialists in the economic analysis of law had come to understand "black markets" in developing countries as informal economies that were insulated from outside investment opportunities because of the absence of secure property rights.[11] Political economists were now reexamining the incentive structure of legislatures, constitutions, and voting systems to try to understand how the workings of these structures affected economic policy decisions and therefore the enhancement of growth and efficiency.[12] Organizational economists, who had long thought of firms merely as "black boxes," were beginning to reconceive of them as constellations of contracts—some formal, others informal—among employers, employees, and suppliers.[13] Development economists had begun to perceive traditional village practices such as strip-farming less as a mysterious folkway than as an insurance system that protects the property of farmers from vandals, animals, and fires through the equivalent of portfolio diversification.[14] Economic historians had begun to understand how contract law and the modern system of international trade had emerged from the evolution of trust and its origins in cross-cultural medieval trade.[15]

I emphasized that "suburban" economics, as characterized by Mancur Olson, was not only analytical, but had a policy side to boot. Game theorists working on the design of auctions for pollution rights were devising clever new pricing schemes for converting previously inefficient state-managed energy sources such as electricity to more efficient and potentially environmentally friendly use.[16] Finance economists had set up the machinery for personal investment accounts to enable average people to partake in the world's expanding capital markets.[17] Transition economists were designing plans for converting previously state-controlled economies to markets through the deployment of vouchers.[18] Development economists had begun to urge the establishment of property rights that would make it possible for people in developing countries to cultivate the kinds of "asset management" practices that have supercharged the economies of western capitalism.[19]

The broader point I tried to make to my listeners was that economists were reengaging culture and politics in the service of economic growth, particularly for underdeveloped and transitional economies, and for the less fortunate corners of our own society. In doing so, they were uncovering the rational underpinnings of otherwise seemingly irrational practices (like strip-farming), while demonstrating why certain time-honored rational institutions, such as the dusty old firm, were not really so efficient after all. Like Adam Smith, these economists were using their new insights to fill in the contours of a better theory of society—not by neglecting or minimizing the influence of either the market or the state, but by better understanding the forces that united them.

Even Mancur Olson, the maverick economist who had spent most of his career explaining why things fall apart, had become possessed of the urge to understand how they could be put back together—how "collective rationality," as he called it, could be galvanized toward the public good.[20]

Olson had become so convinced of the importance of building broad-based social and political institutions as a foundation for economic performance that he dedicated what turned out to be his last years to seeking ways to promote such institutions, especially in underachieving societies that were struggling to enrich their economic well-being.

The economists' suburban journey hardly registered in the canonical left-wing criticisms of the field or even in the free-market celebrations of it. But it represents potentially a huge step forward in the consideration and betterment of our social condition, as well as a gentle step backward toward the reconciliation of the two sides of Adam Smith: wealth, embodied in markets; and moral sentiments, embedded in the political and civic institutions that abet the successful functioning of markets.

The suburbanized economics extolled by Mancur Olson animates Samuelson's Instructions by illuminating its social embeddedness, and it addresses Heilbroner's Warning by indicating how economic society can achieve greater broad-based prosperity without abandoning the growth-producing power of markets. It makes it harder for the social critics of both the Left and the Right to dismiss economics as just so much mathematical meandering.

Rational Fools

Just as economists have begun to colonize Mancur Olson's suburbs, the suburbs have begun to beautify the field's old city structures. For example, the idea of economic rationality, a cornerstone in the edifice of economics, is evolving into something far more sophisticated and subtle than the old greed-and-glory tandem that, however caricatured, had long enabled critics to dismiss economics as a science of the undead. Along this line of research, economists, led by the Indian-born Nobel prize-winning economist and philosopher Amartya Sen, perhaps the leading authority in the world on ethical foundations of economics, acknowledged that economic rationality is highly contingent on its social context.

According to this style of analysis, inner-city kids who see absolutely nothing around them except death and destruction and therefore assume that they won't make it to age 21 years, are not necessarily considered so irrational if they fail to apply themselves in school, or drop out altogether.[21] By the same token, a "yes man"—that all-too-familiar ambitious executive who sees it in his interest to tell his boss what she wants to hear instead of telling her what he knows is right—is acting pretty rationally, given the context, if it means serving the short-term goal of getting ahead in his career.[22]

Alongside the troubling insight that even the most destructive and foolhardy behavior can be deemed rational, depending upon the circumstances, is another intriguing line of research. Recently, economists have suggested that when people are seeking to serve their own self-interest, cooperating with others—rather than merely trying to maximize their own interest at everybody else's expense—is rational.

Economists have traditionally assumed that it is rational for people to maximize their own economic self-interest, and that this compulsion serves the greater interest, "as if by an Invisible Hand." So far, so good. But a caricatured version of this insight suggests that the greater good can reasonably be served by unrepentant avarice: "greed, for lack of a better word, is good," announced Gordon Gekko, the Nietzschean antihero in Oliver Stone's movie *Wall Street,* as if greed were somehow the queen of all virtues.[23]

Not really, say contemporary economists. In his "commitment model" of rational behavior, Cornell economist Robert Frank, another widely respected expert in psychological aspects of economic behavior, suggests that a dose of cooperation actually serves to secure one's self-interest in the long run. The idea is: If I demonstrate an interest in cooperation and team play, this signal will be noticed and I will be called on to participate in rewarding activities over time, thus serving my own greater interests. Given these broadly shared social expectations, it is probably more profitable, over the long run, to get an MBA and *run* a bank than to get a gun, let out a wailing prayer to Adam Smith, and rob one.

The commitment model, when joined with an increasing awareness of social context, has made for a much more widely accepted means of understanding rational behavior than in the days of hypergreed. The insights of Frank and his colleagues into why it is rational for people to tip at out-of-town restaurants they'll never visit again, to pay rather than cheat on their taxes, and to seek compromise rather than burning bridges in organizations, have helped to define modern microeconomics as a more subtle science of social behavior.[24]

But this trend would hardly have seemed strange to Adam Smith, who observed: "In all the middling and inferior professions, real and solid abilities, joined to prudent, just, firm, and temperate conduct, can very seldom fail of success, . . . The success of such people, too, almost always depends on the favour and good opinion of their neighbours and equals; and without a tolerably regular conduct, these can seldom be obtained."[25]

The Crabgrass Enlightenment

So, the Adam Smith of moral sentiments is back, and the suburbs of economics are thriving. But what accounts for the shift in emphasis from markets to other kinds of institutions? I give credit to two factors—one from the school of economic ideas, and the other from the school of hard knocks.

While mid-twentieth-century macroeconomists were fighting the dragons of inflation and unemployment (and, often, each other) and, in the process, hammering out sturdier fiscal and monetary policy principles, microeconomists were quietly revolutionizing—or should I say *suburbanizing*—their part of the field. Douglass North, a Nobel prize-winning economic historian who started his career as a Marxist and learned economic theory while playing chess, is noteworthy among economists who revived the profession's interest in institutions.

North by Northwest

Born in 1920, North, the son of a Cambridge, Massachusetts-based insurance executive, had suffered no vocational ambiguity. "I knew where I was going the day I decided to become an economist. I set out to understand what made economies rich or poor because I viewed that objective as being the essential prerequisite to improving their performance." The man from Massachusetts changed his venue when his father's business relocated him to the San Francisco Bay area. Young Douglass, wishing to stay close to his family, enrolled as an undergraduate, and later as a graduate economics student, at the University of California, Berkeley. Not surprising, North, seemingly obsessed with making the world a better place, found the means of doing so in Marxism, then virtually the official state religion of Berkeley. North learned a lot of economic history at Berkeley, then moved to the faculty of the University of Washington in Seattle. There, he began playing chess with a colleague and theorist, Don Gordon. "In the three years of playing chess every day from noon to two, I may have beaten Don at chess, but he taught me economics; more important, he taught me how to reason like an economist, and that skill is perhaps the most important tool that I have acquired."[26]

North's chess lessons served him well. He married his Marxian passion for changing the world with his acquired skill "to reason like an economist," and the outcome is known as the New Institutional Economics. Why institutions? According to North, "They are the rules of the game of a society and in consequence provide the framework of incentives that shape economic, political, and social organization. . . . Institutions affect economic performance by determining, together with the technology employed . . . the total costs of production. Since there is an intimate connection between the institutions and technology employed, the efficiency of a market is directly shaped by the institutional framework."[27]

In his classic history of western economics, cowritten with Robert Thomas, North:

> . . . considered the economic development of Western Europe from the middle ages to the eighteenth century, and showed that economic incentives, based upon individual property rights, were a prerequisite for

economic growth. . . . The speedier industrialisation in England and the Netherlands depended upon the fact that certain conservative institutions, such as the guilds, were weak. Private property rights were also guaranteed in these countries, as opposed to the case of Spain where the lack of institutional innovation led to a century-long stagnation. Innovations, technical changes and other factors that are generally regarded as explanations, are not considered to be sufficient by North. They are themselves a part of the growth process and cannot explain it. Effective economic organizations are the key to economic change.[28]

North's insight about the relevance of institutions occasioned a minor revolution in economics by encouraging neoclassically inclined economists to peek under the hood of their elegant models and examine the underlying moral, political, social, and legal conditions that helped to produce economic performance. This insight, and the flood of research it unleashed, made economics messier and less self-assured, but they don't call it suburban for nothing.

Two Cheers for Government

To restate the claim made at the beginning of this chapter, the monetary economics of Keynes and his fellow macroeconomists led to the return of Adam Smith. Before moving on to the new initiatives issuing forth from the reunification of wealth and sentiments, it is worth noting how some contemporary economists have come to think about the one institution Smith is least associated with, but which is nevertheless regarded as vital to a progressive economic society—government.

Smith regarded government as necessary for guaranteeing vital public functions, such as defense and education, which could not be relegated to markets. Despite the recent triumph of markets on a grander scale than even Smith himself could have imagined, he would almost surely see the need for a continued economic role for government. Economist Dani Rodrik has been eloquent in reminding other economists of the continued importance of government, not in spite of, but rather *because* of, the explosion of markets.

Dani Rodrik, a native of Turkey, received his PhD in economics at Princeton and now teaches at Harvard's Kennedy School of Government.

He brings economic analysis to bear in an effort to understand some of the most important functions government can play in economic state-craft, and the most effective and efficient ways in which government can perform its role. Rodrik has written on why some states are more suc-cessful than others, and why different models of government interven-tion work in some kinds of economic cultures and fail to fit others.

For example, Japan, despite almost universal advice from critics near and far, has had horrendous problems liberalizing its banking institu-tions, in part because the financial discipline that comes with this kind of reform can create serious unemployment, and Japan, unlike the United States and most Western European countries, has no economic safety net to protect the droves of potential unemployed workers vic-timized by this unavoidable process. Its corporations and *keiretsus are* its safety net, and they depend on the banking system as it is historically constituted.

According to Rodrik, "In their haste to roll back the state, many economists and policymakers have overlooked the fact that the mainte-nance of social safety nets is not a luxury but an essential ingredient to a market economy. Markets are a wonderful thing, but they also expose households to risks and insecurities that have to be contained."[29]

As an example of an artful effort to use government to bolster free markets and growth, Rodrik notes how recent government reforms have worked in Chile. Chile's President Patricio Alwyn, "raised the minimum wage, increased spending on pensions, social subsidies, basic education and health, and launched debt-relief programs (e.g., for housing debt) for lower and middle income groups. Chile has shown that such things can be done in a fiscally responsible manner."[30]

As Rodrik points out, the support for these social programs was paid for by tax reform, not by deficit spending. But Rodrik's overriding point is that, given the economic context, government, in the form of social in-surance, is a necessary structure in policies designed to expand markets, not subvert them; to stabilize the society, not subsidize it. Adam Smith, for his part, put it thus:

> The third and last duty of the sovereign or commonwealth is that of erecting and maintaining those public institutions and those public works which, though they may be in the highest degree advantageous to

a great society, are, however, of such a nature that the profit could never repay the expense to any individual or small number of individuals.[31]

Two Hands Clapping

As mentioned earlier, Adam Smith saw that social institutions—including but not limited to the market—if properly harnessed, held the greatest possible promise for enriching and civilizing a society long bereft of the basic necessities or mercies that are most taken for granted today. As I hope this chapter has demonstrated, the "suburban" economists of the present and the upcoming generations are dusting off Smith's vision as they embrace the importance of civic institutions and social capital.

9

Kitchen Chemists

Rates of growth of real per-capita income . . . are diverse, even over sustained periods. . . . Indian incomes will double every 50 years; Korean every 10. I do not know how one can look at figures like these without seeing them as representing possibilities. Is there some action a government of India could take that would lead the Indian economy to grow like Indonesia's or Egypt's? If so, what, exactly? If not, what is it about the "nature of India" that makes it so? The consequences of human welfare involved in questions like these are simply staggering. . . .

Robert Lucas

For a very small expence the public can facilitate, can encourage, and can even impose upon almost the whole body of the people, the necessity of acquiring those most essential parts of education. The public can facilitate this acquisition by establishing in every parish or district a little school, where children may be taught for a reward so moderate, that even a common labourer may afford it; the master being partly, but not wholly paid by the public: because if he was wholly, or even principally paid by it, he would soon learn to neglect his business.

Adam Smith

Adam Smith's monumental economic achievement was to explain to legislators how to promote commercial activity through markets and thereby increase the purchasing power of the entire society. For this he is justly dubbed "the father of free enterprise." But he also saw in his scheme a crucial place for *public* enterprise. In one of his most quoted passages, he noted that ". . . There are many expenses necessary in a civilized country for which there is no occasion in one that is barbarous. Armies, fleets, fortified palaces, and public buildings, judges, and officers of the revenue must be supported, and if they be neglected, disorder will ensue."[1]

Fat Brains

In addition to Smith's brief laundry list of "expenses," the history of modern public enterprise includes everything from employment programs to highway systems, urban renewal, public housing, social security, power and electrification projects, public broadcasting, and space programs. To say that enterprises such as those, and others like them, have had a mixed reception, is to revel in the obvious. Pundits on the Right have long criticized them for their inefficient means and growth-subverting ends. Critics on the Left complain that public enterprises are too few and far between, and are underfunded.

How might Adam Smith have thought about the structure and function of public enterprise if he were advising governments today? To my mind, his sentiments emerge in the work of a handful of contemporary economists. Their ideas encompass the development of basic scientific research and the delivery of education, projects designed to mediate the economic legacy of racism, employment initiatives for the hardcore unemployed, and tax strategies designed to promote equity and growth. What these initiatives have in common is the fresh integration of market incentives and moral purpose in their design—a formula reminiscent of Adam Smith's plan for the structure and function of public institutions.

If I Had a Hammer

Adam Smith was the original multitasker: a man of ideas and a man of action. He sought not only to draw a blueprint of a civilized commercial society, but, through his meetings and correspondence with legislators, and through his books, to help build the society he had envisaged. He was both chief architect and general contractor. This builder's passion, which has never really left the soul of economic activists like Smith, can be seen in grand public initiatives dating from the German welfare state of the nineteenth century and continuing in the New Deal of the early twentieth century and in enduring public enterprises such as the British national health service, the New Frontier and Great Society crusades of the 1960s, and other efforts, large and small (energy and conservation projects, national education schemes, social security, and transportation systems).

Aside from their intended economic purposes, a singular beauty of certain public enterprises is that, so often, they are born of great social spirit. For example, Britain's national health service rose alongside a war effort that united the hearts and galvanized the soul of an entire nation. The social programs of the 1960s accompanied historic reforms on the part of Americans long riven by racial injustice and hostility. These and similar public enterprises bear the mark of moral sentiments engendered by a sense of solidarity and purpose that is rare in fast-moving, atomized societies like ours. However ineffective or inefficient some of these public enterprises may be, they embody public pride. Canadians appear fiercely proud of their national health service, not so much because of its medical excellence nor certainly for its economic efficiency, but because of the moral sentiment it supports. Americans love public education—despite its unenviable record of achievement in recent generations—at least partly because of its historic role in promoting a sense of citizenship.

These are exactly the kinds of projects that strike horror in the hearts of classical liberals because these critics regard such public enterprises as ineffective and corrupt parasite-structures intended primarily to serve the bureaucrats who administer them while soaking the public that pays for them. According to these critics, public enterprises, from health services through public school systems, ravage the public purse, subvert economic growth, strengthen the hand and fatten the wallet of government, reduce personal freedom, stifle fairness and creativity, and subvert the aspirations of the very people they are intended to help—people who would be better aided by freely functioning markets. The mind races to the indelible images of the drug- and gun-infested public housing projects, the failing schools, and the substandard hospitals in our big cities.

Yet, even Milton Friedman and his coterie of classical liberals, borrowing from Adam Smith, see a place in society for the general provision of education, aid to the poor and infirm, and maintenance of physical infrastructure. Where they draw their line in the sand against welfare-state liberals is in the *design* of such public enterprises. Welfare-state liberals tend to train their eyes on the ends; classical liberals pay attention to the means.

Adam Smith, Social Engineer

In this ongoing battle involving the purpose, scale, and design of public enterprise, compromise presently seems to have carried the day. Even as Big Government has been declared dead, certain economists continue scribbling at their drawing boards, concocting plans for new public enterprises intended to address Big Problems. What is different about these contemporary economists' efforts? They pay as much attention to the incentive structures of public enterprise as they do to the outcomes, thereby returning the architectural franchise of public policymaking to the tradition of Adam Smith, Social Engineer. They know the devil is in the details. They've seen him there in his past incarnations.

Further, the new breed of public economists always keeps one eye on the greater service of economic growth in the design of public enterprise—growth that is not to be confused with the redistribution of wealth, which was the overriding economic goal of many an old public program. The lesson here is: Growth expands the economic pie. Socially, it pays larger long-term residuals by bringing into the mainstream people who are on the economic fringe.

A vital dimension in Adam Smith's revived conception of public enterprise is the advancement of *knowledge,* especially technological research. For Smith, knowledge played a dual function in a civilized commercial society: In the pin factory, the application of specialized knowledge facilitated the expansion of economic prosperity. In schools, knowledge enriched the lives of people throughout all ranks of society, especially the less fortunate, whose days were numbed by the tedium of the brutal work done in that same pin factory. Since Smith's day, and owing largely to the success of the commercial division of labor he described, brain work has gradually outpaced backwork as the most economically productive of activities, thereby increasing the relative value of knowledge. The relationship among the economic function of knowledge, economic growth, and civic purpose is only now emerging in full force.

Digitizing the Pin Factory

Connections between knowledge and economic growth have preoccupied economists since the early days of commercial society two centuries ago, and have had a particularly impressive renaissance recently. No one has been more imaginative or eloquent in framing the link between ideas and growth than Chicago-trained, Stanford-based economist Paul M. Romer, who points out that no amount of fiscal and monetary magic, however clever, can, in and of itself, lead to sustained growth; only new ideas can effectively enlarge the economic pie. Echoing the sentiment that our system of free markets prevails not because of its inherent virtues, but because of its manifest superiority over other systems, Romer, a pragmatist, insists that the "challenge for economists is to understand why markets perform well and then build upon their strengths."[2]

In stating that "everything, including institutions, can always be improved," this economist has refocused the profession's effort to understand and distill the factors that lead to economic growth, including the production of new knowledge. This search for the sources of economic growth—and the defense of its importance in the culture of capitalism—is one of the most vital features of Adam Smith's present legacy.[3]

Economists historically contend that growth depends on a range of factors: demographic shifts, technological change, savings and consumption, the work ethic, levels of trade, legal rules, and educational achievement—among others. Today's approach to understanding growth in advanced societies, and in those moving toward higher industrial levels, emphasizes this notion: freely functioning economic institutions have the inherent capacity to absorb and to synthesize a continuing reconfiguration of ideas, large and small, that drive economic activity, trade, and efficiency.[4] This linkage suggests that economic growth emerges from invention and innovation. Thus does there appear a compelling economic need for public enterprise that supports the creation of new knowledge.

According to Paul Romer, the better an economy absorbs and processes ideas, the more likely it will generate new recipes for goods and services and, ultimately, for greater growth and higher standards of living. Romer makes his point via a compelling comparison. In confronting the wildly disparate levels of economic development that have occurred throughout the world since World War II, he asks why did some economies explode with growth while others sputtered?

The answer lay, at least partly, in the decision of the more successful countries to open up their industrial cultures to ideas from the outside world of transnational corporate capitalism. The emphasis here is on openness to trade not only in products but in *ideas*—managerial techniques, manufacturing processes, labor practices, R&D strategies, organizational forms, legal and bureaucratic innovations.[5] For example, before World War II, Japan had been famously resistant to ideas from the outside world. But all that changed. Postwar Japan opened its economic culture and welcomed ideas from around the world, especially in manufacturing.

For decades, this openness has paid great dividends to Japan and to the world. We witness evidence of it daily in the remarkable proliferation of Toyota cars, Toshiba laptops, and other products of Japanese enterprise that populate our homes, schools, and workplaces. Alternatively, the decision of other countries to protect their industries from capitalist competition and from the influence of the new ideas competition brings, is equally evident in their persistent poverty and public corruption.[6]

Paul Romer takes his conceptual engineering analogy into the kitchen to explain high-growth paths. Japan, a country that cannot boast of an overabundance of natural resources, is given to finding new ways—new recipes, if you will—of combining its limited resources to create useful products that are vastly out of proportion to the value of their natural ingredients. Accordingly, Romer notes:

> Economic growth occurs whenever people take resources and rearrange them in ways that are more valuable. A useful metaphor for production in such an economy comes from the kitchen: To create valuable final products, we mix inexpensive ingredients together according to a recipe. . . . Human history teaches us, however, that economic growth springs from better recipes, not just from more cooking.[7]

The so-called East Asian "Economic Miracle," of which Japan was the prime mover, has run into heavy weather in the past decade. As noted in the previous chapter, some policies, such as the reform of financial infrastructure, much needed in Japan, are more difficult to deploy than others. Nevertheless, Japan's adaptation and application of the economics of ideas to the process of *manufacturing* remains nothing short of remarkable.[8]

Paul Romer conjectures that there are literally tens of thousands of different small and large ways of organizing the production of objects—be they hamburgers, shirts, cars, heart operations, or superconductors. Thus, the true brilliance of the Japanese industrialists has been in their unceasing determination to find the best, most efficient, and most ingenious ways, for manufacturing products. Romer highlights this process as an intriguing source of growth:

> The most important lesson from the study of research and development, economic growth, and the history of technology is that there are more ways to arrange objects of the physical world than humans can possibly imagine. Ultimately, all improvements in standards of living can be traced to discoveries of more valuable arrangements for the things in the earth's crust and atmosphere. . . .[9]

The foregoing claim has never been embodied as compellingly as in the creative combination of the materials needed to make airplanes, which, in turn, have efficiently connected today's modern economies and helped to drive growth forward by facilitating trade among these economies. Because of the precise ways in which airplane parts must be arranged, they are much more valuable, as objects, than is the sum of their parts.

Pins, Kitchens, and Classrooms

The parallels between the humble image of Romer's kitchen and Adam Smith's pin factory are highly suggestive. Because the operators of Smith's pin factory exploit specialized functions, cooperation, and a division of labor, they are able to make pins more efficiently than a single artisan could ever make them. This mode of enterprise constitutes a powerful growth engine that has shaped economic activity throughout the modern world.

Smith's pin factory exists full-blown in tens of thousands of forms around the world, not unlike Minerva issuing from the head of Zeus. But in Romer's kitchen, as opposed to Smith's pin factory, the action is in the mental investment that shapes production—from the organization of work through the design of products. Indeed, as Chicago's Gary Becker and Kevin Murphy have suggested, the division of labor embodied by Smith's pin factory is limited not so much by the structure of the market as by the power of the human brain and its ability to produce new and inventive means of serving society's material needs.[10]

A compelling example of this metamorphosis is Toyota's just-in-time production process, which brought about improvements in the quality control and efficiency of auto production, and represented a seismic advance in efficiency over Henry Ford's ingenious assembly line, itself a magnificent breakthrough. What is important here is that this shift in production technologies—from an assembly line to a just-in-time organization—reflected a change in *thinking,* not material—brainwork, not backwork. This creative reorganization of the way things work helps to explain the success of leading postindustrial capitalist enterprises from Toyota to Microsoft, as well as the economic returns to the larger society.

The idea of economic recombination is hardly restricted to product design and production processes. It has important parallels in the making of policies, expressing itself in creative strategies for designing new public enterprises once constructed only through massive, and often wasteful and ineffectual, government investment projects.[11]

Sixties Wine in Twenty-First Century Bottles

Paul Romer has an exciting proposal to address a perennial issue charged by public-private debate: the provision of large-scale public enterprises too costly for individual businesses to undertake and yet too easy for governments to convert into tax-eating public monstrosities. Although he limits his conceptualization to projects in scientific and technological research and development, Romer's idea has promising implications for large-scale projects in other areas as well.

In his paper, "Implementing a National Technology Strategy with Self-Organizing Industry Investment Boards," Romer proposes a scheme that would enable society to direct substantial financial resources to support innovative technological development and leverage it into large-scale economic benefits for the public without the burden of structural or bureaucratic increases in the size of government.[12]

Romer first identifies the kinds of goods—for example, parallel-processing super computers—that are so costly to produce yet so vital to the well-being of society that they require development through large-scale collective action. The conundrum is that just as the government alone is large enough to undertake such projects, private enterprise alone has the incentive structure needed to carry them out efficiently and without producing a massive self-sustaining bureaucracy—a problem tailor-made for Smith-style analysis. Romer then suggests some clever kitchen chemistry for this new form of public enterprise: an arrangement called a "self-organizing industry investment board" that unites the respective strengths of government and business for the purpose of carrying out the necessary research effectively and efficiently.

Industry investment boards would operate largely by exploiting the respective strengths of both business (an interest in profits, and a ready responsiveness to incentives) and government (the ability to tax, and a large-scale coordination capability). This arrangement represents an effort designed to short-circuit many of the traps that usually accompany such enterprises when they are attempted by government or business alone.

According to Romer's article, the national government would facilitate the research and development necessary to undertake the design and production of these supercomputers, but the financing would come exclusively through taxes levied on the businesses directly engaged in (and most likely to benefit from) the creation of these new products. Progress on this project would be reviewed by the corporate members of industry investment boards, thus balancing each member's agreement to pay the requisite tax with a corresponding incentive to scrutinize and endorse (or, as the case may be, end) the project.[13]

It stands to reason that if self-organizing industry investment boards could be designed to create supercomputers, they could also be organized to tackle a whole range of other large-scale scientific projects, from computational biology to nanotechnologies to robotics.

I came across a particularly compelling potential application in an article by financier Michael Milken. Milken wrote forcefully about the huge positive economic and other implications of finding a cure for cancer: "The main benefit would be an incalculable, but magnificent, reduction in human suffering; and the economic benefit of lives saved would be in the tens of trillions of dollars. . . ." Milken, a world-class champion of freedom from big government, here calls for aggressive *big-government action* on the scale of the heroic public enterprises of the past. He estimates that a public investment of about $20 billion would accelerate cures by about a decade.[14] How would such a large-scale project be carried out? To my mind, this one is custom-made for Romer's industry investment boards.

Nips and Tucks

Romer points out that the self-organizing industry investment board idea is actually a new variation on an old capitalist theme: It evolves out of earlier institutional innovations such as the limited-liability corporation, the modern research university, the scholarly system of peer review, the law of copyright and patents, and the history of industrial research and development. Just like the kitchen chemistry that creates new physical products, it joins elements of the existing institutional environment to solve old problems in novel ways. Romer's proposed investment boards come about through the creative assortment of some of the basic institutional materials of capitalism, reengineered to produce a desired outcome. The economic dynamics are reflected in the market design; the social capital emerges in the public provision of the civic goals—enhanced health care, improved physical infrastructure, streamlined social services, renewed energy sources, revitalized public transportation systems—that these technological innovations are designed to serve.[15]

Repainting the School House

Thanks to Paul Romer and others, the *expansion* of knowledge through public enterprise is now widely acknowledged as a vital ingredient in feeding the large-scale technological initiatives necessary to enhanced economic prosperity. However, the *inculcation* of knowledge—education, in other words—is even more crucial in the direct reduction of persistent public problems (such as inequality and poverty) in which the entire society has a stake. Although Adam Smith promoted the enrichment of knowledge through education primarily to buffer the mental hardship incurred by laborers, it is not unreasonable to imagine that he would have appreciated the direct economic value of education in a society that produces more pixels than pins.

Beyond universities and R&D departments, perhaps the most vital public institutions in the cultivation of knowledge are local elementary and secondary schools—the pride of democratic civil society and a core engine of economic and social progress. Their manifest educational functions aside, neighborhood schools—those that unite the interest and commitment of parents, local educators, civic leaders, and business—have long been invaluable assets for a healthy civil society, and thus carry potent supplies of social capital.

Given the shift in our economy—away from smokestacks and toward knowledge and information-based industry—good neighborhood schools have, if anything, increased in value as wellsprings of human and social capital. But, in the recent generation, the delivery system of public education has come under great stress for its failure to produce graduates who can adequately perform the basics of reading, writing, science, and mathematics, which are needed to support the shift in the economy.

In a sense, the *public* school system represents a cultural feature of market democracy that is an exact opposite of many of capitalism's contemporary *private* enterprises—especially the corporation. Our fast-breaking corporate culture stresses innovation, change, and creativity, and if anything, tends to threaten communal stability through constant upheaval. In contrast, long-entrenched educational structures—school districts, educational bureaucracies, teachers' unions, state education boards, graduate schools of education, and textbook publishers—tend to subvert the very organizational and institutional innovations that promote educational creativity.

Burdened by vestigial features such as centralized administration and uniform regulation, regular public schools have become less effective in serving the interests of the students who struggle to get through them. The underwhelming performance of elementary and secondary schools during the past several decades has become cause for seemingly endless public debate.

Time was when the old "factory model" that defined our public schools served children and communities far better than the system does today, and perhaps for no other reason than *the fit was better.* The educational standards and social values of our society were more uniform, and the educational bureaucracy was less entrenched than it is today. But that was before destabilizing influences—rapid and extensive suburbanization, big government, racial conflict, the mass migration of mothers out of their homes and into the work force, television, and long-range commuting—changed our midcentury industrial society.

When communities functioned as more stable environments, so did community schools. In today's decentralized world, the monopolistic structure of the public school system no longer fits its institutional setting. The result is a system that is effectively reproducing itself and serving its professional constituencies rather than adapting to change and serving the students it is charged to educate. This resistance to change in a rapidly evolving social environment has led to the kind of festival of perverse incentives that Adam Smith lamented when he wrote his early critiques of education at Oxford University.

In Smith's view, the incentive structure of the university favored the interests of the faculty over those of the students. He noted: "The discipline of colleges and universities is in general contrived, not for the benefit of the students, but for the interest, or more properly speaking, for the ease of the masters."[16] Only by changing the incentives would the university achieve the institutional ability to innovate in the delivery of knowledge. Smith expanded this position to cover the entire range of public services:

> The expense of the institutions for education and religious instruction is likewise, no doubt, beneficial to the whole society, and may, therefore, without injustice, be defrayed by the general contribution of the whole society. This expense, however, might perhaps with equal propriety, and even with some advantage, be defrayed altogether by those who receive the immediate benefit of such education and instruction, or by the voluntary contribution of those who think they have occasion for either the one or the other.[17]

As usual, Smith's instruction is revealing. Incentives, organizational adaptability, administrative creativity, informational transparency—the kitchen chemicals of institutional innovation in an educational universe—matter as much in the delivery of grammar and math as they do in new crankshafts or parkas.

It could be argued that Smith's educational challenge for today's commercial society would be to develop a system that promotes greater pedagogical performance by adapting the incentive structure of schooling to better serve students. Only a change that promotes fresh and exciting learning techniques, approaches, and structures—characteristic, it might be noted, of our far more successful and more competitive contemporary system of higher education—will inject new vitality into elementary and secondary schooling. This is where an unlikely pairing of economists enters the picture.

Competition, Education, and Community

Milton Friedman, in the late 1950s, first proposed the then-radical idea of school choice through vouchers as a solution to what he perceived as an ineffective school system. More recently, a young Harvard economist, Caroline Hoxby, has done impressive empirical work that largely confirms the value of a greater measure of parental choice inherent in school reform.

Friedman, in his characteristically direct and incisive manner, began talking about improving education through choice in his larger critique of socialism and the welfare state. For Friedman, the enhancement of choice through vouchers would leverage the power of markets in education by turning parents, and their children, into customers shopping for the best educational product rather than passively accepting whatever the state was serving up. Enhanced market power would enable families to shop for better schools and, by extension, better teachers, better pedagogical ideas and innovation, and better fit for each student rather than the "one-size-fits-all" factory model of modern schooling. In addition, markets would, by necessity, draw parents more fully into the education of their children by encouraging them to actively engage in the choice of schools (just as they are engaged in the choice of, say, clothing stores or autos), and compelling them to make this choice a priority.

By the same token, Friedman argued that markets would help students at the bottom of the socioeconomic ladder by destabilizing the status quo and therefore weeding out bad schools while promoting better ones. Markets would do their selective work. Most importantly for Friedman, markets would serve as a spur to inventive and exciting ideas in the delivery of basic educational skills and information—a vital function that he sees as being subverted by the inertia of the public education bureaucracy. The battle for school choice since then has been fought in seminars and on op-ed pages, as well as in the streets.[18]

Not surprisingly, the entrenched interests in city halls, school boards, the courts, and the teachers' unions have resisted, with all of their might, the encroachment of the Invisible Hand in education. Since Friedman first penned his critique of public schools and called for market-driven vouchers as part of his stirring defense of choice and freedom, spending on schools has gone up precipitously, the bureaucracy has ballooned, and the achievement levels of students have declined. In the inner city, where educational innovation is most needed, it has nose-dived.

Still, as Adam Smith might have predicted, it's hard to keep a strong idea down, regardless of the interests arrayed against it. Over the past two decades, and most notably with the appearance in 1983, of "A Nation at Risk," a widely discussed report on the state of education, the calls for educational innovation in the form of enhanced options have grown louder and have been better informed and more frequent. One of the most eloquent voices is that of Caroline Hoxby, a leading expert in the investigation of elementary and secondary education. Unlike Friedman's early work, which was largely philosophical and inspired by the free-market principles of classical liberalism, Hoxby's contributions all come in the statistical and econometric expression of empirical work. She kicks tires.

Caroline Hoxby holds a master's degree from Oxford (where the incentives have changed vastly since the days of Adam Smith) and a doctorate from MIT. The author of a host of influential publications on the economics of education, she has challenged the conventional wisdom on public education through her statistical studies of the effects of changes in the status quo of schooling on the relative performance of students, the ability of schools to attract good teachers and innovative administrators, the price of elementary and secondary education to taxpayers, and the educational implications of racial balance and diversity among students.

According to Hoxby, commenting on the United States, ". . . countries have improved their education a lot since 1970, whereas we stayed about the same. . . . We're not doing the worst in terms of math and science and reading and writing, but we're certainly not doing the best amongst other nations with similar industrial composition. . . . The other worry is that we've been spending a lot more on education since 1970. Education spending has gone up by about 85% in real dollars since 1970."[19]

Hoxby's painstaking empirical findings generally support policies that make possible the extension of greater degrees of choice and a wider variety of options for parents and students. She sees several positive implications flowing from enhanced educational choice, and she notes that one of the most salient developments is the provision of incentives to the best teachers to forgo other professional options in favor of teaching—and, tellingly, to especially innovative and entrepreneurial administrators who spearhead organizational changes that lead to enhanced performance. This final point resonates most clearly with the legacy of Adam Smith.

School choice has gradually become a greater and more widely accepted reality in elementary public education, especially in view of the options available within the established educational system: common schools, target schools, special schools, home schools, and charter schools (publicly funded schools administered free of most of the regulations that define the overly bureaucratic and inefficient centrally administered public school system).[20] The choice realized through these educational forms enables parents and children to "vote with their feet" and holds parents' feet to the fire to keep them informed and engaged in the education of their children. If they are unhappy with the results, they have the option to move their children into publicly funded schools of their choice without incurring the huge costs commonly associated with private education.

The beauty of this option is fourfold:

1. It affords parents a greater measure of flexibility, thereby harnessing competition in the promotion of both pedagogical creativity and organizational efficiency;
2. It does not require the expense normally associated with traditional educational options, such as independent or religious parochial schools;
3. It *demands* the participation and commitment of parents, thereby stimulating the wellsprings of civic engagement at the level of the neighborhood, town, and city;

4. It provides employers—not only businesses, but governments and nonprofit organizations—with the most important source of capital attainable in the current economy: better educated people. These employers then become the best guarantors of business investment in local communities and of vigorous local participation in civic life.

Many intellectuals who advocate a more vigorous civil society argue that civic participation at the local level is vital to the invigoration of democracy at *all* levels. School choice—especially the novel innovation represented by the charter school option *within the existing public school system*—combines, in profound ways, the strengths of civil society with those of government in serving the public interest.

Inner-City Seminar

Adam Smith insisted that the cultivation of a more decent society was impossible without conditions that ensured the expectation of a steadily expanding economic prosperity that reached all levels of society. Contrary to economists who underplay the significance of inequality, Smith underscored the importance of enhanced economic equity by emphasizing: "No society can surely be flourishing and happy, of which the far greater part of the members are poor and miserable. . . ."[21] Smith combined market forces and government services to help reduce the ranks of the poor and miserable. The recent industrial transformation in the advanced countries has fueled economic productivity, innovation, and prosperity for the present generation, and has helped to spread a great deal of wealth. But this trend has yet to address the pressing problems of poverty and inequality in large parts of our society. New public enterprises are needed to address this difficult problem. Some economists are reawakening the combined moral imperative and incentive structures originated by Adam Smith in such enterprises. Notable among these economists are Glenn Loury and Edmund Phelps.

Social Capitalist of the Soul

A Boston University economist and a prominent African American intellectual, Glenn Loury has been particularly active, among economists, in

making a case for more research and intervention into the tenacious character of poverty, and for giving greater attention to the cultural as well as
the economic difficulties attendant in the reconstruction of communities
among the less fortunate. For Loury, this combination of economic and
social resources is captured neatly in social capital (see Chapter 1).

Loury regards the networks that distribute social capital as a mixed
economic blessing because they include some people while excluding others, thus reinforcing the inequality in society's opportunity structure.
Rerouting the circuitry of social capital into areas beset by poverty, and
thereby dismantling the sources of inequality that divide our society, is thus
a challenge that has economic *and* cultural dimensions.[22]

Loury sees a vital role for educational initiatives that combine economic
and moral resources in dealing with the festering problems of poverty, joblessness, broken homes, drug abuse, and crime, as well as the breakdown of
institutionalized discrimination. He is particularly concerned about the society's beleaguered black communities, which have long labored under the
stigma of race and a legacy of discrimination. His prescriptions for change
offer a little something to upset just about everybody.

Canons to the Right

Contrary to critics on the Right, Loury supports, and argues forcefully for,
greater government involvement in curing the ills of the poor, and measures
to reform and improve established, if ineffectual, programs such as affirmative action through better design. Loury casts grave doubt on the wisdom
of efforts favored by many conservatives and intended simply to move people from the welfare rolls into the labor market through workfare.[23] Pro-
voking the criticism of prominent conservatives, many of whom have long
admired his work for its moral acuity, Glenn Loury has argued that long-
maligned preferential efforts such as affirmative action (in its various
forms) are needed to counteract social division—the calcifying of cross-
racial social networks—caused by the long-entrenched legacy of racism and
industrial dislocation, especially in cities. But just as surely, he has argued
that these programs need to be made more effective and more efficient.

In other words, affirmative action needs some economists' kitchen
chemistry—new recipes for success. This style of thinking unites Loury
with the same incentive-based design mentality that imbues Paul Romer's

thinking on the solution to large-scale public investment projects, and more remotely with Adam Smith, who insisted that the delivery of public services should be cost-effective—a notion that Loury integrates well into his ideas on the alleviation of poverty and social division.

Loury makes a trenchant point about the vital importance of social capital in reversing the historically deleterious patterns of racial discrimination. Ingeniously, he looks for inspiration and instruction in one of the few existing social institutions that has effectively dealt with racial injustice: the military. Loury points out:

> The U.S. Army cares about the number of black captains because it needs to sustain effective cooperation among its personnel across racial lines. That the racial identities of captains and corporals sometimes matters to the smooth functioning of a military institution is a deep fact about our society, one that cannot be wished away. . . . Ironically, the irrelevance of race to a person's moral wealth may be more evident to the members of this institution than elsewhere in our society precisely because the government has taken account of race in the conduct of its military personnel policies.[24]

Drawing on the military model, Loury calls for "developmental" affirmative action: dealing with the long intractable problems of black urban poverty and social isolation through a combination of race-awareness and rigorous training. Consistent with the worthy goals of traditional preferential affirmative action, Loury's approach is designed to target and correct racial discrimination. However, beyond the older and widely criticized preferential approach to affirmative action, condemned by many as reverse racism because it provided jobs for blacks who were often unprepared for them, Loury folds a touch of Adam Smith into his prescription by insisting that it is vital to acknowledge "the fact of differential performance and seek to reverse it directly, rather than trying to hide from the fact by setting a different threshold for the performance of blacks."[25]

Loury's new approach comprises targeted programs for historically disenfranchised people engaged in higher education and also in business and management education. He goes straight to the subjects that promise the greatest possible returns to educational investment: mathematics and science. According to Loury: "[Given] that black students are far scarcer than white and Asian students in the fields of math and science, encouraging their entry into these areas without lowering standards—through summer workshops, support for curriculum development at historically black colleges, or the financing of research assistantships for promising graduate students—would be consistent with my distinction between 'preferential' and 'developmental' affirmative action [as would] the provisional admission of black students to the state university, conditional on their raising their academic scores to competitive levels after a year or two of study at a local community college."[26]

Note the presence of both sides of Adam Smith in Loury's formulation: a burning moral concern for equity, and a jeweler's eye for the fine functioning of incentives. However, as with so much of Smith's legacy, the message cuts in two ways, challenging partisans not only on the political right, but on the left as well. It leaves us wondering: Who's afraid of Glenn Loury?

Canons to the Left

Contrary to critics on the Left, Loury refuses to accept the view that the problems of many poor and disenfranchised people are entirely economic and are therefore entirely amenable to relief through straightforward economic redistribution. Destructive cultural factors—owing to a centuries-old legacy of social isolation, in Loury's view—matter as well. As he has said:

> It may be that social policy, by itself, is not capable of eradicating deeply entrenched patterns of child rearing and social interaction that pass on personal incapacity—criminal violence, promiscuous sexuality, early unwed childbearing, academic failure—from one generation to the next. It is imaginable, is it not, that the moral life of the hard core urban poor will have to be transformed before some of these most marginalized souls will be able to seize such opportunity as may exist.[27]

Glenn Loury believes that cultural reconstruction of poor and blighted communities must go hand-in-hand with economic and educational reconstruction, but he sets himself apart because he is one of the few analysts who thinks hard and creatively about both sides of this enterprise!

Loury's position meshes with Adam Smith's views of the institutional linkage among competitive markets and moral sentiments. In addition to approaches such as developmental affirmative action, which is designed to generate economic capital in pockets of extreme poverty, Loury insists that society must act to understand and support fundamental moral institutions in order to encourage the cultivation of greater social capital.

Civic and moral institutions—schools, churches, hospitals—in areas ravaged by economic underdevelopment and discrimination are few, far between, and, in many cases, as battered as the spindly social fabric that holds these communities together. As a result, the people who are born into these cultures suffer the slings and arrows of this outrageous fortune from birth onward, and they have little recourse to the institutional support system that most of us take for granted throughout our lives. Loury, citing James Q. Wilson, a neoconservative political scientist who insists that the reconstruction of inner-city culture begins with the family, notes that: "Wilson . . . proposed an intensive preschool education . . . , including parent training and home visitation of nurses, along with child care . . . [as well as] residential programs for unmarried teenage mothers, who have no competent adult to oversee their handling of newborns. . . ." Education, to say nothing of the first steps toward economic progress, begins in the home and in the family.[28]

Absent a stable family, if there is one institution that has been called on more than ever in recent years to serve the needs of such strained communities, it is the church, often an island of civility in this sea of desolation. Through synagogues, mosques, parishes, and ministries of all kinds, churches have assumed, as never before, an outsized role with respect to addressing the needs of the poor, the sick, the drug-addicted, the elderly, the homeless, and the helpless, and are strategically better placed than most other civic institutions to reach the needy. Loury's reference to the biblical story of Nehemiah's renewal of Jerusalem resonates with this point:

> Nehemiah, a Jew, was specifically concerned about his people. His work, the reconstruction of civil society, could only be undertaken, as it were, "from the inside out. . . ." We blacks are connected—by bonds of history, family, conscience, and common perception in the eyes of outsiders—to those who languish in the urban slums. Black politicians, clergy, intellectuals, businessmen, and ordinary folk must therefore seek

to create hope in these desolate young lives; we must work to rebuild these communities; we must become our brother's keeper.[29]

This impulse reflects the growing recognition on the part of policymakers that churches are well placed to fight the battles of poverty and social pathology on the local front. Debate continues as to whether national organizations such as the National Council of Churches, the United Jewish Appeal, Catholic Charities, local ministries, or some combination thereof, should be among the primary agents in delivering services to the needy. But many leaders (including the President of the United States) now acknowledge that a civil and personal delivery system represented by a church is a welcome complement to government-led educational initiatives such as those noted by Glenn Loury.[30]

Dismal Performance

As Loury has lamented, economists simply do not spend much time and trouble worrying about poverty. This is a serious criticism of a profession so well positioned to make a difference in the lives and communities of the most unfortunate members of our society. If every economist were to turn his or her attention to the problems of the poor, the emergent solutions would surely include a heavy quotient of new ideas into the social and economic capital of these sorely deprived and long-suffering locales. Glenn Loury's efforts, both as an outspoken public intellectual and as an engaged economic researcher and social scientist, help to keep the issue alive—as does the work of Edmund Phelps.

The Marshall of Morningside Heights

Edmund ("Ned") Phelps, a distinguished Columbia University economic theorist, is known primarily for a large body of work in macroeconomics, the scholarly province of Keynes and Friedman. However, Phelps's idea—using the economic engine of public finance to inject market vitality into the lives of low-waged workers—brings him closely into line with the intellectual style of the worldly philosophers of the past, the thinkers who wanted to extend the growth-enhancing power of private enterprise to include the broadest possible cross-section of society. Phelps notes: ". . . the Enlightenment theorists were philosophers as well as economists. . . . For them it was a moral axiom that running the economy on the principle of free enterprise would lack legitimacy if the system left many people out. The Scots saw the moral imperative of extending free enterprise to the largest number possible, stamping out privilege and democratizing opportunity."[31]

Recall that Alfred Marshall, the great successor to Adam Smith and his fellow Enlightenment philosophers, was led into the study of economics by his concerns about poverty. Marshall insisted that economic aid to the poor was not only morally correct, but politically necessary if poor people were to be able to exercise their political rights and responsibilities as full-fledged members of a modern civilized society. Few economists would question Marshall's motivation on its merits, but policies intended to shore up the economic condition of poor people—from almshouses to welfare checks—have, more often than not, served as traps. Welfare recipients are especially star-crossed because if they succeed in finding a typically ill-paying job in the private market, they are forced to sacrifice what little they receive from public assistance. Therefore, the challenge for economists like Phelps is to design relief policies that leverage the power of markets without simply enhancing the size of government.

Writing from the vantage of Columbia's campus in New York's Morningside Heights, Phelps, in his book *Rewarding Work: How to Restore Participation and Self-Support to Free Enterprise,* urges policymakers to construct a system of strong financial subsidies to businesses in distressed areas—notably, among the few institutions of civil society that exist in many of these areas—as an incentive to hire workers from the ranks of the poor. According to Phelps, the pressure exerted on the labor market would force wages upward, creating a greater demand for goods and services in these areas, and raising the level of economic prosperity. While this program would be expensive to fund at the outset, Phelps argues that the economic gains would eventually offset the costs of crime, violence, drugs, and physical dilapidation that have turned many of our old industrial districts and neighborhoods into places of fear. These economic subsidies would help to leverage other reconstructive efforts—in schools, churches, and complementary nonmarket institutions—to improve the inner city.

Phelps's proposal is one of the most exciting recent ideas to emerge from the economics of public enterprise.

Comparable to Loury's efforts, Phelps's proposal is refreshingly different from many of the inefficient welfare state programs that have merely separated the poor from everybody else, while taxing the public purse and delivering little relief. The proposal, based on well-specified incentives, is intended to exploit initiative, revive free enterprise, and connect impoverished communities to the wealth of the larger society through its primary circuitry: markets. Government financing would be used strategically for rewarding work, as the title of Phelps's book indicates, and as Adam Smith would have approved.

Edmund Phelps's audacious design—infusing economic capital into pockets of poverty through existing businesses—is a long time coming for low-wage and unemployed people and a welcome contribution from an economist who cares about closing the loop between wealth and sentiments.[32]

Matthew Men

In the past few years, Paul Romer has been stressing that if we are to cultivate greater levels of economic growth through the production of knowledge, we need to train more professionals who are dedicated to applying knowledge to the solution of real-world problems; that is, we need more engineers.[33] But the rewards to talented young people from superlucrative fields such as investment banking have made professions such as engineering, medicine, and teaching, to name a crucial few, less attractive.

An intriguing approach to the production of more engineers and researchers—and a seed to greater levels of social capital through high-level education and training—comes from Robert Frank of Cornell University, who, along with Philip Cook of Duke University, has identified a perverse trend in contemporary capitalism called "winner-take-all markets."

Given the huge rewards to success in such professional fields as entertainment, investments, law, telecommunications, advertising, and sports, accruing from the technological and international expansion of markets (movie stars and professional athletes are perhaps the most visible of the great beneficiaries of this trend), Cook and Frank point out that the financially bountiful appeal of these professions has drained a great deal of talent away from many socially productive and valuable pursuits. What's more, the pull of these megamarkets and the money that flows from them have contributed to a culture of conspicuous consumption that has channeled the expenditures of increasing sums of capital away from investment in growth-enhancing goods such as education, and into luxury pursuits.[34]

According to Cook and Frank, these trends exact a double whammy on the economy: they drain growth and they fuel inequality. Beyond these perturbations, exorbitant wealth—the kind that drives winner-take-all markets, caught the eye of Adam Smith, who was then wearing his moral philosopher glasses. Referring to the outsized wealth produced by the monopolies of his own day, Smith observed that easy wealth tended to "destroy the parsimony which in other circumstances is natural to the character of the merchant. When profits are high, the sober virtue seems to be superfluous, and expensive luxury to suit better the affluence of his situation."[35] Smith saw another serious moral problem associated with easy money. The lifestyles of the rich and famous had deleterious effects on the behavior of the working classes. Smith was no fan of the ostentatious.

Frank takes a page from the tax economists' playbook when he proposes a progressive consumption tax for the purpose of changing the incentive structure that has driven the economy into such lopsided excess. The idea is: If consumption is taxed at high rates at the highest levels, people will have less incentive to gamble their talents by competing for the tiny percentage of jobs that allow for super-rich consumption, and greater incentive to follow potentially less lucrative, though no less satisfying, career paths; in other words, more Volvos, fewer Ferraris. By better distributing talent—and, thereby, human capital—into more productive pursuits, this tax would have a salutary effect on economic growth.[36]

Progressive consumption taxes have their downside—driving people to spend abroad, encouraging black markets, and permitting governments to make inappropriate moral judgments, to name just a few.[37] But at least the proposal represents a start toward replenishing growth-producing careers and professions, and reducing the extreme degrees of inequality that now beset the economy. As with other such institutions, the rules of taxation, as we have discovered, are always subject to debate and—more to the point—innovation.

Means and Ends

Owing largely to the rediscovery of the importance of knowledge as a well-spring of economic growth, of higher levels of public health and well-being, and of progress in the war against poverty and inequality, the cultivation of knowledge through new and ambitious forms of public enterprise has become a matter of great social concern and debate. Yet, often overlooked in this conversation is a purpose every bit as important to a society as smarter computers and sharper mathematicians: the education of the soul, both individual and collective. That note unequivocally carries an ancient echo of the author of *The Theory of Moral Sentiments*.

10

Egg Men

I first began to develop the ideas . . . during the real estate boom of the 1980s. I knew people who rushed into buying homes because they thought they'd miss the opportunity if they waited. Then values plummeted and many of these people lost their equity. I thought: Wouldn't it be a good idea if the financial markets could alleviate such misfortune?

Robert J. Shiller

I still don't think the road to salvation is through old-fashioned welfare state policies, . . . something more radical is needed. Some of my conservative friends sometimes call the radical solution citizen capitalism. Some of my left-oriented friends call it propertied socialism. But, as Jim Tobin says, it don't matter what you call it . . . liberalism, conservatism, progressivism, a new New Deal or a new fair deal or whatever tickles your fancy. Let's keep pushing solutions and who knows? If Evander Holyfield can knock out Mike Tyson, the United States can knock out the scourge of the new inequality.

Richard B. Freeman

Given the monastic character of my job as a book editor, I spend blessedly little time traveling, compared to most of my road-riddled white-collar colleagues. Fortunately, when I do travel, my beat includes, for the most part, the pleasant streets, squares, and quads of the campuses where I visit my authors—places much like Nassau Street, the leafy main thoroughfare of Princeton, New Jersey, where I work and live. But every now and then I leave these familiar groves for some more unusual venues.

For instance, in working with my finance economists, I frequently have occasion to visit New York's Wall Street, a money bazaar on steroids. On other occasions, when I return to my hometown to see my family, the trip often takes me across an equally remarkable, if more desolate thoroughfare, Diamond Street in Philadelphia. Had Adam Smith accompanied me on my trips, I believe he would have been intrigued by the streets of Lower Manhattan and North Philadelphia, but for deeply different reasons. His reaction to these streets would have sent him back once more to his writing desk.

Early in *The Wealth of Nations,* Smith noted that, with the advent of the division of labor, "Every man thus lives by exchanging, or becomes in some measure a merchant, and the society itself grows to be what is properly a commercial society."[1] On our imaginary trip via New Jersey Transit to New York's financial district, Smith, after recovering from the shock of Wall Street's computerized offices and trading rooms, I'm convinced would have been impressed and not a little pleased by the embodiment of his vision of a place where "every man thus lives by exchanging. . . ." Wall Street is, after all, nothing if not an exchange. Smith would have discovered that the financial transactions that represent the daily output of Wall Street's bankers and traders reflect the sedulous management of the world's wealth, and thus a free society's investment in commerce, science, industry, and civilization. Not a bad day's work in the eyes of the great designer of commercial society.

However, during our ride in my more than gently used 1984 BMW through decidedly noncivil North Philadelphia into Diamond Street, Smith—after making sure that his door was locked—might wonder aloud where his civilizing project had gone awry, and how terribly far from its noble origins Diamond Street had fallen. Diamond Street, ironically enough, was named by educator and social evangelist Russell Conwell, who exhorted his fellow Philadelphians in 1915 to find their fortune in the "acres of diamonds" beneath their feet.[2]

Unless the value of bullet shells, used syringes, and broken wine bottles has risen recently, the denizens of today's Diamond Street are out of luck. No man, or woman, is a merchant here; each person is severed from

any connection with the commercial society—wealth, civility, sentiments, the works—that Smith saw as the great hope of all ranks of people.
What would give Smith greater pause would be a look at the numbers:
moving closer to the fates of Diamond Street are the millions of marginal
Main Street workers who have seen their incomes and earning power diminish as the technological base of the economy and the distribution of
income have shifted in the past generation.

The tale of these two streets, one racing with fortune and possibilities,
the other rife with desperation, would set Adam Smith's mind astir. In his
characteristically philosophical way, he would worry first about Diamond
Street. He would think about how to make every North Philadelphian a
merchant, for in doing so he would provide the key not only to greater
wealth for the unlucky and deprived, but also the basis for community—
for enriched social capital and for greater democratic engagement. The key
he would identify would be that of new ownership—of homes, of jobs and
businesses, of financial assets. What Russell Conwell failed to note in his
"acres of diamonds" homily was that the diamonds beneath the Philadelphians' feet were not worth much if they didn't own at least some of them;
if they did not bestow economic citizenship on residents.

Smith, in his economist's intellectual style, would set himself to figuring how to leverage the financial horsepower of Wall Street in the interest
of Diamond. The disparity that separates these streets, as if on two different planets, has challenged some clever economists to think, in Smithian
style, of using the prosperity of Wall Street to power the return of Diamond Street by turning the undeveloped assets of Diamond into potential
profit for Wall. This impulse springs from a new twist on one of the central social inventions of modern economic thinking: *financial engineering*.

Sidewalk Securities

Though we tend to associate financial engineering with stocks, bonds, and
the various exotica of the investments business, policy journals are brim-
ming these days with news of the creation of new kinds of assets for the
working class and the underprivileged. Among these instruments are: individual housing accounts for poor families; individual savings accounts for
the working poor, modeled on middle-class investment plans; innovative

educational and medical accounts for working families; shared ownership of public utilities for local communities; futures markets for the value of homes, jobs, cities, and even countries; and all manner of new asset-based policy innovation.

Contrary to earlier government-administered welfare-state programs, such as the notorious high-rise rental housing projects that pocked the urban landscape of the 1960s, and consistent with Adam Smith's insistence on the strategic delivery of public services, these new financial innovations are designed to create property ownership for their constituents, without adding wasteful and corrupt bureaucracy to the public purse. But that is not all.

As one critic remarks, "The challenge for economists is not to create a system of 'workfare' that is yet another mode of welfare, but to provide incentives—economic and moral—that will revive the work ethic and stimulate the spirit of independence."[3] Economists' ideas for stimulating property ownership through financial innovation meet this challenge by providing people not only with access to hard assets, but also with access to social capital—a means of partaking more fully in the social networks that contribute to a healthier civic culture. Property bestows empowerment on its owners, and ownership enhances civic participation, the mother's milk of social capital. In the words of one of the architects of this movement, ". . . assets are a key to family and community development based on capacity rather than maintenance. . . . In order to develop capacity, families and communities must accumulate assets and invest for long-term goals."[4]

Before turning to the asset-building financial engineering ideas that promise to better align the corners of Wall Street and Diamond, a bit of background is in order on the improbable intellectual origins of financial innovation and the revolution it spawned on Main Street. Invariably, these origins are associated with the economist who provided the analytical justification for the long-held sentiment that you should never put all your eggs in one basket: Harry M. Markowitz.

The Egg Man Cometh

Harry Markowitz is an American, Chicago-born in 1927. As a child, he was a self-described nerd who played chess and the violin, and dabbled in cryptography. The only child of a grocer and his wife, Markowitz studied economics at the University of Chicago, but, even well into his years as a graduate student during the mid-1950s, he had little idea of what to do with his life. Markowitz eventually made the bizarre decision to study the stock market, which was then a little understood, and even less scrutinized, feature of the economy. It fell neatly in none of the clear-cut categories of microeconomics or macroeconomics. But it managed to provide Harry Markowitz with the wealth of statistical information he needed to test his big idea: the proposition that one could reduce the risk in one's stock holdings through asset diversification.[5]

Markowitz wrote a PhD thesis titled, "Portfolio Selection" at the business school in Chicago, under the direction of a celebrated trio: Jacob Marschak, Tjalling Koopmans, and Milton Friedman. This brief and spartan statement, in which the equations overwhelmed the words, provided the mathematical justification for the view that to protect and enhance one's financial holdings, it was best to spread those holdings over a portfolio of securities balancing risk and return. Safety in the long run could be secured only through diversification.

Friedman said of the thesis, "It's not math, it's not economics, it isn't even business administration." But as the subsequent half-century's obsession with the financial markets attests, Markowitz's probing insight into the relationship between risk and return has been as influential as any idea to emerge from modern economics.[6]

"Portfolio Selection" became for investment capitalists what *The Communist Manifesto* had been for Marxists: part instructions booklet, part *cri de coeur*. The Markowitz message, "Go forth, and diversify," would ring down the decades, transforming Wall Street, corporate finance, and the world's monetary economy in its echo. It finally drew the attention of the Nobel Committee in Stockholm. They awarded Harry Markowitz, the erstwhile nerd, the Nobel prize in 1990.

Following the deregulation of financial markets in the late 1970s, Markowitz's insight would open the floodgates to an explosion of new investment instruments through employer-managed personal investment plans and their many variations. It reawakened the fusty old futures and options markets. It would beget the derivatives revolution and make possible the financial restructuring of big business in the 1980s. It fueled the capital markets that led to the stakeholder revolution, which then gave new life to a bloated, punch-drunk corporate sector and indirectly delivered hundreds of billions of dollars into the hands of middle-class people through pension fund management, an act of antielitism that would have amazed and impressed Marx himself.

Further, and most importantly in any consideration of the legacy of Adam Smith, the prospect of making every man and woman all the way to Diamond Street a merchant has been revived by these asset-generating financial technologies. One analyst notes that, ". . . asset-building accounts . . . are the most rapidly growing form of domestic policy. Asset accounts may become a primary form of domestic policy during the twenty-first century."[7]

Diversify by All Means

In the wake of Harry Markowitz and his diversifier's dream came a small army of economists who extended the new theory of finance in a multitude of directions. William Sharpe drew on a footnote in Markowitz's thesis to define quantitatively the relationship between risk and return in financial instruments. Merton Miller and Franco Modigliani made the claim that capital structure is of secondary importance to future earnings in revolutionizing the theory of corporate finance. Eugene Fama confronted (or should I say, affronted) Wall Street with the proposition that financial markets are efficient and therefore resist the kind of unscientific stock picking that most investment managers had practiced proudly and innocently for decades.

The 1970s witnessed the second great wave of financial research. A trio of young MIT economists—Robert C. Merton, the late Fischer Black, and Myron Scholes—lit the fire that fueled the derivatives revolution that would redefine financial scholarship and practice into the next century. Following this seminal MIT-based development, Berkeley economists Hayne Leland and Mark Rubinstein used the conceptual raw materials of asset diversification to create the technology for portfolio insurance. The result of this research has revolutionized the way the world manages its wealth.[8]

Grafting Growth

The first impressive economic returns from the application of the new production technology of financial innovation expressed itself in the improved
strength of America's capital markets during the 1980s. Despite a steady
infusion of investment from the 1950s through the shattering recession of
the early 1970s, these markets had fallen flaccid because of the inefficient
way in which this growing wealth was then managed. According to Peter
L. Bernstein, in his book *Capital Ideas,* "The merry game of just picking
the best stocks and tucking them into the client's portfolio had worked
well enough when portfolio management organizations were small."[9]

But, as Bernstein goes on to explain, a heavy price was paid by Wall
Street professionals and their clients when "stormy economic weather
overwhelmed the optimistic markets of 1971 and 1972." Casting about
for new ideas to rescue their business, money managers turned to the ex-
otic theories of finance economists, whom they had earlier maligned as
"academia nuts" for advice.[10]

Bernstein recounts that Wall Street's network of old boys got more
than they had bargained for. The academics equipped a new generation of
Wall Street professionals—"rocket scientists," in the popular parlance—
with the means of managing portfolios with greater scientific precision.
These new financial engineers adapted the theories of Harry Markowitz
and his fellow economists into the mighty production technology of modern portfolio management. This social invention, emanating from the
chalk-dusted offices of MIT, Berkeley, and the University of Chicago, has
since made possible heretofore-unheard-of levels of competition and efficiency in the modern capital markets. It has attracted steadily greater levels of investment along the way, dissolved cross-national economic
barriers, broadened stock ownership through pensions and mutual funds,
and laid the financial groundwork for prosperity in the developing world.
Commenting on the social implications of this phenomenon, one observer
has noted:

> Over the last third of the 20th century, control of capital in America has
> shifted away from private institutions and toward public markets, mak-
> ing the prospect of financing growth more forward-looking and more

democratic. Entrepreneurs are no longer limited to a few institutions that used to control the money spigot. The turning point was 1974, when interest rates spiked, the stock market fell 45%, and large financial institutions, faced with their own problems, stopped lending to all but the highest-rated borrowers. . . . Leaders of small and medium-sized firms with good prospects, who had been dependent on relationships with individual banks and insurance companies, could now turn to a market-based system with thousands of institutional buyers, including mutual funds, which . . . would eventually grow larger than the banks.[11]

The shock of this revolution reverberates throughout society and around the globe. Leveraged buyouts, spin-offs, management buybacks, and other forms of restructuring helped restore the financial health of corporations by returning the active management of these companies to the people most able to make economically informed decisions about their direction—shareholders. Meanwhile, comparable industrial behemoths, in socialist countries such as the USSR, buckled at the knees and dragged their governing orders down with them.

The effects of corporate restructuring in capitalist society have echoed through the ranks of management, steadily pushing power and responsibility for decisions to the level at which executives possess the best information for making these decisions. Meanwhile, derivative financing has been used to secure massive investment in sprawling sectors of the economy, from education through medical research through housing. The record of this revolution registers itself daily on financial pages. Despite several highly publicized corporate bankruptcies associated with the revolution in finance, the overwhelming success of modern portfolio management is now a fact.

This revolution has not stopped at any of the usual geographical or political borders. The production technology of financial engineering is now among this country's most valued export products. It is studied and adopted in corporations, banks, financial institutions, business schools, and governments around the world.[12]

The triumph of asset-building financial technology in the corporate and institutional sectors begs the question of how far it can be extended and adapted to serve civic communities. Can financial capital beget social capital? Many commentators have their doubts and have registered a great deal of criticism at the wave of downsizings and uprootings that have followed in the wake of financially driven restructuring. Some of this criticism is justified. Restructuring, particularly in the guise of downsizing, has played havoc by disrupting companies, towns, neighborhoods, and the lives of employees and their families—especially those at the low end of the income scale. But overlooked just as readily are the bad old days of the fatty and inefficient conglomerates of the 1950s and 1960s, which sent many leading companies, and even whole industries, into nosedives, exposed entire sectors of the economy and sections of the country to hard times, and turned more than a few vital communities into ghost towns. Except for the coming of flexible financial markets, our own corporate crack-up could have come closer to the fate of Soviet industry.

The financial revolution and its resultant corporate restructuring have changed a once dire situation, by and large, for the better. Following the great wave of financial engineering initiated by Harry Markowitz and his successors, America not only recovered its industrial footing but experienced the greatest decade of prosperity in its recent history. Its flexible and broadly diversified financial markets, expanded pool of venture capital, highly dispersed shareholder investment culture, and heavily reformed managerial practices have enabled the country to stay competitive even in the face of global competition and cyclical downturns. In the words of the late Merton Miller, who received the Nobel prize (for his work on capital structure) in the same year as Harry Markowitz, "That the U.S. economy did not freeze up into depression in 1989–90, as it had in 1931 and so often before that, can be credited, I believe, to the rich variety of nonbank financial markets and institutions available to American firms and households."[13]

Furthermore, financial engineering has proved to be an invaluable technology for rethinking the expansion of social capital, and it can be adapted to an enormous range of purposes. Whether the goal is to raise funds for a new power plant, privatize a state-run industry, finance a health care system, design a social insurance program, or pay for a new biology lab or football stadium, applied financial innovation represents the production technology that synthesizes the mix of financial instruments and markets that is needed to underwrite centrally important social goals.

A Random Walk Down Diamond Street

The contrast between our two unusual streets—Wall and Diamond—could not be starker. The good financiers of Wall Street have long had reason to be cheerful, if not exuberant, even if the market dips and ducks. The Markowitz-led financial revolution has given Wall Street great life, and government insurance programs such as FDIC have provided the brakes needed to prevent the kind of calamity witnessed in 1929.

But the poor devils of Diamond Street have reason to be nothing but depressed and very rationally so, even on those days when the sun shines on their squalid dominion. Nobody there, except maybe the local drug dealer, is thriving. Yet the vitality that drives Wall Street and the futility that suffuses Diamond Street may have an intriguing connection.

Broad financial diversification—as opposed to lopsided portfolios—made a big comeback when the tech bubble burst in the spring of 2000. The volatility that characterized the fevered financial markets at the millennium prompted virtually every responsible media commentator and economist to intone a single cautionary point: In a stormy environment, investors, and particularly small investors, should be sure that their portfolios are properly diversified. Burton Malkiel, author of the finance classic, *A Random Walk Down Wall Street,* writing in the *Wall Street Journal,* was most emphatic on this note, as have been other economists, investment advisers, pundits, and journalists. Economist Paul Krugman, in the *New York Times,* and UCLA finance economist Michael Brennan, in the professional journals, called for a futures market in dividends as a means of diversifying away some of the tremendous momentum trading that contributes to this volatility.[14]

In a stroke of Adam Smith–style intellectual innovation, Yale's Robert Shiller framed the argument for greater diversification as an imaginative public policy proposal: a creative twist on asset diversification designed to transform financial capital into a more socially productive resource, while expanding the investment options open to financial professionals. Shiller suggested not only that investors place their eggs in more than one basket, *but that the number and kind of baskets be expanded* beyond the usual offerings, in order to cover a vastly greater array of risky economic assets, including homes and jobs—and even streets.[15]

The Unheavenly City Secured

Referring to the plight of small investors, Shiller noted that "while financial experts today are typically extolling diversification, they do not stress
what genuine diversification really means." Shiller proposes a far-reaching
expansion of the idea of diversification, with implications for Diamond
Street as well as Wall:

> New institutions or markets should also be created that would make it
> easier to get out of their exposure to the stock market. The institutions
> we have—such as short sales, stock index futures, and put options—are
> not user-friendly and most investors do not avail themselves of
> these. . . . The proposed international markets I call macro markets
> would include markets for long-term claims on the income of specific
> occupational groups; and markets for currently illiquid assets such as
> single-family homes . . . retail institutions such as home equity in-
> surance or pension plan options that correlate negatively with labor
> income or home values will help people make use of such risk manage-
> ment tools.[16]

Shiller designed a class of securities based on futures contracts in job
income and housing values now known as *macromarkets*. As one analyst
notes, in describing the logic of Shiller's scheme: If you are worried that
your job as a computer programmer may be eliminated by competition
from India, then you buy shares in the Indian economy. This would give
you insurance because, if the feared competition materializes, you might
lose your job, but the value of your shares would go up."[17]

In other words, Shiller wants to expand the number of baskets in which
we place our eggs by creating new markets for managing a whole range of
previously undiversifiable risks, from our homes through our careers and
through our communities.[18] His call for macromarkets would provide the
artful hedgers of Wall Street with a whole new galaxy of products to ply on
their ever-expanding universe of clients. But what, one may reasonably ask,
does this bode for the tattered sentinels of Diamond Street?

By providing some protection for homes and livelihoods, and the
neighborhoods they collectively comprise, these new financial instruments
can potentially help cities ride out the short-term damaging effects of

demographic shifts, industrial dislocations, or economic downturns that occasionally beset them, thereby blunting the downward spiral that results in the creation of ghoulish precincts like Diamond Street. In other words, the financial innovation proposed by Shiller would supply a bulwark for ensuring some greater measure of economic stability for our cities.

Particular applications of financial innovation might also have profound regional, as well as local, implications. For if a system of markets can be forged to offset financial losses for towns and central cities, it could possibly help to stabilize entire regions by thwarting the destruction of local housing and job markets in periods of economic convulsion. More to the point, this heightened stability might provide crucial new incentives for investors and developers interested in reviving inner-city neighborhoods and other locales now considered too risky in the absence of a capital market capable of hedging the risks. Thus working backward, in the manner of Adam Smith, Shiller proposes a way of shaping socially beneficent outcomes by exploiting the creative power of the market itself.

Other financial instruments then could be deployed to address the specific maladies of struggling areas like Diamond Street. For example, no less aggressive a buccaneer capitalist than Michael Milken has proposed the creation of such instruments: securities designed to help entrepreneurs in inner-city businesses raise the capital they need to sustain and expand their operations. According to Milken, ". . . many of our two million minority-owned businesses struggle in 'domestic emerging markets' because they don't have access to financial technology. We need creative new approaches, such as securitizing packages of loans to establish a secondary market for their debt, much as mortgage-backed securities strengthened the housing market by separating borrowers and lenders."[19]

Hard as Diamonds

Much of the credit for the idea of injecting asset-building capital into our city streets goes to the wizards of academia and Wall Street who provided the vital research—on the corner where Milken's town meets Shiller's gown. But the economic creativity behind these moral sentiments is only just taking shape. Meanwhile, the wind still blows hard as diamonds down the Diamond Streets of this world. And with the ending of the era of big government, streets like Diamond have fallen increasingly out of the protective yoke of state agencies which, however inefficient, once provided a modicum of support. Hence, action is needed sooner rather than later.

Michael Sherraden, who spawned many of the ideas for asset-based development for the poor and disenfranchised, notes that because the majority of asset-based policies benefit mostly well-to-do households and are, "considerably more regressive than the social insurance and means-tested transfers that were the mainstays of social policy in the twentieth century," it is not only morally desirable, but vital, to intensify the design and creation of assets for the poor and the working class. According to Sherraden, "If the benefits were distributed progressively (more for the poor), they could provide every low-income person in the country with a decent home and health insurance coverage, plus a fully funded IRA."[20]

Diamond Street needs social capital, but it must come in the form of increased assets if it is to have any lasting social effects. It needs Wall Street if it is to thrive again. And what holds for the people of Diamond Street has a message for the middle- and working-class people who populate the Main Streets of our cities and neighborhoods. Few economists speak directly on their behalf, but two such economists, Martin Weitzman and Richard Freeman, do so eloquently.

Every Man a Micromerchant

Adam Smith would be pleased to observe that private firms remain the real economic engine of the wealth of nations. No matter how effective the public programs designed to tackle large-scale economic problems such as health care or transportation, or highly targeted economic difficulties such as urban poverty, companies employ the great majority of people and make the great mass of useful things (to say nothing of many useless, if popular, things). Keeping firms—the pin factories of the present, and the jobs, families, and communities that thrive on them—vital, while preventing them from fleeing the precincts of their host cities for other climes, is an eternal challenge for civic leaders. An economist who is well known for helping to address this problem, through a deft turn of social invention called employee stock ownership, is Martin Weitzman of Harvard.

"Best Idea Since Keynes"

Weitzman's thunderbolt of an idea—dubbed by the *New York Times,* at the moment of its birth in 1984, as the "Best idea since Keynes," is the now-familiar ESOP—the Employee Stock Option Plan.[21] ESOP does what the name implies; it reduces the rate of escalation in workers' pay in return for a share of the profits, thereby encouraging greater efficiency and productivity by keying everyone's attention on the bottom line. By making every worker in some measure an owner (an extension of Adam Smith's conceit of making each man in some measure a merchant), ESOPs are designed to provide most employees with a higher expected return than wages, some voice within the firm, and some added power over their own futures.

ESOPs provide the economy with a way of heading off inflationary pressures that are structurally built into industrial sectors by wage agreements. In this way, ESOPs help check the vicious spiral of cost-driven inflation and unemployment. The downside is that they entail risk especially if shares of employee-owned stock are not balanced with other financial holdings. That is, if they are not diversified. Still, ESOPs have become a standard feature of the industrial landscape.

Since Weitzman's article appeared in the 1970s, ESOPs have become established institutions throughout North America and elsewhere. According to the National Center for Employee Ownership, there are now some 11,400 ESOPs. Meanwhile, the gradual decline in unemployment and control of inflation have neatly paralleled the restructuring of corporations along the lines of Weitzman's remarkable reengineering idea.[22]

Consistent with the civic adaptation of financial innovation, the concept of the ESOP is now being recast to promote expanded public ownership of local utilities and natural resources. Advocates see ESOPs and their spin-offs as correctives for the persistent problem of inequality in capitalist societies because these instruments introduce a broader dispersal of authority over decisions affecting local and regional public economic resources.

Referring to Adam Smith as a source of inspiration for this institutional innovation, one analyst conjectures:

That famous Scot envisioned a "self-designed" system informed by a complex range of overlapping values reflecting the purpose, aspiration and motivation that make humans so uniquely human. He recognized that the moral foundation of markets, like that of democracies, is grounded in the notion that they are systems of widely distributed control—thus the deference granted consumers in the case of markets and constituents in the case of democracies, which are routinely seen as a marketplace of ideas.[23]

More distant variations of this kind of ownership innovation have emerged in the form of proposals for portable insurance and for savings plans that enable workers to transfer from one job to another without a loss of their capital as may be occasioned by economic downturns and convulsions.

Thus, in an ironic twist that only a lover of unanticipated consequences could appreciate, Weitzman's ESOPs and their extensions have saved a remnant of socialism, decentralized worker ownership, through an ingenious sleight of the Invisible Hand.

Exiles on Main Street

Say the name Richard Freeman among economics watchers, and you would likely get the following reaction: "Stalwart labor economist intent on fighting inequality." The economics watchers would be right, particularly with regard to Freeman's long-standing goal of addressing the inequalities that mark our society. But their characterization would have missed the means that Freeman has recently recommended to achieve his stated ends. Freeman is quick to reaffirm his reading of our social condition, and the picture he paints is not a pretty one. He observes:

> . . . income inequality in the United States has massively increased. This jump owes to the unprecedentedly abysmal earnings experience of low-paid Americans, income stagnation covering about 80 percent of all families, and an increase in upper-end incomes. The rise in inequality—greater than in most other developed countries—has reversed the equalization in income and wealth we experienced between 1945 and 1970. The United States has now cemented its traditional position as the leader in inequality among advanced countries.[24]

As noted previously, it is hardly surprising to hear Richard Freeman intone the time-honored criticism of inequality. He is a labor economist and a man of the Left. What is new? Some of his proposed solutions, which sound less like the ruminations of a traditional labor economist intoning the historical remedies of Karl Marx than the precepts of a finance scholar drawing on the new-world technologies of Harry Markowitz. Freeman has proposed, essentially, an asset-based plan for the working class. His proposal gives a whole new meaning to the term "working capital." Freeman proposes to:

> . . . give workers control of the assets they already "own" but do not control—the $5 trillion in deferred wages now residing in pension and other retirement funds. . . . The same goes for the worker equity tied up in employee stock option plans (ESOPs), which already claim some 11 million employee participants. . . . If labor's capital were more firmly under control of its worker owners, we would expect it would be used to help foreclose the "low road" on industrial restructuring that has disrupted American labor markets and depressed family incomes. . . . We would also expect . . . investment in metropolitan cores—where many workers with pension assets reside and where their investment would bring the double bounce of an income return and an improved community—and here it can be expected to benefit poor urban minority populations.[25]

Who says economists are bereft of moral sentiments and ideas for addressing the inequities of capitalism? Freeman's proposal not only speaks to the plight of lower middle-class workers and the working poor, who occupy the fringes of today's finance-driven capitalism, but focuses on cities, those most vital incubators of social capital. Freeman rings a particularly Smithian note when he says that "cities are centers of hope as well as despair. By concentrating people, skill, and resources, they create 'agglomeration' benefits—new ideas and production techniques generated through the interaction of their residents and communicated outward; externalities from environmental improvement that spur economic growth."[26]

Why Should Wall Street Care about Diamond Street?

Perhaps the whole notion of asset-based solutions to poverty and widening inequality still rings false to readers. The thought of inner-city denizens rebalancing portfolios, renegotiating mortgages, and all that, is a strange one. After all, if Wall Streeters wanted to trade with Diamond Streeters, why would they not be doing so already? The reason these streets don't meet is simple: Wall Street financial professionals are in the business of getting the best return on their clients' money. You don't have to be the president of Merrill Lynch to know that you make more from investing in Microsoft and General Electric than in a check-cashing cheese-steak joint in North Philly.

However, new opportunities for high returns, particularly in the wake of the tech stock bubble, are no longer so easy to come by. Finance professionals need to dig deeper to develop new businesses as sources of customers for their own services and for the products made by their corporate clients. Recall Michael Milken's remark about developing a secondary market for securing minority-owned businesses. What is true of the healthy potential purchasing power of developing countries identified by Hernando De Soto is equally true (and perhaps more easily accessible) of the Diamond Streets and the working class neighborhoods—the "domestic emerging markets"— of this country.

As the costs of energy and transportation increase, the supply of oil shrinks, the availability of arable countryside diminishes, the press of suburban sprawl intensifies, cities—even inner cities—will become more attractive. Economist Edward Glaeser has argued that today's information economy favors cities much as manufacturing served them in the past. He notes that cities are gaining in their economic utility. "Cities are about information and skills, so it shouldn't be a surprise that cities are getting more valuable."[27] Wall Street's wisest may yet discover that they, too, are likely to find their future fortune in the "acres of diamonds" beneath Diamond Street.

Part of the challenge in attracting big money to Diamond Street is to initiate some economies of scale in the financing of the inner city, a project that economist Peter Tufano of the Harvard Business School has undertaken. Accordingly, "Tufano, working with teams of students and industry volunteers, has been attempting to design a partnership of governments, businesses and community-based organizations to make this successful demonstration program available to the 40 million eligible American families."[28] This seems a small step, but if it works like the other ideas mentioned in this chapter, it is a step in the direction of higher social purpose.

Why Should Government Care about Asset-Based Policies?

If Wall Street's incentives for using financial innovation to reach inner cities through secondary loans to business and other such measures are just becoming clear, governments' incentives, from Washington to Westminster and beyond, should be much more apparent. First, the prospect of asset-based development strategies promises to relieve fiscally stressed governments of some of the immensely expensive entitlement programs of the welfare state, such as Social Security and Medicare. Second, if asset-based development strategies can be made to work, they will begin to regenerate the tax base in the cities where the assets themselves are being seeded, through incipient property taxes and business taxes alike. Thereby, Wall Street helps not only Diamond Street, but Capitol Street.

Government is no longer a stranger to modern finance. Dynamic capital markets now serve as repositories for much of the wealth of average citizens. By the introduction of mass-marketed retail investment instruments—IRAs, 401(k) plans, and countless other large and small innovative variations—the capital markets have begun to absorb increasing amounts of wealth being steadily directed by the middle classes as a *supplement* to demographically burdened state-supported programs such as Social Security. As for government's more mainstream economic reform activities, it is impossible to imagine the ongoing efforts to restructure the economic foundations of social insurance—from child care to old-age pensions—without the guidance of the applied theory of modern finance. As we have seen, imaginative uses of this theory are just beginning to come to the fore.[29]

Acres of Derivatives

On that note, one could probably do worse than recall the evangelistic spirit from which Diamond Street earned its name in the early twentieth century. Now the twenty-first century is upon us. Old inner cities, as well as rural areas and vast parts of the developing world, are still in need of initiative and investment, but they are far more likely to find their revival in weightless acres of derivatives and secondary markets than in Russell Conwell's acres of diamonds. Harry Markowitz's template for asset diversification,

Robert Shiller's big idea for using financial innovation to secure the vitality of homes and jobs, Michael Milken's proposal for financing minority businesses, Michael Sherraden's initiative in proposing individual development and housing accounts for the poor, Martin Weitzman's ESOPs and their spin-offs, and Richard Freeman's proposal for turning the control of workers' pension funds to their owners, comprise the raw material of this job. These ideas, and their progenitors, are worthy of their Scottish Enlightenment legacy.

This is precisely the kind of social innovation that motivated Adam Smith to devise the institutions for expanding prosperity and civility more than 200 years ago. Leaders who would turn their backs on the opportunity to incorporate Diamond Street and similarly misbegotten thoroughfares and venues into the present wealth of nations, would do well to recall Adam Smith's counsel on the country of Ireland, the Diamond Street of its day, quoted earlier in this book:

> To crush the Industry of so great and so fine a province of the empire is equally unjust and unpolitic. . . . Nothing, in my opinion, would be more highly advantageous . . . than this mutual freedom of trade. It would help to break down that absurd monopoly which we have most absurdly established against ourselves in favour of almost all the different classes of our own manufacturers.[30]

Now, who's afraid of Adam Smith?

11

Urban Outfitters

Subsidiary trades grow up in the neighbourhood, supplying it with implements and materials, organizing its traffic, and in many ways conducive to the economy of its materials. . . . For subsidiary industries devoting themselves each to one small branch of the process of production, and working it for a great many of their neighbors, are able to keep in constant use machinery of the most highly specialized character.

Alfred Marshall

. . . the enduring competitive advantages in a global economy lie increasingly in local things—knowledge, relationships, motivation—that distant rivals cannot match.

Michael Porter

Robert Putnam has it down to a mantra. As noted earlier, he argues in his book, *Bowling Alone,* that the decline of social capital (or moral sentiments, as Adam Smith might have described it) could be traced by a triangle that connects the places where people live, where they work, and where they shop. As the past several decades have worn on, this triangle, separating home from work from marketplace, has continued to expand, and as it widens, the quality of our social life contracts. Putnam notes that each additional 10 minutes spent in daily commuting cuts involvement in local life by 10 percent.[1]

He backs up his claim with a mini-blizzard of facts, but none is as revealing as a testimonial he gleaned from a California woman: "I live in Garden Grove, work in Irvine, shop in Santa Ana, go to the dentist in Anaheim, my husband works in Long Beach, and I used to be the president of the League of Women Voters in Fullerton." If, as seems pretty reasonable, we assume that this person spends at least part of her time in her car (e.g., driving from Irvine to Santa Ana) talking on a mobile phone to somebody in another car (e.g., en route from Fullerton to Long Beach), it could be said that she is not so much a suburbanite as an earthbound space-traveler.[2]

For the best of reasons—those having to do with the cultivation of civic culture and moral sentiments—Putnam hopes that we "will spend less time traveling and more time connecting with our neighbors than we do today, that we will live in more integrated and pedestrian-friendly areas, and that the design of our communities and the availability of public space will encourage more casual socializing with friends and neighbors."[3]

Lofty, sweet, and sensible as Putnam's sentiments are, I find it hard to believe—but for one hitch—that our Californian autonaut would be the least bit inclined to sacrifice her sports utility vehicle, mobile telephone, two-car garage, auto CD player, monthly parking spaces, and other appurtenances just to be able to commune more closely with her neighbors. But that one hitch is the kicker: When she reaches her various destinations, social contact—lunching with her friends, schmoozing with her neighbors, working with her colleagues and clients, chatting with her grocer, or even exchanging nervous quips with her dentist—is probably what gives her the greatest satisfaction in her day.

If Robert Putnam could magically reduce the distances that separate our Californian's various social encounters, thereby giving her more time to enjoy the things that really matter (except perhaps for the dentistry), he might be able to sell her on some new and more efficient real estate. But he is a political scientist, not a prestidigitator nor even a real estate salesman. He might need the less than magical ministrations of our last group of economists to help sell us on the comforts of a more citified life. Those economists see the return of the city less as a democratic ideal than as a competitive opportunity. For them, sidewalk society will thrive again because people will see it is in their *interest* to recreate it.

The following policy initiative, the last to be discussed in this book, is about that: an effort, on the part of a handful of economists, to demonstrate the continuing economic advantage and social appeal of cities and, more generally, of city life. This impulse goes all the way back to Alfred Marshall, the first economist who understood the economic power of cities. But it finds its modern origins in a slightly incongruous-sounding activity: *market design*. The founding father of market design was a glorious transplant from Marshall's London to Milton Friedman's Chicago: Nobel laureate Ronald Coase.

Capital Socialist

According to journalist David Warsh, "People who are still mystified by the transformation in global politics in favor of markets since, say, 1980 would do well to pay a little extra attention to . . . Ronald Coase. . . . [Coase] achieved something a good deal more far-reaching and less partisan than the writing of *The Road to Serfdom,* the creation of the Institute for Economic Analysis, the founding of *The National Review,* the launching of the Goldwater campaign or any other events usually hailed as turning points in the intellectual history of present-day conservative politics."[4]

Ronald H. Coase, the winner of the 1991 Nobel prize in economics and a professor in the law school of the University of Chicago, was born in London in 1910 and came to intellectual maturity far outside the arc of the monetary and macroeconomic fireworks that had preoccupied his generation of economists both in England and in America. His first major contribution to the lore of economics appeared in 1937 in his article, "The Nature of the Firm," published in the journal *Economica.*

This article, which would have cascading consequences in subsequent economic thought, was inspired by, of all people, Vladimir Lenin. Coase, himself then a young socialist, was seduced and struck by Lenin's claim that the Soviet economy would be run as one big factory, and by no means a pin factory. Coase set out to test the viability of so bold a claim.[5]

Idea Factory

Coase began to ask himself: If one could conceive of an economy in terms of one big factory, why did firms in capitalism exist at all? Coase reasoned that firms came into being in order to solve an economic problem. He deduced that, under some circumstances, economic efficiency favored markets as a form of organization, whereas under other circumstances, economic efficiency favored firms. The preferred form of organization was dictated by costs. But these costs had nothing to do with the typical factor and production costs accounted for in standard microeconomics. The costs that Coase identified accounted for which form of organization, such as markets or bureaucracies, was most efficient. These particular costs came to be known as transaction costs.

The transaction costs (or costs associated exclusively with business, apart from overhead and production costs) of, say, providing society with, say, refrigerators are lower if production is organized within a relatively small number of large firms than if they are spread across 10,000 tiny garages, each making a single part. By the same token, the transaction costs incurred in providing society with legal services are lower if these services are organized in 100,000 different law practices, each serving its clients, than through three gigantic Orwellian law firms.

Technological, managerial, and financial forces affect transaction costs; thus, the ratio of firms to markets, from time to time, will depend on the available technology. Seen in the light of erstwhile socialist Ronald Coase, Lenin's idea for an economy based on one big factory is about as crazy as the other extreme: an economy in which people buy washing machine parts from 1,000 different vendors and assemble the machines in their basements. Transaction-cost analysis would provide economists with a whole new way of understanding how the governance structure of corporations and other organizations evolves, how industries develop and change, and how the welfare state becomes a means of delivering public services.

Ronald Coase moved to America in the 1950s and was once again struck with a protean contribution to the economic style of thinking. This one was even more powerful and had direct implications for the welfare state. As with his consideration of Lenin's One Big Factory, Coase set himself once again to pondering the very nature of economic activity. This time, he reflected on the question of why government had to be the provider of public services—a notion that was not only sacrosanct, but, until Coase got a hankering, unquestioned. Maybe this question occurred to Coase because he was by then living in Chicago, where the government resembled one big factory—a corrupt one, at that.

In his 1958 study, "The Federal Communications Commission," Coase posed the proposition that the economic value of a service—in this case, the radio spectrum—had little to do with who owned the rights, once they were legally established, and everything to do with the economic potential of how the service in question was used. In other words, if private individuals and firms could achieve greater economic efficiency from the use of services such as the radio spectrum or airlines or telecommunications, why should government not license user's rights to these private individuals? This issue could be addressed by the invention of tradable markets through public agencies, or, as it is known today: privatization.[6]

Just Desserts

David Warsh recounts how all this got started. A dinner party for Coase was hosted by George Stigler and attended by a group of Chicago economists who were interested in, but then highly skeptical of, Coase's idea. According to Warsh:

> The Chicagoans had gone into the room believing, along with liberals, that there were certain indispensable services that government had to provide because markets couldn't be made to offer them. They had walked out with a new vision of what government might accomplish through the clever establishment of property rights. Over the next 30 years, they persuaded most liberals of the acuity of their intuition.[7]

The effect on public policy of the ideas of Ronald Coase has been nothing less than seismic. Not only did his heat-seeking mind locate the mortal flaw in Soviet economic orthodoxy (much to the surprise of generations of left-leaning Western social critics), he also showed the way to save the Western welfare state: reengineer it by overlaying it with markets—that is, by creating a useful incentive structure for delivering public goods and services and thus by making it more efficient.

Whenever we see newspaper accounts of the creation of new charter schools, or the sale of pollution rights, or the subcontracting of local construction contracts, or the provision of school lunches, or the spinning off of huge national utilities, the trenchant mind of Ronald Coase is never far behind. Markets and privatization have their limits, especially when matters of national security are concerned, and they are often difficult to achieve. But now it would be hard to imagine a smoothly functioning public sector without markets and privatization. This is especially true in Western market democracies where contract law, private property, and robust financial markets make smoothly functioning privatization possible.

The political catch phrase for Coasean economics, "reinventing government," has echoed through the halls of government from Washington and Ottawa through Peking and Lima.[8] Cities, for generations the bastions of centralized and sometimes even corrupt political administration, have recently begun to reinvent themselves more along the lines of Ronald Coase than those of Vladimir Lenin (or Al Capone). Meanwhile, back at the blackboard, economists have been refining and extending Coase's social engineering arts, and applying them to firms, nations, and, increasingly, cities. Indeed, the spirit, if not exactly the letter, of Coase's work has breathed life back into the idea of long languishing cities as competitive, productive places.

Boston Borne

A quarter century after the Hyde Park dinner that ushered the ideas of Ronald Coase into the mainstream of economic discourse, a young economist, then an assistant professor at the Harvard Business School, did something unheard of among young economists, most of whom were obsessed with producing articles: he wrote a book. Michael Porter's *Competitive Strategy* (1980) became an instant classic.

By introducing the idea that all businesses operated according to a given strategy, whether explicit or implicit, and explaining that a firm's strategy depended not only on competition with its direct opponent—say, Hertz versus Avis—but on competition with the five forces in its strategic environment (buyers, suppliers, entrants, rivals, and substitutes), Porter revolutionized the way in which business leaders thought about their companies.[9]

Coase had demonstrated that an industry was dependent, for its size and structure, on the basis of its transaction cost environment. Porter applied a similar style of analysis to the internal structure of the firm by demonstrating how the prospects of a company within an industry depended on how well it understood the dynamic forces that defined its economic environment. In other words, whereas Coase showed how Lenin got caught napping by assuming that his One Big Factory could produce a nation's income efficiently, Porter showed how Hertz could get caught napping by assuming that it had outplayed Avis, while failing to consider the other competitive forces impinging upon it.

Twenty years and a dozen books after The Free Press published *Competitive Strategy,* Michael Porter had managed to explain not only the strategic principles of competition, but why certain firms achieved competitive advantage over others, why nations did so, and finally, for our purposes, *how cities could do so.*[10]

Michael Porter's Moral Sentiments

As noted before, Alfred Marshall was the original urban economist. His urban economics began with this hard-headed insight: "Employers are apt to resort to any place where they are likely to find a good choice of workers with special skill which they require; while men seeking employment naturally go to places where there are many employers who need such skill as theirs and where therefore it is likely to find a good market."[11] Thus, it is hardly a surprise today that chipmakers flock to Silicon Valley; moviemakers, to the Hollywood Hills; book publishers, to New York's Third Avenue; insurance executives, to Zurich; and investment professionals, to Wall Street and the City of London. Nor is it a surprise that all this congregating produces knowledge spillovers that create additional economic strength.

Michael Porter updated Marshall's insight through a series of extensive studies that culminated in his book, *The Competitive Advantage of Nations.* In it, Porter confirmed the insight that for all the globalization that has marked the recent past, productivity still occurs around clusters of firms, and the better a municipal area or region supports the competitive features that make it attractive, the more prosperous its clusters will be.[12]

As a natural extension of his interest in competitive clusters, and as a considered expression of his genuine passion—his moral sentiments—for cities, especially inner cities, Porter has developed his urban analysis into an active and ongoing advocacy project: The Initiative for Competitive

Cities. Reviewing Porter's project, it is clear that when he undertakes something, he does so with a commitment and resourcefulness characteristic of, say, the pharaohs of ancient Egypt. Dispatching himself, his associates, and his researchers into a dozen cities around America since 1994, Porter has taken it upon himself to advance the conviction that flows forth from his scholarship: Cities must compete.[13]

The City Strategic

Contrary to many urban analysts before him, Porter takes a tough-love approach to the economic renewal of cities. He stresses their competitive economic advantages and insists that cities use these advantages as competitive weapons. For Porter, the economic strength of cities is to be found, as they say on Wall Street, in their long-term fundamentals. According to Porter, "Today, the enduring competitive advantages come from local things: a unique network of suppliers, a unique network of specialized skills, leading educational institutions. These are the kinds of advantages that cities inherently enjoy over other locations."[14]

Further, and perhaps most importantly, Porter notes that the global shift to a sophisticated service economy, which is now leading job growth, also favors cities: "In services, proximity is much more important than in manufacturing. Companies must be near their customers. . . . 'Just-In-Time' and responsiveness are the governing rules." Porter cites a dozen crucial industrial clusters where cities have strengths—everything from education and knowledge creation through health technology and financial services. Cities rate high on all of these relevant indexes, and thus are ready to rock.[15] So, what's holding up the show?

One Big Unhappy Factory

Michael Porter indicts the urban leadership of the past generation for undermining the very institutions that need to be supported if cities are to realize their natural potential. He notes that urban leaders have "needlessly driven up the cost of doing business. Business infrastructure has been neglected. Business taxes have increased while the quality and efficiency of public services have been allowed to badly deteriorate. Regulation has made business growth and expansion in cities next to impossible."[16] After pondering Porter's list of indictments, a reader could come away wondering whether the leaders of our cities had decided to forgo Alfred Marshall's insights into the character of industrial districts, and Ronald Coase's ministrations on transaction costs, in order to build Vladimir Lenin-style One Big Factory theme parks. State and federal governments conspired in this civic perversity by passing destructive zoning and transport laws.

To get cities to realize their potential, Porter starts by identifying the competitive advantages of inner cities themselves: first, proximity (they are conveniently located); second, a large, underserved local market (they are the core of their regional economies); and third, an "available, loyal workforce." Contrary to the views of other analysts, Porter and his researchers see tremendous potential in the inner-city labor market. He notes that, in the next decade, 80 percent of the American workforce growth will come from among minorities, and a large percentage of these workers will be city and inner-city residents.[17]

Porter then calls for:

1. City leaders to hammer out competitive strategies for their respective cities;
2. The national government to modify the skewed incentives and policies that seem to favor economic activity in the suburbs;
3. More capital to be directed toward improving business sites and infrastructure;
4. A reduction to zero for capital gains taxes in cities, in order to stimulate entrepreneurial activity;
5. An "aggressive national strategy" of workforce development.

He sees the nation's growth rate tied directly to workforce development, and insists that the greatest possible gains in this area are to be had among inner-city minority workers.[18]

Porter calls on business leaders to recognize "the genuine business opportunities in inner cities"; to learn to adapt their strategies, products, and practices to the needs of city markets; to build business-to-business connections with existing urban businesses and other economic institutions; and to get directly involved with inner-city workforce development. Porter himself has put his money where his mouth is by using his organization, The Initiative for a Competitive Inner City, as a market maker between mainstream businesses and inner-city workers and businesses.[19]

Beyond the dynamic civic economics of Michael Porter, other economists, far from his quarters in Boston and Coase's in Chicago, are also contributing to the idea of a city revived.

When Companies and Communities Tango

Recall again Robert Putnam's powerful claim that the diminution of social capital in the past couple of generations is reflected in an expanding geographical triangle wherein the three points represent where people work, shop, and live. The more time we spend traveling the long distances between these points, the less time we have in our various communities, and the weaker our social networks become.

One way to help reverse this trend and shrink the triangle is to coordinate the commitment of capital to communities through the strategic integration of companies and municipalities—or, as economists say—through economic complementarity (an idea that made its debut in the work of Alfred Marshall).

Stanford economists Paul Milgrom and John Roberts have looked at the problem of complementarity between companies and communities in a hard-headed way, as dismal scientists do. First, they examine the interests and incentives of all the parties involved. They note that a given company and its host community have certain cospecialized assets, "each of which is more productive when used with the other." For example, both the plant and the town have joint interests in investment in "roads, sewage-treatment facilities, schools, and other assets whose value depends on the plant's continued operation."[20]

The challenge, according to Milgrom and Roberts, is for the town to safeguard these assets from corporate opportunism at the time of investment, perhaps by "agreeing on restrictions on plant closings," and other such measures. The corporation, for its part, receives commitments from the town in terms of needed road and sewage projects, housing, and other resources.[21]

This strategic approach amounts to a kind of corporate/communal prenuptial agreement. The assurances arrived at would also encourage the plant to invest in the cospecialized assets it holds with the town, thereby improving their complementarity. In effect, this approach extends the contracting character of the firm to its dealings with its hometown. For example, the broadly dispersed local ownership structure of the Green Bay Packers, limited as it is to Green Bay residents, effectively serves as a cospecialized asset shared by the local citizens and their beloved team. The loyalty and love between town and team may be deep, but it doesn't hurt to have a strong strategic tie on which to build these sentiments.[22]

The beauty of the idea of cospecialized assets—everything from power stations through occupational training schools—is that they can be designed to fit distinctive situations, in the way that the Packers' charter was specified to meet the needs of a football team *and* a small Wisconsin town.

Economists Go to Town

Also flowing out of some of Ronald Coase's ideas about the flexibility of economic institutions is a stream of new research in economics that touches directly upon the business institutions so vital to cities and inner cities—notably, corporations.

Corporations are crucial to the fulfillment of a newly competitive city, but a chorus of critics will charge that the transnational corporation, the mother ship of restless capital, is actually working at cross purposes with civic sensibility; it is sideswiping communities on the reckless road to high returns. As the critics have it, the corporation is wreaking havoc, not so much on the old Left's welfare state, dead by its own hand, but rather on Edmund Burke's haven of traditional values and civility. The corporation swerves from one source of profits to the next, sucking communities dry—or so the story goes.[23]

And as these critics further attest, the transnational corporation is an institution teeming with Edmund Burke's detested economists, sophisters, and calculators, in the bespoke roles of managers, accountants, and consultants. Seldom do social critics reach a rhetorical pitch of greater fervor than in their condemnations of corporations as the killers of culture.

Yet, as Adam Smith might have advised, the challenge is not to condemn but to acknowledge the commercial motives of corporations—including the free movement of capital—accept the continued influence of the institutions of corporate capitalism within communities, and find ways to coordinate the interests of the firm with those of the town, neighborhood, or city that provides businesses with the human and social capital that enables corporations to thrive. This approach is evident in the commentary of several contemporary economists.

Emperors of Ice Cream

Discussions about the social responsibility of corporations always bring to mind the anecdote Californian journalist Warren Hinkle tells of his friend and fellow 1960s counterculturist, Howard Gossage, a reformed advertising man who decided, late in life, to preach truth-in-advertising to other advertising executives. According to Hinkle, Gossage complained that preaching truth-in-advertising to ad executives is like trying to tell "an eight-year-old kid that sexual intercourse is more fun than a chocolate ice cream cone."[24]

If Gossage had taken a cue from Adam Smith, perhaps an appeal to the self-interest of the ad men would have worked better; eight-year-olds do grow up. The lesson for intellectuals who are interested in the socially responsible behavior of corporations is that corporations ultimately are dependent upon the towns and neighborhoods they sometimes seem so willing to exploit. In the long run, communities are still there, both as sources of human capital (employees) and social capital (civic institutions), and as markets (customers). In the longer term, it makes as much sense for corporations to treat communities well, as it does for communities to accommodate corporations.

UCLA economist Sanford Jacoby makes a case in point. In 1998, Jacoby wrote an article—a corporate eulogy, if you will—about ousted Sunbeam chairman "Chainsaw Al" Dunlap, upon Dunlap's firing from Sunbeam.[25] Dunlap had gained fame as a corporate turnaround "artist." His artistry was comparable to that of, say, a tree surgeon. He distinguished himself by his capacity to fire large numbers of employees with extreme prejudice in the service of greater cost-competitiveness. These staff reductions allegedly led to greater efficiency, profitability, and value for shareholders, and sunnier futures for the companies in turnaround.

Restructurings through downsizing of this kind—some of them needed—became standard operating procedure during the 1980s, when American businesses stripped down from bloated levels of excess capital to fighting form, in order to contend in the increasingly competitive global economy. Downsizing, generally speaking, came to be looked upon by Wall Street as something beyond a necessary evil—a spare, spartan sign of corporate health because less fat equaled more muscle equaled greater profits. Capital began to follow the downsizers with heat-seeking excitement.

Dunlap took the efficiency movement an extra step. At Sunbeam, which he took over as chief executive officer in 1996, apparently he fired staffers for no other reason than to please Wall Street and without any subsequent improvement in efficiency or productivity. The fixer failed to fix the right problem. Sunbeam failed to shine and Dunlap's number was called. The game was up and Dunlap was out.

According to economist Jacoby, the moral of the story for Wall Street as well as for embryonic Dunlaps all over, is that there is a high road and a low road by which companies can share risks with their employees. The low road is the one Chainsaw Al blazed and eventually torched: Fire employees, drive up the share price, and ask questions later. The high road is more Adam Smith's style—and is better business, to boot. As Jacoby says in another article:

> The high road, associated with companies like IBM and Hewlett-Packard, recognizes that a company has a moral obligation to employees and their families. These employers rely on layoffs only as a last resort. . . . What seems the ethical thing to do also makes good business sense. At high-road companies, management realizes that the company's human assets are an inimitable source of competitive advantage. . . . Moreover, when high-road companies do turn to layoffs, they try to be fair because they know they're in business for the long haul. If and when business improves, companies with good reputations will have an easier time getting the best and brightest workers.[26]

Jacoby's description of the high road squares nicely with Robert Frank's recently reconceived economics of moral sentiments in that the downsizing action that may seem most rational on the surface, given the profit-maximizing behavior of firms, actually is the less rational option in the long run.

There is another advantage to firms that take the high road. If a company makes clear its policy to fire employees as an efficiency measure only after it has reasonably exhausted most other cost-cutting possibilities, that policy makes it harder for managers to execute unfair or otherwise indiscriminate firings behind the veil of economic prudence. If anything can be said in defense of Chainsaw Al, it is probably that, in cutting staff at Sunbeam, he was certainly not the first executive to fire otherwise productive, experienced, collegial employees for apparently unjustified reasons. This kind of action is much more difficult to effect in a high-road firm, where firings are carried out only as a measure of last resort, than in a low-road firm, where firings due to political or other expediency can be covered by the broad brush of cost-efficiency.

The Australian Firewall

Short of efforts to coordinate the interests of a firm and a town, and in the face of irresponsible and irrepressible practitioners of low-road management, ultimately the only real coercive force society has at its hand against corporate adventurism is government. Perhaps the best firewall government has against the profligate exercise of corporate power is a tax that serves as a disincentive to such behavior. Such a tax was devised by two economists at the Evatt Institute in Australia, Christopher Sheil and Peter Botsman.

Sheil and Botsman have proposed that "banks and financial institutions would have to pay a special tax to offset the social costs of mergers." This tax, if properly implemented, would serve not only as a compensatory measure providing some financial insurance to towns hit by downsizing as a result of mergers or other restructuring actions, but would also build some cautionary disincentives into the culture of restructuring, which sometimes gets the better of companies that would sacrifice their own long-term prospects and those of their employees for short-term gain.[27]

The aforementioned tax carries with it all the potential inefficiencies of any kind of corporate tax, and thus—like downsizing—should be considered only after other, more positive, measures are exhausted in the effort to secure the fit between a firm and a town.

The Civic Complementarities of Corporations

One critic makes the point that the economic boom of 1990s America is probably unrepeatable.[28] But the fact that the revolution in corporate restructuring is probably unrepeatable also means that much of the most unsettling social disruption it has brought to communities is also likely to be lessened. Revolution has given way to restoration, at least for the time being, and perhaps a period to reflect on the ongoing relationship between firms and communities.

Economist John Kay makes a singularly important point. He notes that corporations are *themselves* communities. Alas, perhaps the first defense against corporate adventurism is recognition, on the part of executives, that corporations as communities within communities must be governed as such if they are to thrive.

Kay adds economic sense to the discussion of the moral dimension of firms. He contends that because a corporation is itself a community, it deserves to be treated with the understanding we hold out for all other kinds of community. Kay uses the example of General Electric and its famous former CEO, Jack Welch, to make his point: "General Electric is an organization with personality, vitality, and values of its own; these values would be stifled by state ownership, have nothing to do with stockholders, existed before Jack Welch and will exist after him . . . the successful firm is the one whose characteristics are well-adapted to the environment in which it trades."[29] Corporate leaders who fail to acknowledge this do business at their own economic risk.

Echoing Kay, an American executive, fresh from a new reading of *The Wealth of Nations,* notes: "Adam Smith would certainly have said that if western capitalism is to have a truly lasting victory it must be based not only on free markets but on the responsible behavior of those operating in such markets."[30] By recognizing the communal character of the corporations they lead, executives embrace the very brand of behavior that Adam Smith's moral sentiments prescribed as consistent with the wealth of nations.

Corporations Go Native

Getting the fit right—by understanding the internal culture of the firm as well as the external culture in which it operates—is, as Kay points out, a real challenge to capitalists. Now, at a time when technological innovation, financial engineering, democratic politics, and media imagery are collectively washing through societies like some sort of futuristic tsunami, getting the fit right between local culture and global innovation should take special precedence, particularly in the plans of executives whose actions have serious consequences for the creation of economic as well as social capital in remote venues. Economist Jeffrey E. Garten, dean of the Yale School of Management, provides a useful example:

> John Browne, Chairman of British Petroleum Co., . . . believes that for BP to thrive, so must the communities in which it does its business. To make that happen, Browne has insisted that the economic and social health of the villages, towns, and cities in which BP does business be a matter of central concern to the company's board of directors. He has also made social investment for the long term an important variable in compensating BP employees around the world.[31]

Nobody is going to mistake British Petroleum for the Little Sisters of the Poor, nor should they. But the sentiments that Mr. Browne incorporates in his business strategy, when combined with avid attention to the bottom line, which keeps the company strong, simply yield a much smarter allocation of financial capital, and a much wiser leveraging of human capital, than the slash-and-burn tactics of the great downsizers.

For corporate executives, high-road behavior is not only smart business in the sense that it helps sustain the firm's long-term prospects through its connection with present and future employees, but also in the sense that it helps to preserve communities, including the churches, schools, hospitals, and satellite businesses that deliver services and help to keep social pathologies at bay. Critics may or may not overstate the cause-and-effect relationship between the rapaciousness of corporate capitalism and the rise of broken families, abortions, drug use, and various forms of criminality, but it would be hard to argue against the more positive view that organizations which support local social stability, including high-road businesses and high-road governments alike, have a salutary effect on the culture, as well as the economies, of towns, neighborhoods, and central cities.

City Limits

As noted throughout this book, the driving focus of many of the present generation of intellectuals is the challenge of "making democracy work" through the cultivation of social capital. The splendor of our finest cities and the civility of our most livable towns, each embodying the highest elements of human culture, reflect social capital in rich quantities. As noted, Italy's Emilia-Romagna is full of social capital; lively commercial centers from Barcelona to Boston to Bangkok hold impressive reserves of it; California's Silicon Valley has it aplenty; Diamond Street and New Jersey's Camden sadly have almost none. Successful cities and towns prosper at least in part because of the social capital contained in the networks of their universities, businesses, foundations, educational institutions, shopping, and neighborhoods; others languish because they lack not only material wealth, but the moral sentiments that social capital cultivates.

Today's intellectuals are duly justified in urging society to retain the high degrees of social capital in the civic cultures where it exists, regain it where it is lost, and extend it to the most unfortunate among us who have never had it. Hence has the study of social capital drawn the attention of such a diverse and otherwise contentious group of thinkers—political scientists, theologians, sociologists, feminists, conservatives, urbanists, architects, philosophers, journalists, civil engineers—everyone but economists, or so it has seemed.

And yet, as was also true in the days of Adam Smith, the challenge of nurturing civic culture is incomplete without the contribution of his erstwhile successors, economists. Smith regarded the cities of Europe in his time as the central nodes of international trade and thus as crucial for expanding economic capital, the equal partner of social capital in creating a fair and prosperous civil society. As the past few chapters have demonstrated, economists from Caroline Hoxby through Richard Freeman through Michael Porter and beyond are working to develop exactly the kinds of economic ideas worthy of Adam Smith; ideas needed to complement the goals so boldly proclaimed by the new Tocquevillians intent on enriching democracy through social capital.

Epilogue: Go with the Flow

If economists could get themselves thought of as humble, competent people, on a level with dentists, that would be splendid.

John Maynard Keynes

Get this [economic plan] passed. Later on, we can all debate it.

President George Herbert Walker Bush

In *The Godfather*, Peter Clemenza, erstwhile rotund *capo regime* of the Corleone criminal organization, may just as well have been talking about macroeconomists when he said, in reference to the impending war of the New York crime families, "This sort of thing has to happen every five or 10 years. It clears out the bad blood."[1] Indeed, every 10 years or so, macroeconomists, the intellectual issue of John Maynard Keynes and Milton Friedman, seem compelled to go to war over the state of the field and the direction in which research should be going. (The microeconomists, for their part, like to gloat that they got it right the first time.[2])

These macrobattles typically take place in journal articles and in books, but occasionally the principals meet and the fur flies in person. The most recent meetings of the macroeconomic families took place in New York, in October 2001, on the fifteenth floor of Columbia University's international studies building. That location, with its magnificent Gotham views, served as a constant and bittersweet testament to a vista that had been stolen from the skyline only a few weeks before, when the towers of the World Trade Center were cut down by the flaming planes of terrorists—and also as a reminder that progress can never be measured against abstractions but too often must be gauged against the unsettling reality of tragedy.

In the wake of the catastrophic events of September 11, 2001—"The Day the World Changed," in the words of *The Economist*—the turnout for the 2001 macroeconomics conference was all the more impressive. The participants and attendees included dozens of the most celebrated macroeconomists in the world, including seven Nobel prize winners and probably as many future Nobelists. These economists had suffered airport ordeals all over the United States and Europe—from San Francisco to Stockholm—but, symbolically, they had all changed flights in one of two scholarly ports of call—the classical Chicago of Milton Friedman and the Keynesian Cambridge of Paul Samuelson. The "brackish" standoff (noted earlier in this book) between the freshwater Chicago economists and the saltwater Cambridge economists was still very much in force on most policy matters; however, for an occasion like this, when a special premium fell on the combative argumentation that pushes science forward, the old competitive juices flowed freely once more.

At stake on the fifteenth floor was claim to the better and more compelling explanation of two protean forces that seldom recede from the minds of macroeconomists and were acutely on their minds during the autumn of 2001: unemployment and inflation. The Chicago economists came up with clever new angles to defend their view that less government is better for the health of the economy in times of economic trouble. The Cambridge economists (many of them from Europe) were equally determined to show that engaged, carefully targeted, activist fiscal and monetary policies were the way to go when the economy fell into a ditch and unemployment grew.

What had changed most in the old Classical versus Keynesian conflict were the words that were used to define the battle lines. In the old lexicon of macroeconomics, sturdy terms like *liquidity, consumption, velocity, investment, government expenditures,* and *the multiplier* were used to explain the economy's collective performance. However, Macroeconomics 2001 came equipped with a new and bewildering set of concepts that included slinky terms like *non-Walrasian microfoundations, menu costs, information cascades, adaptive behavior, market friction, diffusion rates,* and other such exotica.

The two most important words in the new contretemps were *expectations* and *knowledge.* *Expectations* (as in *rational expectations*) comes from an insight made in the late 1970s in Chicago and its scholarly suburb, Minnesota. If government tried to revive a flagging economy by standard Keynesian countercyclical measures such as easing money or increasing government spending, the public, rationally enough, would anticipate these moves, adjust its economic behavior accordingly, and neutralize the policy's intended effects, potentially pushing the business cycle back into its own tracks.

The Keynesians—or neo- (meaning younger) Keynesians—struck back on schedule, about 10 years later. They acknowledged the importance of expectations, but claimed that the public's expectations were not nearly as rational as those of the Chicago or the Minnesota economists—or at least not as mechanical. The *knowledge* held by the public in responding to government measures reflects, according to neo-Keynesians, "imperfect information" that blurs the rational response of all-too-human consumers and businesses to policy initiatives. Hence, society's response to weakened economic conditions might be to further withdraw from investing, consuming, and trading, thereby fueling the liquidity trap that sucks a poorly behaving economy into recession and even worse. To do nothing, argue the neo-Keynesians, would only bring harm. The unemployed would be left high and dry and their ranks would potentially swell.

So, all those years after the monetary economists of the Depression and War years had defined the debate over macroeconomics as a fight over government's role in reviving a flagging economy, this same problem had been transformed into an infinitely more complicated puzzle about the behavior of information: how people respond when they get it, how to interpret their response, and how timing matters in government's response. I'm already reserving my seat for the next macrorumble a decade from now.

The level of discourse at this meeting quickly got to be very technical. It was like watching a foreign-language movie without subtitles—I could figure out who was trying to poison whom, but I couldn't quite tell the arsenic from the cyanide. I would have destroyed the binding of even a well-bound English-to-Economics/Economics-to-English dictionary by lunchtime of the first day of this conference. Mere familiarity with Samuelson's Instructions did not suffice. Awash in numbers and jargon, I decided to fall back to a more anthropological stance and read the signs a bit differently than most of my fellow observers.

A Case of Uncertain Identity

My first observation had to do with the ostensible purpose of this meeting. The high priests of macroeconomics had come from near and far to salute the career of Columbia economist Edmund (Ned) Phelps (whom we met in Chapter 9, "Kitchen Chemists"). Phelps is neither a card-carrying Chicago or Cambridge economist, but tellingly, has contributed to *both* the Chicago and the Cambridge perspectives. Perhaps his most widely cited contribution to economic theory, the nonaccelerating inflation rate of unemployment (NAIRU), is one that he shares with that most bracing of freshwater Chicagoans, Milton Friedman. Both Phelps and Friedman claim that the trade-off between inflation and unemployment is strictly limited. In other words, countercyclical Keynesian measures intended to stimulate employment through activist fiscal and monetary policy can get policymakers only so far, an impulse hardly treasured by Keynesians and absolutely rejected by those economists who are farther Left. And yet, Phelps's favored solution to the problem of hard-core unemployment—the bold employer tax credits discussed earlier—is pretty ambitious even by the standards of the most activist Keynesians. So, in effect, the classicists and the Keynesians appeared to have come together to praise an economist who had, effectively, delivered a potent mixture of fresh water and salt water through the circular flow of economic ideas. Both sides of Adam Smith were in the air.

Theorems for the Common Man

The other anthropological observation that I made, amid all the mathematical and theoretical acrobatics, had to do with the common man—or, as the case may be, woman—a personage who gets little face time during mathematical economics jamborees. One celebrated Chicago economist came to the spirited defense of a fellow economist who, though bereft of any of the celebrity that adorned most of the attendees of this august gathering, had made a seminal contribution to an important current in the field without receiving due credit for it. I liked this expression of support for an odd-economist-out, and the concomitant contempt for the star system that defines the sometimes stultifying celebrity culture of modern academic economics.

Just as I was savoring this defense, a prominent Keynesian economist, and a scholar only too happy to engage the classical opposition, made what seemed like an almost inadvertent comment that, for me, captured the purpose behind the entire, 200-year-long modern economic enterprise. He talked about the plight of the people on a street in Gary, Indiana, the small deindustrialized and now rust-riddled working-class town in which he had grown up. In making this reference, this great economist was echoing a sentiment stressed ages ago by Adam Smith, whose passion for the masses of people drove him to his obsessive preoccupation with what it took to stimulate the wealth of nations—still the goal of economists everywhere.

Of Streets and Sentiments

After having witnessed two days of high-wire scholarly stunts by macro-economists—old and young; more or less libertarian, and more or less socialist; American and European; classical and Keynesian; incomprehensible and downright impenetrable—I said my thanks and excused myself early. I wanted to get home for a special Saturday evening roast chicken dinner that, I confess, had long since replaced the economics of information and expectations in my imagination. I grabbed my bag and hopped on the elevator. Fifteen flights beneath all the buzz, I stretched my legs and walked out into the fresh, cool, rain-cleansed air of Amsterdam Avenue. Then across Columbia's Harlem campus, and into the subway to catch the downtown Broadway Local to Penn Station, where I would board a train to Princeton.

As I hustled myself along, I could not help but hope that Ned Phelps and his contentious friends, fifteen floors up, would, amid all the theoretical fireworks, succeed in finding new ways to fend off the dragons of joblessness and inflation. For, if they did, it would bring new hope to these streets. I am convinced that it will be in these streets, the Amsterdam Avenues and the Diamond Streets; the South Side of Chicago and the spectral venues of Gary, Indiana, and Camden, New Jersey—that the newly revived civic economics of Adam Smith—the stuff of moral sentiments, of civil society, of Jane Jacobs' social capital, and of Robert Putnam's era of civic renewal—must be deployed if our society is to take the necessary next step toward realizing the magnificent vision of Heilbroner's worldly philosophers. A century ago, Alfred Marshall made this point at a conference probably much like the one on the fifteenth floor that day:

> The end before us is a great one. It calls for a steady, searching analysis, and for a laborious study of actual conditions. Economists cannot do it alone. Perhaps it may be found that their share in it will not be large, but I myself believe it will be very large. I submit, then, that a most pressing immediate call on us is to associate in our minds and those of others economic studies and chivalrous effort.[3]

Notes

NOTE

The quotations by Deirdre McCloskey and Jonathan Sacks in the front matter first appeared, respectively, in McCloskey's great 1995 *American Scholar* article, "Bourgeois Virtues," and in Sacks' trenchant *First Things* piece, "Morals and Markets," two of my favorite articles. I chose these quotations to keynote this book because both blend, so well, a respect for the centrality of the market in our society with an acute sensitivity to the need for leavening the market with cultural consideration—with just the right touch.

PREFACE: SYMPATHY FOR THE DISMAL

I opened this chapter with two quotations—from Thomas Peacock and Walter Bagehot, respectively—that I found in David Whynes' learned and enjoyable *Invitation to Economics,* published originally by Martin Robertson, and then by Blackwell's. It is a wonderful combination of economic basics and historical lore. I discovered this book when I worked for Blackwell's in the mid-Eighties.

    1. Kevin O'Rourke and Jeffrey Williamson, 1999. *Globalization and History* (Cambridge, Massachusetts: MIT Press).

    2. Alan S. Blinder, January, 2000. "How the Economy Came to Resemble the Model," *Business Economics.*

    3. John Maynard Keynes, 1936 [1989]. *The General Theory of Employment, Interest and Money* (New York: Harvest Books).

CHAPTER 1:   LETTER MAN

1. Gary Burke, personal conversation with my former Harcourt colleague in 2001. Since this story goes back several decades, has several parts, and has been passed through several sources, it may be apocryphal, but I doubt it. It's too improbable to have never happened.

2. Alfred Marshall, 1890. *Principles of Economics an Introductory Volume,* 8th Ed. (London: Macmillan, 1920), p. 1.

3. Mario Puzo and Francis Ford Coppola, 1972. *The Godfather* (New York: Paramount Pictures).

4. Adam Smith, 1759 [1984]. *The Theory of Moral Sentiments,* eds. A. L. Macfie and D. D. Rafael (Indianapolis, Indiana: Liberty Fund), p. 231.

5. Glenn Loury, March, 2000. "Who Cares about Racial Inequality?" *Journal of Sociology and Social Welfare,* Vol. XXXVI, No. 1.

6. Robert Putnam, 1992. *Making Democracy Work* (Princeton, New Jersey: Princeton University Press).

7. Alexis de Tocqueville, 2000. *Democracy in America* (New York: Bantam Classics).

8. Robert Putnam, 2000. *Bowling Alone* (New York: Simon & Schuster), p. 19.

9. Jane Jacobs, 1961 [1993]. *The Death and Life of Great American Cities* (New York: Vintage Books).

10. Loury, op. cit., p. 141.

11. Putnam, op. cit., p. 211.

12. There is no dearth of critical assessments of (and occasionally, savage assaults on) economics. Some of the more prominent include: Paul Omerud, 1977, *The Death of Economics* (New York: John Wiley & Sons); Alan Ehrenhalt, "Keepers of the Dismal Faith," *New York Times,* February 23, 1997; Robert Heilbroner and William Milberg, 1996, *The Crisis of Vision in Modern Economic Thought* (Cambridge, Massachusetts: Cambridge University Press); Lester Thurow, *Dangerous Currents* (New York: Random House); The Post-Autistic Economic Web site, http://www.paecon.net/ and *The Post-Autistic Economic Review.*

13. Adam Smith, [1978]. *Lectures on Jurisprudence,* eds. R. L. Meek, D. D. Rafael, and G. P. Stein (Indianapolis, Indiana: Liberty Fund), pp. 538–539.

14. Adam Smith, 1984. *The Theory of Moral Sentiments,* eds. A. L. Macfie and D. D. Rafael (Indianapolis, Indiana: Liberty Fund), p. 304.

15. Jerry Z. Muller, 1993. *Adam Smith in His Time and Ours* (New York: The Free Press), p. 8.

16. Michael Jensen, Summer, 1994. "Self-Interest, Altruism, Incentives, and Agency Theory," *Journal of Applied Corporate Finance,* Vol. 7, No. 2, p. 43.

17. There are many extant criticisms of the basic market model of Adam Smith, from the notion that the modern corporation has distorted the simple dynamics of the market economy to the presence of inevitable market failures, to the idea that atomized market interactions of the great mass of people fail to capture individual strategic motives. However, no economic analyst I know of rejects out of hand completely the idea that the pursuit of self-interest mediated by markets serves the public good, the fundamental building block of Adam Smith's modern market economy. Some of the more prominent and informed challenges to Smith's model appear in the following works: Bradford DeLong, the *Wall Street Journal;* Leonard Nakamura, *Bulletin of the Philadelphia Federal Reserve Bank;* Joseph Stiglitz, *On the Economic Nature of the State* (Blackwell Publishers); Robert Heilbroner, *The Worldly Philosophers* (New York: Simon & Schuster); and Sylvia Nasar, *A Beautiful Mind* (New York: Simon & Schuster).

18. D. N. McCloskey, Spring, 1994. "Bourgeois Virtues," *The American Scholar.*

19. John Kay, 1996. *The Business of Economics* (New York: Oxford University Press), p. 141.

20. Putnam, op. cit., p. 401.

21. Hernando DeSoto, 2000. *The Mystery of Capital* (New York: Basic Books), pp. 6–7.

22. Adam Smith, 1759 [1981]. *An Inquiry into the Nature and Causes of the Wealth of Nations,* eds. R. H. Campbell and A. S. Skinner (Indianapolis, Indiana: Liberty Fund), Book V, p. 759.

23. John Maynard Keynes, 1991. *Essays in Persuasion* (New York: W.W. Norton & Co.), p. 319.

CHAPTER 2:   THE INSTRUCTIONS

The opening quotes in this chapter are from Paul Samuelson and William Nordhaus's textbook *Economics,* 13th Ed., which I had a hand in bringing to publication during my employment at McGraw-Hill in the early 1980s, and from William Breit and Roger Ransom's book *The Academic Scribblers,* a popular supplementary textbook published by Holt, Rinehart, and Winston, from my years as a college book salesman. In 1999, I published a reprint of this book at Princeton University Press.

1. Ethan Coen and Joel Coen, 1987. *Raising Arizona.* Twentieth Century Fox Film Corporation.

2. Jacob Viner. My sources report that Viner made his famous comment in conversation.

3. Todd Bucholz, 1989. *New Ideas from Dead Economists* (New York: Penguin, A Plume Book), p. 96. For a brief and enjoyable introduction to economics, few books are better than Bucholz's witty account. His book is instructive because Bucholz is more generous in his treatment of the free-market ideas of classical economists than is Robert Heilbroner in his canonical *The Worldly Philosophers*. Bucholz's view of the world reflects the post-Vietnam generation's rediscovery of Chicago-style classical liberalism and coolness toward the welfare-state Keynesianism of the Sixties and Seventies.

4. Mark Skousen, Spring, 1997. "The Perseverance of Paul Samuelson's *Economics*," *The Journal of Economic Perspectives*, Vol. 11, No. 2, p. 145. Skousen is, if anything, a more zealous free-market economist than is Todd Bucholz, but in his assessment of the history of Samuelson's unabashedly Keynesian textbook, Skousen is admiring of Samuelson's achievement.

5. *The Economist*, August 23, 1997, p. 58. This article appeared during the fiftieth anniversary of the publication of Paul Samuelson's textbook. I thought the article reflected a surprising ambivalence on the part of *The Economist's* editors for a book that did more to advance the modern principles of economics than any ten of its kind since World War II.

6. Michael Barone, 1990. *Our Country, a History of America from Roosevelt to Reagan* (New York: The Free Press). I edited and published this book by Michael Barone, the Baedeker of modern American politics, as James Q. Wilson described him in *The New Republic*, while I was at The Free Press. For me, the most memorable point made by Barone was his characterization of the economic progress made in the American middle class since the years following the Depression and the New Deal.

7. The 1992 Clinton for President campaign, attributed to Clinton political advisor James Carville. If Carville didn't actually say, "It's the economy, stupid," the phrase still has done more for his reputation as the most fatalistic of contemporary political consultants than perhaps anything that he actually did say.

8. William Styron, 1979. *Sophie's Choice* (New York: Random House). I drew my recounting of the Samuelson celebration dinner in this portion of Chapter Two from a dog-eared, yellowed copy of a typewritten speech that I delivered at MIT's Endicott House in suburban Boston that evening in December, 1981. Much of the research for this talk was inspired by my reading of the unusually interesting history of McGraw-Hill, *Endless Frontiers*.

9. "The Economist with a Bestseller," February 14, 1959. *Business Week*, pp. 73–74.

10. Bennett Kremen, November 1, 1970. "Speaking of Books: Samuelson's *Economics*," *New York Times Book Review*, p. 2.

11. Michael Elia, personal conversation. Mike Elia was a development editor at McGraw-Hill who, at the time of the Samuelson dinner, had worked on several editions of Samuelson's great textbook. Now associated with Prentice Hall, Mike was helpful to me in commenting on early drafts of this book.

CHAPTER 3:   THE WARNING

The quotations by John Maynard Keynes and Robert Heilbroner that open this chapter seem to me to reflect the same sentiment: that capitalism could be made to work only if political solutions could be designed to check the unruly market forces that threatened to undo the very prosperity that these forces brought into being. This was a major theme in the work of Adam Smith, brought back into currency since the 1990s in works by Jerry Muller, Emma Rothschild, Deirdre McCloskey, and other thinkers, but largely absent in the literature of mainstream economics.

1. *The Economist,* August 23, 1997, p. 58. This note refers to the sales of Samuelson, not Heilbroner. Reference to Mr. Heilbroner's sales figures is noted on his Website at the New School University.

2. Robert Heilbroner, 1992. *The Worldly Philosophers,* 6th Ed. (New York: Touchstone), p. 8.

3. Ibid.

4. Robert Heilbroner and William Milberg, 1995. *The Crisis of Vision in Modern Economic Thought* (New York: Cambridge University Press), p. 6.

5. Partha Dasgupta, September 1998. "Modern Economics and Its Critics," working paper. Dasgupta's paper is an extraordinarily harsh assessment of the work of Robert Heilbroner.

CHAPTER 4:   LITTLE PLATOONS

1. Robert Heilbroner, 1992. *The Worldly Philosophers,* 6th Ed. (New York: Touchstone), p. 317.

2. Diane Coyle, 1998. *The Weightless World* (Cambridge, Massachusetts: MIT Press). This book is a deeply informed, deftly written characterization of the modern information-based economy with a particular emphasis on the connection between information technology and growth.

3. Adam Smith, 1759 [1981]. *An Inquiry into the Nature and Causes of the Wealth of Nations,* eds. R. H. Campbell and A. S. Skinner (Indianapolis, Indiana: Liberty Fund), Book I, p. 7.

4. Avner Greif, 1998. "Self-Enforcing Political Systems and Economic Growth: Late Medieval Genoa," *Analytic Narratives,* eds. Robert Bates, Avner Greif, Margaret Levi, and Jean-Laurent Rosenthal (Princeton, New Jersey: Princeton University Press), Chap. 1, p. 23. Greif's work, applying game theory

to his explanation of the evolution of trade across unfamiliar Mediterranean cultures in the Middle Ages marked a new departure in the style of economic history by introducing strategic considerations into economic decision-making in the evolution of political and economic institutions. Also, the name "social invention" used to describe contracts and other such institutional innovations, is taken from the late James C. Coleman.

5. Peter Bernstein, 1996. *Against the Gods: The Remarkable Story of Risk* (New York: John Wiley & Sons). Peter Bernstein recounts the origins of modern insurance in the contracts written in eighteenth century English coffee houses for the purpose of insuring sea-faring merchant ventures.

6. Hernando DeSoto, 2000. *The Mystery of Capital* (New York: Basic Books). De Soto argues with great persuasiveness that a prime missing link in the development of poor and transitional economies is the lack of useful and legitimate titles to property ownership.

7. Paul M. Romer, 1993. "Implementing a National Technology Strategy with Self-Organizing Industry Investment Boards," Brookings Papers, Microeconomics 2. This quote from Paul Romer aptly summarizes his view, developed in the Eighties and now widely held, that economic growth is attributable at least in part to advances in knowledge and technological breakthroughs.

8. Ibid. Romer emphasizes the necessity of technological advancement over shifts, however necessary, in macroeconomic policy measures. I think he is trying to make the point that policy modifications at the margins of economic activity are second order to the central role played by industrial and technological innovation in the advancement of economic growth.

9. Max Weber, 1930. *The Protestant Ethic and the Spirit of Capitalism.* Tr. by Talcott Parsons. (London: HarperCollins Academic), p. 17. This is perhaps the most famous, widely cited, passage from Weber's classic commentary on the culture of market society.

10. Robert Putnam, March 21, 1993. "The Prosperous Community," *The American Prospect,* Vol. IV, No. 13.

11. Edmund Burke, 1790, "Reflections on the Revolution in France."

12. Ferdinand Mount, 1990. *The Subversive Family* (New York: The Free Press).

13. Adam Smith, 1759 [1984]. *The Theory of Moral Sentiments,* eds. A. L. Macfie and D. D. Rafael (Indianapolis, Indiana: Liberty Fund), p. 244.

14. Smith, op. cit., Book IV, p. 612.

15. Francis Fukuyama, 1995. *Trust: The Social Virtues and the Creation of Prosperity* (New York: The Free Press), p. 11.

16. Deirdre McCloskey, Spring, 1994. "Bourgeois Virtue." *American Scholar,* Vol. 63, No. 2.

17. Gary Becker. This is a theme developed consistently throughout the Nobel Prize-winning work of Gary Becker on human capital and noted most emphatically in his 2000 work with Kevin Murphy, *Social Economics* (Cambridge, Massachusetts: Harvard University Press).

18. Mancur Olson, Spring, 1996. "Big Bills Left on the Sidewalk: Why Some Nations Are Rich and Others Are Poor," *The Journal of Economic Perspectives,* Vol. 10, No. 2, pp. 3–24.

19. "New Economists: Journey Beyond the Stars," December 19, 1998. *The Economist,* pp. 143–146.

CHAPTER 5:   ENLIGHTENMENT WONK

I chose quotations for this chapter on Adam Smith from his books, *The Theory of Moral Sentiments* and *The Wealth of Nations.* These quotes stress seemingly contradictory virtues of love and self-interest, but Smith showed how these impulses actually complement each other in serving as the necessary foundations for a civilized and prosperous society.

1. Robert Heilbroner, 1992. *The Worldly Philosophers,* 6th Ed. (New York: Touchstone). Heilbroner's book, along with those of Todd Bucholz (1989, *New Ideas from Dead Economists,* New York: Penguin) and especially Jerry Muller (1993, *Adam Smith in His Time and Ours,* New York: The Free Press) form the foundation of this chapter—and of much of my knowledge of Adam Smith. Sometimes I had trouble distinguishing the source of specific materials because they are cited in two, or even all three, of these books and because they are part of the canonical lore of the 200 year-old biographical and intellectual history of Adam Smith. I wish to attribute my *general* appreciation of Smith to the three main sources cited in this chapter in the following way: I have gleaned most of my knowledge of Smith's intellectual style and his insights into the integration of markets and moral sentiments from Muller; most of the biographical history from Heilbroner, and certain insights on Smith's economics (and witticisms) from Bucholz.

2. Heilbroner, op. cit., pp. 42–46.

3. Adam Smith, 1759 [1981]. *An Inquiry into the Nature and Causes of the Wealth of Nations,* eds. R. H. Campbell and A. S. Skinner (Indianapolis, Indiana: Liberty Fund), Book I, pp. 25–26.

4. Muller, op. cit., pp. 62–76.

5. Muller, op. cit., pp. 16–27.

6. Ibid., p. 48.

7. Smith, op. cit., Book V, p. 772.

8. Muller, op. cit. Muller is at his best when revealing Smith's insights into the unanticipated consequences of faulty incentive structures. See his Chapter Six, "Social Science as the Anticipation of the Unanticipated." The

modern notion of unanticipated consequences is a centerpiece of contemporary sociological theory as developed by the celebrated Columbia University sociologist Robert K. Merton in his classic 1948 book, *Social Theory and Social Structure.*

9. Muller, op. cit., p. 20.

10. Peter Bernstein, personal conversation. In reading this manuscript many times over, Bernstein often filled in (and straightened out) my history of economic ideas. This is but one example.

11. Heilbroner, op. cit., p. 74.

12. Smith, op. cit., Book I, pp. 25–26.

13. Ibid., p. 15.

14. Smith, op. cit., Book IV, p. 456.

15. Muller, op. cit., p. 69.

16. Heilbroner, op. cit., p. 68.

17. Bucholz, op. cit., p. 28.

18. Ibid., p. 30.

19. Adam Smith to Henry Dundas, November 1, 1779 [Letter]. *Glasgow Edition of the Works and Correspondence of Adam Smith,* eds. E. C. Mossner and I. S. Ross (New York: Oxford University Press), pp. 241–242. Quoted in Jerry Z. Muller, 1993. *Adam Smith in His Time and Ours* (New York: The Free Press), p. 26.

20. Muller, op. cit., p. 136.

21. Ibid., pp. 6–7. This is perhaps the most vital point Muller makes about the social architecture on which market civilization depends and its elucidation in the thinking of Adam Smith.

22. Adam Smith, 1759 [1984]. *The Theory of Moral Sentiments,* eds. A. L. Macfie and D. D. Rafael (Indianapolis, Indiana: Liberty Fund), p. 204.

23. Ibid.

24. Muller, op. cit., p. 94.

25. Ibid., p. 100, and personal conversation. Muller's effort in tracing Smith's Impartial Spectator through Freud's super-ego through contemporary sociological role theory begun by Mead and Cooley and evolved through the work of Robert Merton is ingenious.

26. John C. Mueller, 1999. *Capitalism, Democracy, and Ralph's Pretty Good Grocery Store* (Princeton, New Jersey: Princeton University Press), p. 25. I don't know what it is about people variously named "Muller" or "Mueller," but they certainly seem to know more about the culture of capitalism than the rest of us. John C. Mueller is a political scientist at the University of Rochester and the author of a fine Princeton University Press book published by a former colleague, *Capitalism, Democracy, and Ralph's Pretty Good Grocery Store.* In it, Mueller makes the convincing argument that democracy, for all its promise and celebrity,

is overrated as a system, whereas capitalism, for all the criticism levelled at it, is underrated.

27. Mueller, op. cit., p. 21.

28. Adam Smith, [1978]. *Lectures on Jurisprudence,* eds. R. L. Meek, D. D. Rafael, and G. P. Stein (Indianapolis, Indiana: Liberty Fund), p. 239.

29. Adam Smith, [1978]. *Lectures on Jurisprudence,* eds. R. L. Meek, D. D. Rafael, and P. G. Stein (Indianapolis, Indiana: Liberty Fund), p. 239.

30. Robert J. Samuelson, December 2, 1996. "The Spirit of Adam Smith," *Newsweek,* p. 63. *Newsweek*'s economics writer, Robert Samuelson (no relation to Paul), wrote the words cited in his article on Jerry Muller's Adam Smith book. It was a fitting commentary and wise acknowledgment not only of Smith's grand civilizing system but of Muller's brilliant explication of it.

CHAPTER 6:   SOUL SURVIVORS

Readers of a certain age will see immediately that I owe an intellectual debt to Sixties Philadelphia singing group, the Soul Survivors, whose one hit song, "Expressway to Your Heart," sounds in retrospect as much a homage to rush-hour traffic as it was to romantic love. The opening quotes, from Victorian economist Alfred Marshall and contemporary social philosopher Michael Novak, take very different avenues to make the same point: that it is it is frustrating, and ultimately impossible, to discuss the structural aspects of economic matters without paying attention to their moral aspects.

1. Robert Putnam, 2000. *Bowling Alone* (New York: Simon & Schuster).

2. John Kay, May, 1998. "The Third Way," *Prospect.*

3. Edmund Burke, 1790 [1987]. *Reflections on the Revolution in France,* ed. J. G. A. Pocock (Indianapolis, Indiana: Hackett Publishing Co.).

4. Paul Gigot, December 27, 1996. "Why Edmund Burke Is a Packer Fan," The *Wall Street Journal.*

5. Daniel Bell, 1996. *The Cultural Contradictions of Capitalism,* Twentieth Anniversary Ed. (New York: Basic Books), p. 330.

6. John P. Diggins, speech, NYC. Intellectual historian John P. Diggins made this point about the philosophers of the Enlightenment setting power against power, as in the system of checks and balances designed by the American founders, in a talk at the West Side Barnes and Noble in New York City during a discussion about the continuing relevance of classic political texts for contemporary debate. Other panelists included David Denby, Jean Cohen, and Mitchell Cohen, co-editor of *Princeton Readings in Political Thought,* a book that served as a discussion point during this session.

7. *The Internationale.* Deirdre McCloskey once noted that socialists have better songs than capitalists. This is proof-positive. I thank Peter Bernstein for providing me with the lyrics.

8. David Whynes, 1983. *Invitation to Economics* (Oxford: Martin Robertson), p. 55.

9. Anatoly Sobchak, 1992. *For a New Russia* (New York: The Free Press).

10. Todd Bucholz, 1989. *New Ideas from Dead Economists* (New York: Penguin, A Plume Book), pp. 148–150.

11. Peter L. Bernstein, 1996. *Against the Gods: The Remarkable Story of Rise* (New York: John Wiley & Sons). Discussion of Galton, pp. 152–157.

12. Bucholz, op. cit., pp. 147–148.

13. Alfred Marshall. I first heard the phrase, "economic chivalry," in a talk delivered by historian Gertrude Himmelfarb, later to appear in her comment in Robert M. Solow's, 1998, *Work and Welfare,* ed. Amy Gutmann (Princeton, New Jersey: Princeton University Press), pp. 77–78. Steve Medema was kind enough to send me a copy of Marshall's "The Social Possibilities of Economic Chivalry," his 1907 address to the Royal Economic Society.

14. Gertrude Himmelfarb, 1992. *Poverty and Compassion: The Moral Imagination of the Late Victorians* (New York: Vintage Books), p. 294.

15. Alfred Marshall, 1907. "The Social Possibilities of Economic Chivalry," *The Economic Journal,* Vol. XVII, pp. 7–29.

16. Bell, op. cit., p. 25.

17. Milton Friedman, 1963. *Capitalism and Freedom* (Chicago: University of Chicago Press).

18. Whynes, op. cit., p. 10.

19. Martin Reisebrodt. "Max Weber's 'Protestant Ethic.'" Class notes from his course on Max Weber at the University of Chicago Divinity School. Reisebrodt is Professor of Sociology at the University of Chicago.

20. Richard Swedberg, 1998. *Max Weber and the Idea of Economic Sociology,* Chap. 1 (Princeton, New Jersey: Princeton University Press).

CHAPTER 7:   DRAGON SLAYERS

The quotations that open this chapter, from Robert Skidelsky's discussion of Cambridge economist Richard Kahn and William Breit and Roger Ransom's chapter on Milton Friedman, were chosen to keynote the direction of economics during the early and middle decades of the twentieth century. Then the field was characterized by a dual obsession with mathematics and monetary principles, the latter being the lone intellectual lifeline available to policy economists for staying unemployment and inflation.

1. Frank Press and Raymond Siever, 1994. *Earth* (New York: W.H. Freeman and Company). Press and Siever attribute this quote to Will Durant.

2. Jerry Z. Muller, 1993. *Adam Smith in His Time and Ours* (New York: The Free Press), pp. 183–184.

3. Erwin Glikes. The late Erwin Glikes, president and publisher of The Free Press, made this point in a personal conversation. Erwin claimed that he learned this from the learned Washington economist Herbert Stein, sadly, now also deceased.

4. Robert Skidelsky, 1992. *John Maynard Keynes: The Economist as Savior, 1920–1937* (New York: Penguin Books).

5. The quote, "Madmen in power . . ." is from Keynes' 1936 masterwork, *The General Theory of Employment, Interest, and Money* (London: Macmillan), pp. 383–384. The characterization of Keynes as an eminent modernist come primarily from the Skidelsky biography, but also from many other writings on Keynes, including chapters in Heilbroner, Bucholz, and Breit and Ransom.

6. Peter L. Bernstein, personal conversation. My thanks again to Peter Bernstein for his deft tutorials on developments in macroeconomic history.

7. David Frum, 1996. *What's Right: The New Conservative Majority and the Remaking of America* (New York: Basic Books), p. 177.

8. Gertrude Himmelfarb, 1991. *Poverty and Compassion* (New York: Random House), pp. 301–303.

9. The Citizen's Income Trust. London: www.citizensincome.org.

10. Skidelsky, op. cit., p. xviii.

11. Ibid.

12. Muller, op. cit., p. 520.

13. Skidelsky, op. cit., p. 425.

14. Frum, op. cit., p. 177.

15. Skidelsky, op. cit, p. xx.

16. John Dryzek, 1987. *Rational Ecology* (Cambridge, Massachusetts: Basil Blackwell), p. 67.

17. I thank Peter Bernstein for this discussion of Milton Friedman's monetary economics.

18. Muller, op. cit., pp. 183–184. Muller repeatedly makes the point that Smith began his view of society from the top down, as it were, by specifying the moral architecture of the good society and fitting the incentive and institutional features to support this architecture. The beauty of this structure is that it is based not on political coercion, but on a constellation of complementary social and economic institutions. Hence, this coercion-free architecture came to be known as a system of "natural liberty." Milton Friedman's contemporary libertarianism emphasizes the importance of freedom as a central feature of natural liberty, as an end in itself as well as a bulwark against the encroaching effects of what Friedman considers an ever-omniverous government.

19. Muller, op. cit. This insight goes straight back to Adam Smith. See Chapter 12, "Applied Policy Analysis: Adam Smith's Sociology of Religion." It

is indeed the basis for the distinction between contemporary neoconservatives who believe in the strategic uses of government to influence the moral behavior of people (political scientist Peter Skerry has used the term, "conservative welfare state" as an apt label for this position) and libertarians such as Friedman who see government structures as encroaching encumbrances in the human quest for freedom.

20. Jackson Toby, personal conversation. This is one of those neat characterizations gleaned from conversations with scholars, in this case the distinguished Rutgers University sociologist Jackson Toby. I met him on an editorial visit to Rutgers' New Brunswick campus many years ago.

21. Lester Thurow, 1989. *The New Pallgrave Dictionary of Economics,* Vol. 2 (New York: The Stockton Press), p. 455.

22. Paul A. Samuelson, 1982. "Economics in a Golden Age," *Paul Samuelson and Modern Economic Theory,* eds. E. Cary Brown and Robert Solow (New York: McGraw-Hill).

23. Dudley Luckett, personal conversation. Luckett, an Iowa State University economist, many years ago regaled me with stories of Samuelson gleaned from the time when he, Luckett, spent a year as a visiting professor at MIT. The image of Samuelson conveyed by Luckett is that of a *wunderkind* speaking tongues.

24. Peter L. Bernstein, 1990. *Capital Ideas: The Improbable Origins of Modern Wall Street* (New York: The Free Press), pp. 112–114.

25. William Breit and Roger L. Ransom, 1998. *The Academic Scribblers* (Princeton, New Jersey: Princeton University Press), p. 110.

26. David M. Kreps, 1997. "Economics—The Current Position," *Academic Culture in Transition,* eds. Thomas Bender and Carl E. Schorske (Princeton, New Jersey: Princeton University Press), p. 100.

CHAPTER 8:   COMEBACK KID

I chose quotes from two of the more unorthodox members of the contemporary economic profession, Albert Hirschman and Mancur Olson, to keynote this chapter. To my way of thinking, their intellectual styles resonate with the moral agenda of Adam Smith and mark the return of his sociological sensibility in contemporary economics—an agenda purchased through the efforts of the previous chapter's dragon slayers.

1. Alan S. Blinder, January, 2000. "How the Economy Came to Resemble the Model," *Business Economics,* pp. 16–25.

2. Attributed to Kenneth Boulding from the Finnish Web site containing economists' jokes, JokeEc.

3. Interview with Kenneth Arrow, December, 1995. *The Region,* Federal Reserve Bank of Minneapolis.

4. Lester Thurow, 1983. *Dangerous Currents: The State of Economics* (New York: Random House).

5. D. N. McCloskey, 1996. *The Vices of Economists: The Virtues of the Bourgeois* (Amsterdam: Amsterdam University Press), pp. 21–61.

6. Paul Craig Roberts, April 24, 1995. "A Minimum-Wage Study with Minimum Credibility," *Business Week.*

7. Conversation with a very mainstream economist.

8. Mancur Olson and Satu Kähkönen, eds., 2000. *A Not-So-Dismal Science,* Preface (New York: Oxford University Press).

9. Ibid. Oliver Williamson, "Economic Institutions and Development: A View from the Bottom."

10. Amartya Sen, 1999. *Development as Freedom* (New York: Alfred A. Knopf). This theme is characteristic of Sen's great work and appears as a master theme in this book. The same is true for the themes mentioned in reference to the other works cited in this section of Chapter Eight.

11. Hernando DeSoto, 2000. *The Mystery of Capital: Why Capitalism Triumphs in the West and Fails Everywhere Else* (New York: Basic Books).

12. Allan Drazen, 1999. *Political Economy in Macroeconomics* (Princeton, New Jersey: Princeton University Press); and Robert Cooter, 1999. *The Strategic Constitution* (Princeton, New Jersey: Princeton University Press).

13. Oliver Hart, 1995. *Firms, Contracts, and Financial Structures* (New York: Oxford University Press).

14. Robert Townsend, 1992. *The Medieval Village Economy* (Princeton, New Jersey: Princeton University Press).

15. Avner Greif, 1998. *Analytic Narratives,* eds. Robert H. Bates, et al. (Princeton, New Jersey: Princeton University Press).

16. Robert B. Wilson, 2001. "Architecture of Power Markets," Research Paper 17 of Graduate School of Business, Stanford University.

17. Robert C. Merton, 1995. "A Functional Perspective of Financial Intermediation," *Financial Management,* No. 24.

18. Roman Frydman and Andreas Rapacynski, 1994. *Privatization in Eastern Europe* (London: Central European University Press).

19. DeSoto, op. cit.

20. Mancur Olson, Spring, 1996. "Big Bills Left on the Sidewalk: Why Some Nations Are Rich, and Others Are Poor," *Journal of Economic Perspectives,* Vol. 10, No. 2, p. 22.

21. Amartya Sen, Summer, 1977. "Rational Fools: A Critique of the Behavioral Foundations of Economics," *Philosophy and Public Affairs,* Vol. 6, No. 4, pp. 317–344.

22. Canice Prendergast, September, 1993. "A Theory of Yes Men," *American Economic Review,* pp. 757–770.

23. Oliver Stone, 1987. *Wall Street*. Twentieth Century Fox Film Corporation.

24. Robert H. Frank, 1988. *Passions within Reason: The Strategic Role of the Emotions* (New York: W.W. Norton & Co.).

25. Adam Smith, 1759 [1984]. *The Theory of Moral Sentiments,* eds. A. L. Macfie and D. D. Rafael (Indianapolis, Indiana: Liberty Fund), p. 63.

26. Douglass North, 1997. *Lives of the Laureates,* eds. William Breit and Roger W. Spencer (Cambridge, Massachusetts: MIT Press), p. 254.

27. Ibid., p. 258.

28. Press release, October 12, 1993. The Bank of Sweden Prize in Economic Sciences in memory of Alfred Nobel.

29. Dani Rodrik, 1997. "The Paradoxes of the Successful State," *European Economic Review,* Vol. 41, Nos. 3–5, pp. 411–442.

30. Ibid.

31. Adam Smith, 1759 [1981]. *An Inquiry into the Nature and Causes of the Wealth of Nations,* eds. R. H. Campbell and A. S. Skinner (Indianapolis, Indiana: Liberty Fund), Book V, p. 723.

CHAPTER 9:   KITCHEN CHEMISTS

1. Adam Smith, [1978]. *Lectures on Jurisprudence,* eds. R. L. Meek, D. D. Rafael, and P. G. Stein (Indianapolis, Indiana: Liberty Fund), p. 239.

2. Paul M. Romer, 1993. "Implementing a National Technology Strategy with Self-Organizing Industry Investment Boards," Brookings Papers, Microeconomics 2, p. 388.

3. Ibid.

4. See Paul M. Romer, 1992. "Economic Growth," for an excellent presentation of the ideas behind economic growth theory. In *The Fortune Encyclopedia of Economics,* ed. David R. Henderson, New York: Warner Books. My discussion of economic growth and of Paul Romer's general ideas on growth are based on this essay.

5. Ibid.

6. Ibid.

7. Ibid.

8. Ibid.

9. Romer, 1993, op. cit., p. 345.

10. Gary S. Becker and Kevin M. Murphy, 1992. "The Division of Labor, Coordination Costs, and Knowledge," Working Paper No. 79 (Chicago: University of Chicago Center for the Study of the Economy and the State).

11. Romer, 1992, op. cit.

12. Romer, 1993, op. cit. My full discussion of self-organizing industry investment banks is based on this article.

13. Ibid.

14. Michael Milken, June 23, 1999. "Prosperity and Social Capital," The *Wall Street Journal*, p. A26.

15. Romer, 1993, op. cit.

16. Adam Smith, 1759 [1981]. *An Inquiry into the Nature and Causes of the Wealth of Nations,* eds. R. H. Campbell and A. S. Skinner (Indianapolis, Indiana: Liberty Fund), Book V.

17. Ibid.

18. Milton Friedman, 1962. *Capitalism and Freedom* (Chicago: University of Chicago Press), Chap. 6.

19. Caroline M. Hoxby, 2000. "The Battle over School Choice," *Frontline.* Public Broadcasting Service.

20. Chester E. Finn Jr., Brunno V. Manno, and Gregg Vanourek, 2000. *Charter Schools in Action* (Princeton, New Jersey: Princeton University Press). See this book for a general discussion of charter schools.

21. Smith, op. cit., Book I, p. 96.

22. Glenn C. Loury, March, 2000. "Who Cares about Racial Inequality?" *Journal of Sociology and Social Welfare,* Vol. XXXVI, No. 1.

23. Ibid., p. 149.

24. Ibid., p. 148.

25. Ibid.

26. Ibid.

27. Glenn C. Loury, "Comment." Robert M. Solow, 1998. *Work and Welfare,* ed. Amy Gutmann (Princeton, New Jersey: Princeton University Press), pp. 53–54.

28. Glenn C. Loury, 1999. "State of Morality in America." Speech, Michigan State University, p. 8.

29. Glenn C. Loury, 1996. "The Divided Society and the Demoractic Ideal." Lecture, Boston University.

30. John J. DiIulio Jr. DiIulio was the director of the Bush White House's faith-based initiative. He has written extensively on the virtues of supporting churches in the inner city.

31. Edmund C. Phelps, April, 1997. "A Strategy for Employment and Growth: The Failure of Statism, Welfarism, and Free Markets," *Rivista Ltaliana Degli Economista,* Vol. 2, pp. 121–128.

32. Edmund C. Phelps, 1997. *Rewarding Work* (Cambridge, Massachusetts: Harvard University Press).

33. Paul M. Romer, 2000. "Should the Government Subsidize Supply or Demand in the Market for Scientists and Engineers?" Working Paper No. 7723 (Cambridge, Massachusetts: Bureau of Economic Research).

34. Philip Cook and Robert Frank, 1995. *The Winner-Take-All Society* (New York: Basic Books).

35. Smith, op. cit., Book I, p. 98.

36. Cook and Frank, op. cit.

37. Susan Lee, 1992. *Hands Off, Why the Government Is a Menace to Economic Health* (New York: Simon & Schuster).

CHAPTER 10:   EGG MEN

1. Adam Smith, 1759 [1981]. *An Inquiry into the Nature and Causes of the Wealth of Nations,* eds. R. H. Campbell and A. S. Skinner (Indianapolis, Indiana: Liberty Fund), Book I, Chap. 4.

2. Russell Conwell, 1915 [1995]. *Acres of Diamonds* (New York: Berkley Publishing Group).

3. Gertrude Himmelfarb, "Comment." Robert M. Solow, 1998. *Work and Welfare,* ed. Amy Gutmann (Princeton, New Jersey: Princeton University Press), p. 84.

4. Michael Sherraden, March–April, 2000. "Building Assets to Fight Poverty," *National Housing Institute Shelterforce Online,* p. 2.

5. Peter L. Bernstein, 1990. *Capital Ideas: The Improbable Origins of Modern Wall Street* (New York: The Free Press), p. 44.

6. Ibid., p. 60.

7. Sherraden, op. cit.

8. Bernstein, op. cit., p. 44.

9. Ibid., p. 10.

10. Ibid.

11. Michael Milken, June 23, 1999. "Prosperity and Social Capital," *Wall Street Journal,* p. A26.

12. Bernstein, op. cit.

13. Merton Miller, Fall, 1998. "Financial Markets and Economic Growth," *Journal of Applied Corporate Finance,* Vol. 11, No. 3, p. 8.

14. Many economics writers and analysts called for prudence on the part of investors during the dot.com crash of spring, 2000. Among them were Burton Malkiel in his *Wall Street Journal* review of Robert Shiller's *Irrational Exuberance;* Paul Krugman in the *New York Times;* and earlier Michael Brennan, 1998, "Stripping the S&P 500," *Financial Analysts' Journal,* Vol. 54, No.1.

15. Robert J. Shiller, 2000. *Irrational Exuberance* (Princeton, New Jersey: Princeton University Press), pp. 228–230.

16. Ibid.; and Robert J. Shiller, 1993. *Macro Markets: Creating Institutions for Managing Society's Largest Economic Risks* (New York: Oxford University Press).

17. Michael J. Mandel, 1996. *The High-Risk Society, Peril and Promise in the New Economy* (New York: Times Business), p. 186.

18. Shiller, op. cit., 1993.

19. Milken, op. cit.

20. Sherraden, op. cit.

21. Martin Weitzman, 1984. *The Share Economy* (Cambridge, Massachusetts: Harvard University Press).

22. "A Statistical Profile of Employee Ownership," 2002. National Center for Employee Ownership (Oakland, California: NCEO).

23. Jeff Gates, 1999. "Peoplized Ownership Patterns—A Missing Ingredient in a Self-Designed Capitalism," *Pai de USIS–JICS,* Vol. 2, Colentina, Romania.

24. Richard B. Freeman, December–January, 1996–1997. "Solving the New Inequality," New Democracy Forum. *Boston Review,* p. 4.

25. Ibid., p. 5.

26. Ibid., p. 9.

27. Edward Glaeser, May 4, 1998. "Brighter Lights for Big Cities," *Business Week,* p. 88.

28. Peter Tufano, 2001. *Finance Faculty Research* (Boston: Harvard Business School).

29. Lillian Chew, April, 1994. "Modelling the Institution: An Interview with Robert C. Merton," *Risk,* Vol. 7, No. 4.

30. Adam Smith to Henry Dundas, November 1, 1779 [Letter]. *Glasgow Edition of the Works and Correspondence of Adam Smith,* eds. E. C. Mossner and I. S. Ross (New York: Oxford University Press), pp. 241–242. Quoted in Jerry Z. Muller, 1993. *Adam Smith in His Time and Ours* (New York: The Free Press), p. 26.

CHAPTER 11:   URBAN OUTFITTERS

1. Robert Putnam, 2000. *Bowling Alone* (New York: Simon & Schuster), p. 213.

2. Ibid., p. 211.

3. Ibid., p. 408.

4. David Warsh, 1993. *Economic Principals* (New York: The Free Press), p. 113.

5. Ronald H. Coase, 1997. *Lives of the Laureates,* eds. William Breit and Roger W. Spencer (Cambridge, Massachusetts: MIT Press), p. 233.

6. Ibid., p. 240.

7. Warsh, op. cit., p. 115.

8. David Osborne, 1992 (Ted Gaebler, contributor). *Reinventing Government* (Washington, DC: Perseus Press).

9. Michael Porter, 1980. *Competitive Strategy* (New York: The Free Press).

10. Michael Porter, 1990. *The Competitive Advantage of Nations* (New York: The Free Press).

11. Alfred Marshall, [1998]. Quoted in *The Weightless World,* ed. Diane Coyle (Cambridge, Massachusetts: MIT Press).

12. Porter, 1990, op. cit.

13. Michael Porter, 1997. "The Next Agenda for American Cities: Competing in a Global Economy," James W. Rouse Lecture, Fannie Mae Foundation. This is a terrific summary of Michael Porter's ideas on the economic condition of cities and the possibilities of their reinvigoration through enhanced competitive strategies.

14. Ibid.

15. Ibid.

16. Ibid.

17. Ibid.

18. Ibid.

19. Michael Porter. http://www.icic.org.

20. Paul Milgrom and John Roberts, 1992. *Economics, Organization, and Management* (Upper Saddle River, New Jersey: Prentice-Hall), pp. 318–319.

21. Ibid.

22. Paul Gigot, December 27, 1996. "Why Edmund Burke Is a Packer Fan," *Wall Street Journal.*

23. John Gray, 2000. *False Dawn* (New York: The New Press). This is a scalding indictment of the social consequences of the new economy in the United States.

24. Warren Hinckle, 1974. *If You Have Lemons, Make Lemonade* (New York: G.P. Putnam).

25. Sanford Jacoby, June 18, 1998. "'Chainsaw Al' Gets His Due," *Los Angeles Times.*

26. Sanford Jacoby, September 7, 1998. "Most Workers Find a Sense of Security in Corporate Life," *Los Angeles Times.*

27. Peter Botsman and Christopher Sheil, 1997. "The Great Wheel of Circulation: The State of Australia's Finance," *Turning Point: The State of Australia,* ed. Christopher Sheil (Sydney, Australia: Allen & Unwin), pp. 56–57.

28. Gray, op. cit.

29. John Kay, May, 1998. "The Third Way," *Prospect.*

30. Thomas W. Synott III, 1998. *Monday Morning Comments.* U.S. Trust.

31. Jeffrey Garten, February 9, 1998. "Globalism Doesn't Have to Be Cruel," *Business Week,* p. 28.

EPILOGUE: GO WITH THE FLOW

1. Mario Puzo and Francis Ford Coppola, 1972. *The Godfather* (New York: Paramount Pictures).

2. Personal conversation. I thank Professor Dominick Salvatore for this comment.

3. Alfred Marshall, 1907. "The Social Possibilities of Economic Chivalry." Address to the Royal Economic Society.

Bibliography

Barone, Michael. 1990. *Our Country: A History of America from Roosevelt to Reagan*. New York: The Free Press.

Bates, Robert, Avner Greif, Margaret Levi, and Jean-Laurent Rosenthal. 1998. *Analytic Narratives*. Princeton: Princeton University Press.

Bell, Daniel. 1996. *The Cultural Contradictions of Capitalism. Twentieth Anniversary Edition*. New York: Basic Books.

Bender, Thomas, and Karl E. Schorske, 1997. *Academic Culture in Transition*. Princeton: Princeton University Press.

Bernstein, Peter L. 1996. *Against the Gods: The Remarkable Story of Risk*. New York: John Wiley & Sons.

Bernstein, Peter L. 1992. *Capital Ideas: The Improbable Origins of Modern Wall Street*. New York: The Free Press.

Breit, William, and Roger W. Spencer, eds. 1997. *Lives of the Laureates*. Cambridge, MA: MIT Press.

Breit, William, and Roger L. Ransom. 1998. *The Academic Scribblers, Third Edition*. Princeton: Princeton University Press.

Brown, E. Cary, and Robert M. Solow, eds. 1982. *Paul Samuelson and Modern Economic Theory*. New York: McGraw-Hill.

Bucholz, Todd. 1989. *New Ideas From Dead Economists*. New York: Penguin. A Plume Book.

Conwell, Russell. [1915] 1995. *Streets of Diamonds*. New York: Berkley Publishing Group.

Cooter, Robert. 1999. *The Strategic Constitution*. Princeton: Princeton University Press.

Coyle, Diane. 1998. *The Weightless World.* Cambridge, MA: MIT Press.

DeSoto, Hernando. 2000. *The Mystery of Capital.* New York: Basic Books.

Drazen, Allan. 1999. *Political Economy in Macroeconomics.* Princeton: Princeton University Press.

Dryzek, John. 1987. *Rational Ecology.* Cambridge, MA: Blackwell Publishers.

Eatwell, John, Murray Milgate, and Peter Newman. 1989. *The New Pallgrave Dictionary of Economics,* vol. 2. New York: The Stockton Press.

Finn, Chester E., Bruno Manno, and Gregg Vanourek. 2000. *Charter Schools in Action.* Princeton: Princeton University Press.

Frank, Robert. 1988. *Passions within Reason: The Strategic Role of the Emotions.* New York: W.W. Norton and Company.

Friedman, Milton. 1963. *Capitalism and Freedom.* Chicago: University of Chicago Press.

Frum, David. 1996. *What's Right: The New Conservative Majority and the Remaking of America.* New York: Basic Books.

Frydman, Roman, and Andreas Rapacynski. 1994. *Privatization in Eastern Europe.* London: Central European University Press.

Fukuyama, Francis. 1995. *Trust: The Social Virtues and the Creation of Prosperity.* New York: The Free Press.

Gray, John. 2000. *False Dawn.* New York: The New Press.

Hart, Oliver. 1995. *Firms, Contracts, and Financial Structures.* New York: Oxford University Press.

Heilbroner, Robert. [1953] 1992. *The Worldly Philosophers, Sixth Edition.* New York: Touchstone.

Heilbroner, Robert, and William Milberg. 1996. *The Crisis of Vision in Modern Economic Thought.* New York: Cambridge University Press.

Himmelfarb, Gertrude. 1992. *Poverty and Compassion: The Moral Imagination of the Late Victorians.* New York: Vintage Books.

Hinckle, Warren. 1974. *If You Have Lemons, Make Lemonade.* New York: G.P. Putnam.

Jacobs, Jane. [1961] 1993. *The Death and Life of Great American Cities.* New York: Vintage Books.

Kanter, Rosabeth Moss. 1997. *World Class: Thriving Locally in the Global Economy.* New York: Touchstone.

Kay, John. 1996. *The Business of Economics.* New York: Oxford University Press.

Keynes, John Maynard. [1931] 1991. *Essays in Persuasion.* New York: W.W. Norton and Company.

Keynes, John Maynard. 1936. *The General Theory of Money, Interest, and Employment.* London: Macmillan.

Lee, Susan. 1992. *Hands Off: Why the Government Is a Menace to Economic Health*. New York: Simon & Schuster.

Mandel, Michael J. 1996. *The High-Risk Society: Peril and Promise in the New Economy*. New York: Times Books.

Marshall, Alfred. [1890] 1920. *Principles of Economics: An Introductory Volume, Eighth Edition*. London: Macmillan.

McCloskey, D. N. 1996. *The Vices of Economists: The Virtues of the Bourgeoisie*. Amsterdam: Amsterdam University Press.

Milgrom, Paul, and John Roberts. 1992. *Economics, Organizations, and Management*. Upper Saddle River, NJ: Prentice-Hall.

Mount, Ferdinand. [1983] 1990. *The Subversive Family*. New York: The Free Press.

Mueller, John C. 1999. *Capitalism, Democracy, and Ralph's Pretty Good Grocery Store*. Princeton: Princeton University Press.

Muller, Jerry Z. 1993. *Adam Smith in His Time and Ours*. New York: The Free Press.

Olson, Mancur, and Satu Kähkönen, eds. 2000. *A Not-So-Dismal Science*. New York: Oxford University Press.

O'Rourke, Kevin, and Jeffrey Williamson. 1999. *Globalization and History*. Cambridge, MA: MIT Press.

Osborne, David with Ted Gaebler. 1992. *Reinventing Government*. Washington, DC: Perseus Press.

Porter, Michael. 1980. *Competitive Strategy*. New York: The Free Press.

Porter, Michael. 1990. *The Competitive Advantage of Nations*. New York: The Free Press.

Phelps, Edmund C. 1997. *Rewarding Work*. Cambridge, MA: Harvard University Press.

Press, Frank, and Ray Siever. 1994. *Earth*. New York: W. H. Freeman and Company.

Putnam, Robert. 2000. *Bowling Alone: The Collapse and Revival of American Community*. New York: Simon & Schuster.

Putnam, Robert. 1992. *Making Democracy Work: Civic Traditions in Modern Italy*. Princeton: Princeton University Press.

Sen, Amartya. 1999. *Development as Freedom*. New York: Alfred A. Knopf.

Shiller, Robert J. 2000. *Irrational Exuberance*. Princeton: Princeton University Press.

Shiller, Robert J. 1993. *Macro Markets: Creating Institutions for Managing Society's Largest Economic Risks*. New York: Oxford University Press.

Skidelsky, Robert. 1992. *John Maynard Keynes: The Economist as Savior, 1920–1937*. New York: Penguin Books.

Smith, Adam. [1776] 1981. *An Inquiry into the Nature and Causes of the Wealth of Nations.* eds., R. H. Campbell and A. S. Skinner. Indianapolis: Liberty Fund.

Smith, Adam. 1977. *The Correspondence of Adam Smith.* eds., E. C. Mossner and I. S. Ross. New York: Oxford University Press.

Smith, Adam. [1766] 1978. *Lectures on Jurisprudence.* eds., R. L. Meek, D. D. Rafael, and G. P. Stein. Indianapolis: Liberty Fund.

Smith, Adam. [1759] 1984. *The Theory of Moral Sentiments.* eds., A. L. Macfie and D. D. Rafael. Indianapolis: Liberty Fund.

Sobchak, Anatoly. 1992. *For a New Russia.* New York: The Free Press.

Solow, Robert M. 1998. *Work and Welfare,* ed., Amy Gutmann, Princeton: Princeton University Press.

Styron, William. 1999. *Sophie's Choice.* New York: Random House.

Swedberg, Richard. 1998. *Max Weber and the Idea of Economic Sociology.* Princeton: Princeton University Press.

Townsend, Robert. 1992. *The Medieval Village Economy.* Princeton: Princeton University Press.

Thurow, Lester. 1983. *Dangerous Currents: The State of Economics.* New York: Random House.

Warsh, David. 1993. *Economic Principals.* New York: The Free Press.

Weber, Max. [1920] 1930. *The Protestant Ethic and the Spirit of Capitalism.* Translated by Talcott Parsons. London: Harper Collins Academic.

Weitzman, Martin. 1984. *The Share Economy.* Cambridge, MA: Harvard University Press.

Whynes, David. 1983. *Invitation to Economics.* Oxford: Martin Robertson.

Index